INSIDE PALM SPRINGS

DON FLOOD

TEXT BY
PETER HALDEMAN

A STEPHEN DRUCKER BOOK

VENDOME

NEW YORK · LONDON

Introduction 12
RANCHO MIRAGE I 14
ANDREAS HILLS I 32
LITTLE TUSCANY 48
TWIN PALMS 60
MUSEUM WAY 70
TAMARISK I 82
RANCHO MIRAGE II 106
THE MESA I 118
TAMARISK II 134
RACQUET CLUB 152
INDIAN CANYONS I 164

VISTA LAS PALMAS 170
INDIAN WELLS 182
THUNDERBIRD HEIGHTS I 196
MOVIE COLONY 216
THUNDERBIRD HEIGHTS II 228
MARRAKESH 244
INDIAN CANYONS II 258
THUNDERBIRD 270
ANDREAS HILLS II 280
THE MESA II 298
SOUTHRIDGE 318

Acknowledgments 334

INTRODUCTION

**OON AFTER ARRIVING IN PALM SPRINGS,** something will come over you. I've seen it happen many times.

You'll start doing things you wouldn't normally do—wearing bright colors, listening to Frank Sinatra, ordering espresso martinis. You'll start saying "Cool!" easily and often.

It's just a matter of time before you drop in on a house for sale, a giddy midcentury house, and see the possibility of a whole new you. This new you will need new furniture, so you'll start exploring vintage furniture shops (cool!) and tossing around names like George Nelson and Paul McCobb. The only question is how far you will take it. In Palm Springs it's perfectly normal to see furniture matched to the year of your house, which is matched to the year of your car, which is matched to the color of your front door.

Just twenty-five years ago Palm Springs was, as one of the better jokes went, "where old people go to visit their parents." People retired, played golf, and faded away while air conditioning hummed in the background.

Then design woke Palm Springs up, house by house, neighborhood by neighborhood. Retirees are coming faster than ever, but there's no fading away anymore. Now they come to relive an idealized version of their midcentury childhoods—houses, furniture, cars, clothes, music—alongside hordes of young newcomers discovering it all for the first time. The fever peaks every February during Modernism Week, when more than 100,000 people from around the world vie for tickets to visit the best of the houses, attend throbbing parties around pools where movie stars once swam, and take three-hour architecture tours on London-style double-decker buses. Always the first tours to sell out are led by a drag queen named Bella da Ball.

At times it's a bit of a circus, but underneath, make no mistake, people here are serious about design. Palm Springs has become one of the world's great architecture destinations because you won't see what you see here anywhere else. This isn't the take-your-medicine modernism that was dispensed in prewar Europe. This is modernism American-style, and here it has always been about pleasure.

Palm Springs is the result of a long list of what-ifs. What if Hollywood's early stars, whose contracts required them to stay within 100 miles of their studios, hadn't brought glamour to this remote desert outpost? What if European architects hadn't emigrated to escape Hitler, fallen in love with California, and found a laissez-faire town that welcomed their unconventional buildings? What if postwar prosperity hadn't made it possible for even middle-class people to own a desert vacation home and fueled a building boom at the peak of the modernist moment?

The first seeds were planted by what's now called the Palm Spring School, a group of local architects—notably Albert Frey, E. Stewart Williams, Donald Wexler, and William Cody—who had a restrained modernist ethos. But with money, Hollywood people, and real estate developers in the mix, "less is more" became simply "more," with bolder houses and fantasy interiors, and big new ideas about living. The American obsession with leisure was fully realized when the gated country club, where you live on a golf course, was invented here in the late 1940s. Detroit named cars after the two most prestigious of them: Thunderbird and Eldorado.

Today the once-small city of Palm Springs has burst its seams; it's a region. The romantic downtown where it began, where some streets were still unpaved as late as the 1950s, now extends twenty-five miles through the suburbs of Rancho Mirage, Palm Desert, and Indian Wells to La Quinta and beyond, where the newest gated city-states are scaled for the biggest egos on the planet. In between there are nearly 400,000 people living year-round in a valley where the summer temperature reliably hits 120 degrees, grass and roses are grown without a thought, and reality has been suspended until further notice.

Palm Springs is also now a style—a staple of fashion, advertising, TV, and movies. A turquoise sofa, orange pillows, a yellow pool umbrella, and you're on your way. Even the most conservative country clubs are flirting with the look to lure the next generation. Don Flood, Peter Haldeman, and I all thought it was time to dig deeper into this style, past its kitschy surface, to find the taste makers who are pushing beyond the formula—people with their own strong design point of view, people who are collecting what the rest of us will be buying ten years from now. The *Inside* series was created by Vendome Press so you could meet them.

—Stephen Drucker

RANCHO MIRAGE I

N 2017 LISA BROWNELL WENT TO LOOK AT a house for sale in Rancho Mirage, a glassy, pool-hugging pavilion built in 1957 by the renowned Desert Modernist E. Stewart Williams. The listing agent met her at the door with an old issue of *W* magazine bookmarked on a moody fashion spread, ironically titled "Domestic Bliss," featuring Brad Pitt and Angelina Jolie acting out scenes of marital discord against the serene backdrop of the Kenaston House, as it's known. The pictures intrigued Brownell, a retired psychotherapist from Los Angeles—but the house itself would change her life. "What hit me when I walked in were the rock wall on one side of the living room and the metal wall on the other, and then all the glass in between," she says. "I just loved that combination of the sleek and the rough."

When it came to decorating the almost-five-thousand-square-foot house, Brownell channeled some of the moodiness of the *W* pictorial but none of the discord. The colors tend to be desaturated. Vintage pieces Brownell acquired online or at local shops were left unrefinished. Peter Stichbury portraits appear in several rooms, his wide-eyed subjects staring at the viewer impassively—or are they upset about something? "As a therapist I was always looking for meaning in people's faces," Brownell offers. "I find it energizing to live with a houseful of interesting ones."

Everything's a little brighter outside (it *is* Palm Springs). A persimmon-orange wall vibrates against the Popsicle-blue pool. Three high-chroma medallion sculptures by Stan Bitters, a recent acquisition, edge the lawn. "They make the whole backyard," observes Brownell, who moved to the desert full-time a few years ago. She uses the yard for everything from Modernism Week fundraisers to playdates for her "daughter," Spencer, an eleven-year-old labradoodle. True domestic bliss.

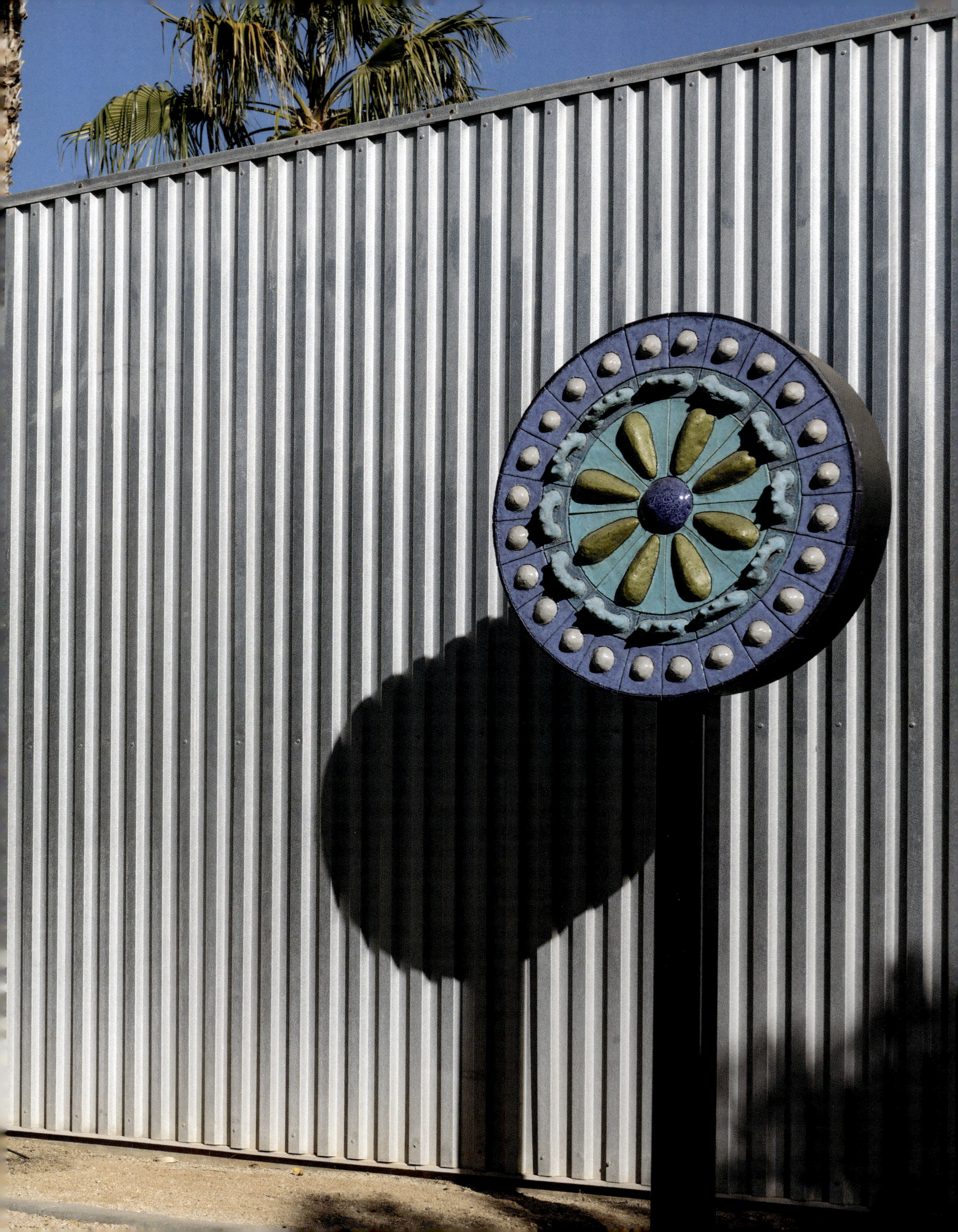

ANDREAS HILLS

THE FLAT-ROOFED, GLASS-WALLED BOX remains the *ne plus ultra* of Desert Modernism, but architecture aficionados are rediscovering the freewheeling designs of the '70s, a period better known for soaring pitched roofs and high, angled plaster walls. The work of John Walling is a prime example. Well represented in the South Palm Springs neighborhood of Andreas Hills, Walling's efforts here include Stonehedge, a five-thousand-square-foot house built for a Chicago businessman that features bisecting rooflines, three interior atriums, and those bachelor pad essentials, a sunken living room and a bar.

As it happened, the bachelor only used the pad a couple of weeks a year, so it was in mint condition when interior designer Sean Gaston and his husband and business partner, Jim Jewell, discovered it in 2017. The couple was stoked to find the rough-sawn ceiling beams unmolested, the mosaic kitchen and bathroom tiles intact. They were also impressed with the house's carefully orchestrated views. "Being in a white, shiny glass box is cool," says Gaston, "but what I love about this place is that it embraces you." Gaston sourced most of the furniture and artwork at consignment shops in the area. "If you look carefully," he says, "you'll see Art Deco, chinoiserie, Arts and Crafts." You'll also see a number of designs by the late great Palm Springs decorator Steve Chase: the chenille sectional in the living room, the Lucite and white oak dining table, the primary bedroom suite. Another Palm Springs legend is conjured outside, where a sculpture from Liberace's estate overlooks the pool.

Chasing their own rainbows, Gaston and Jewell are preparing to retire soon, selling their house in the Bay Area to move to southern California and get more use out of the desert refuge built for a man who barely used it at all.

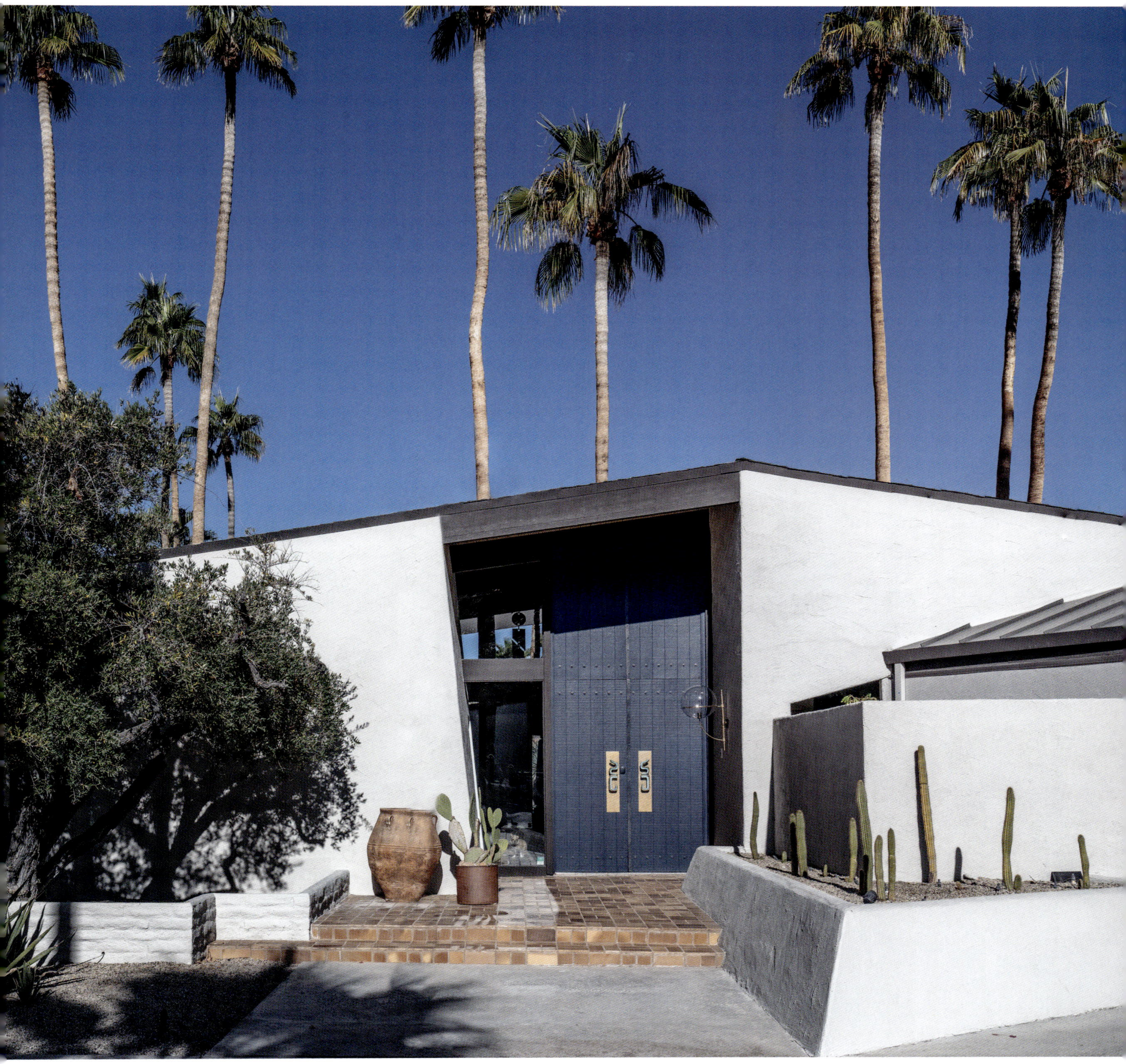

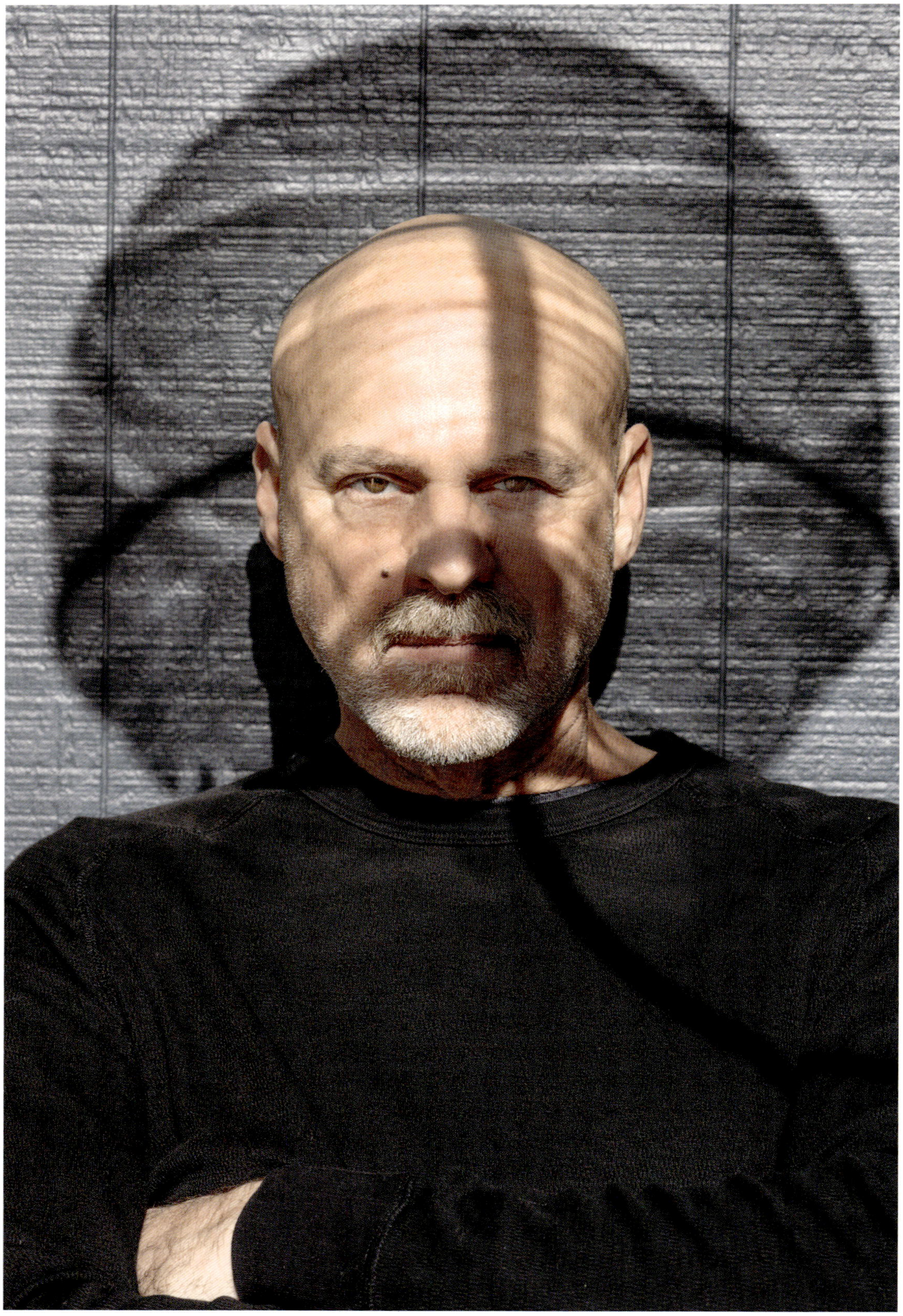

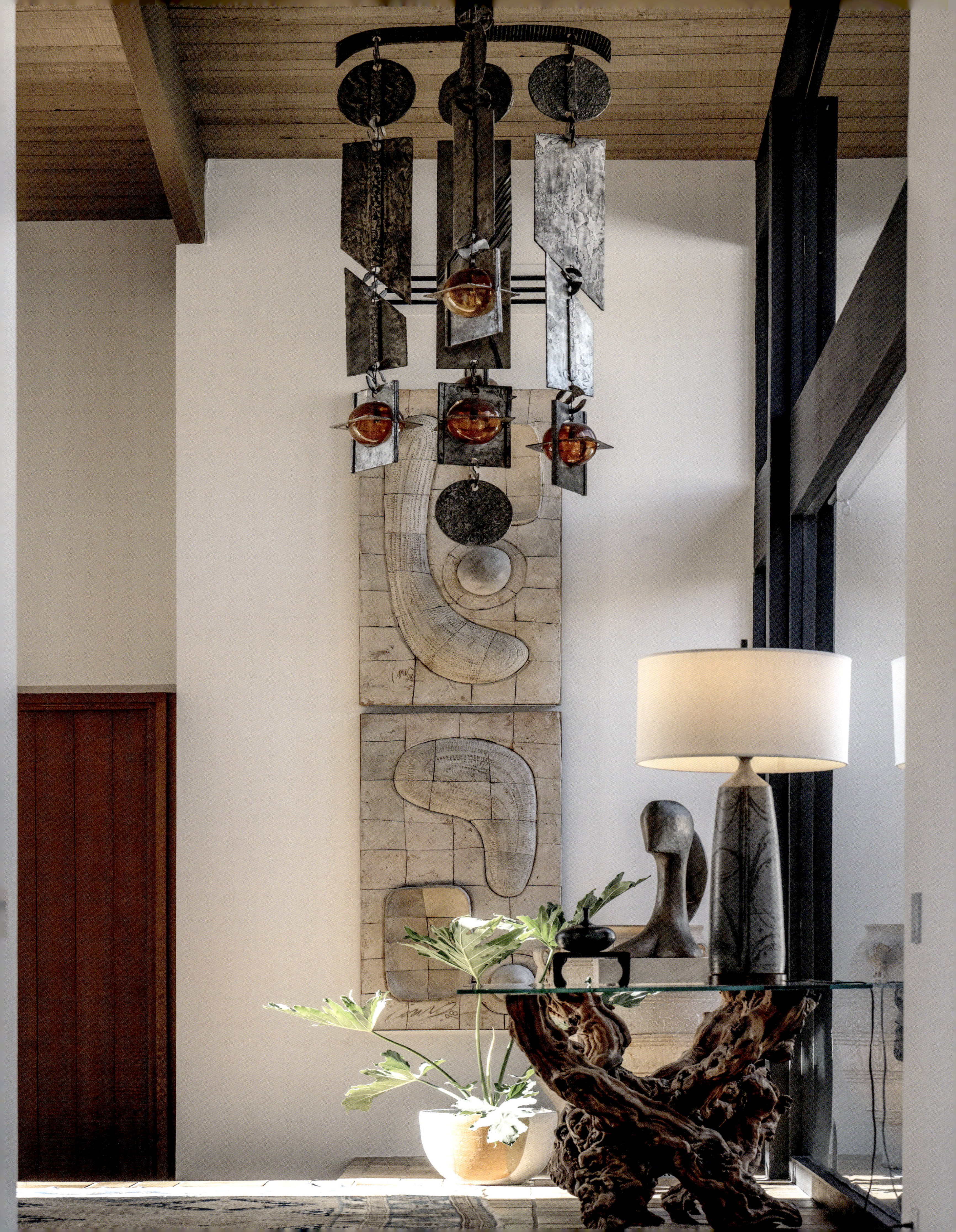

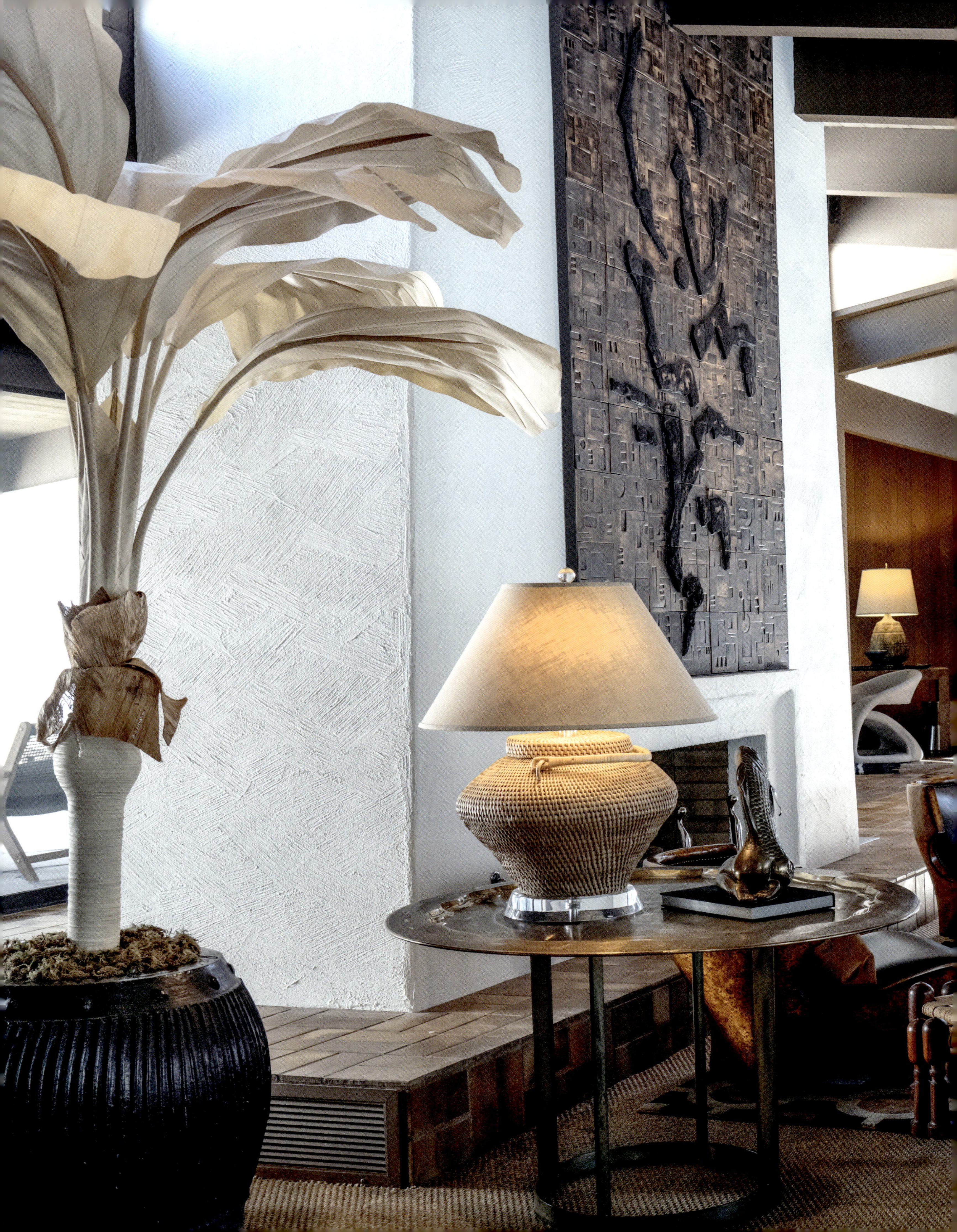

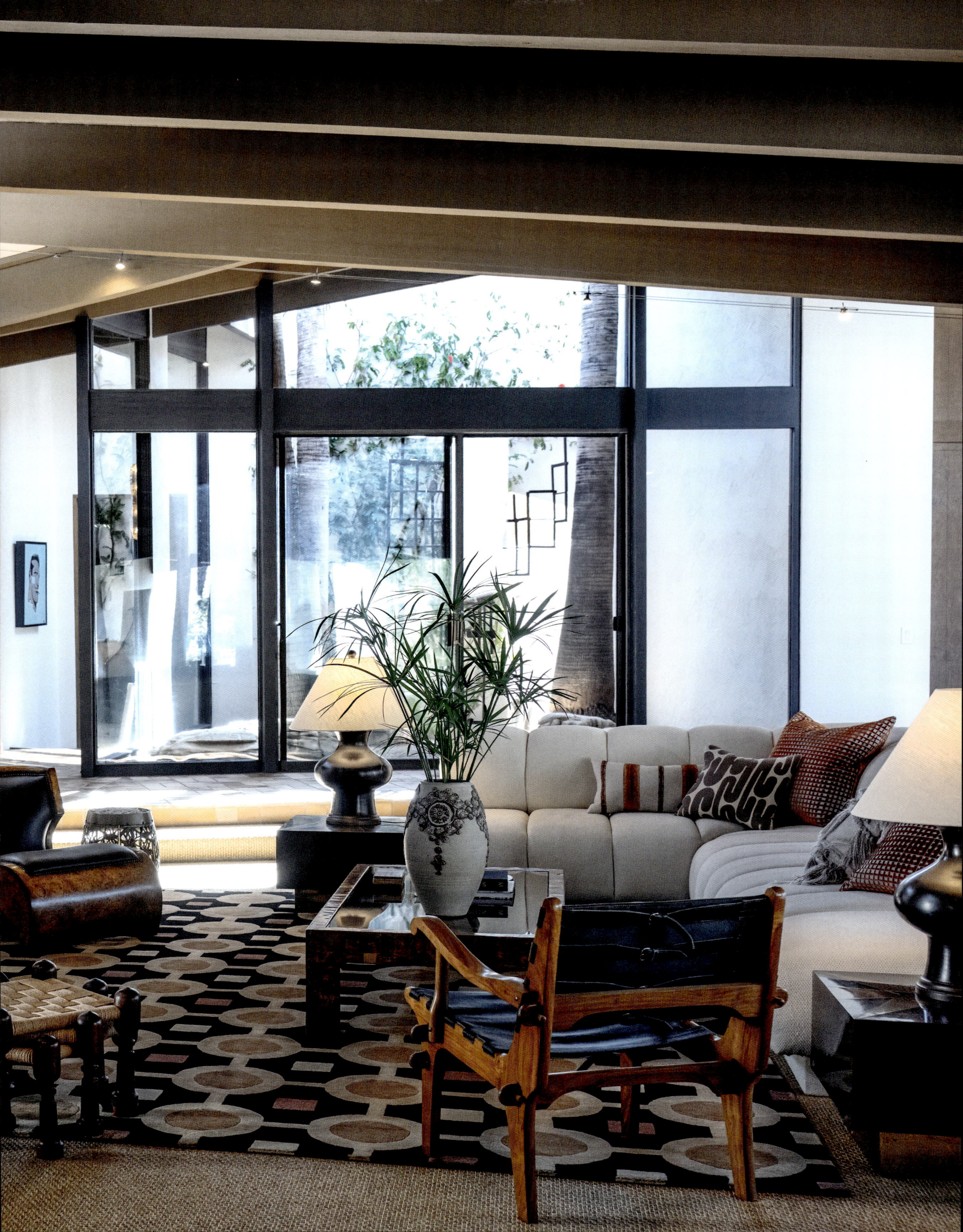

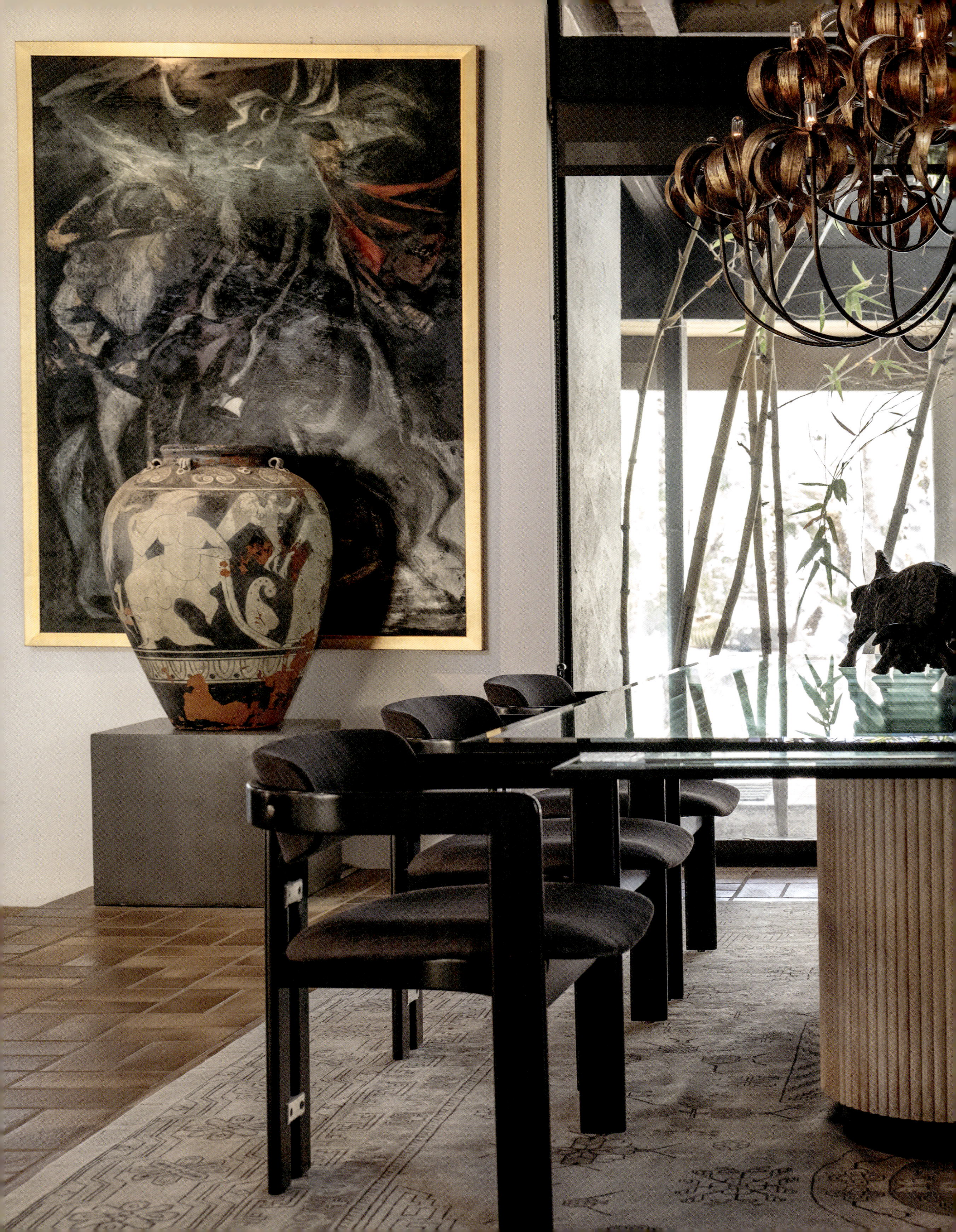

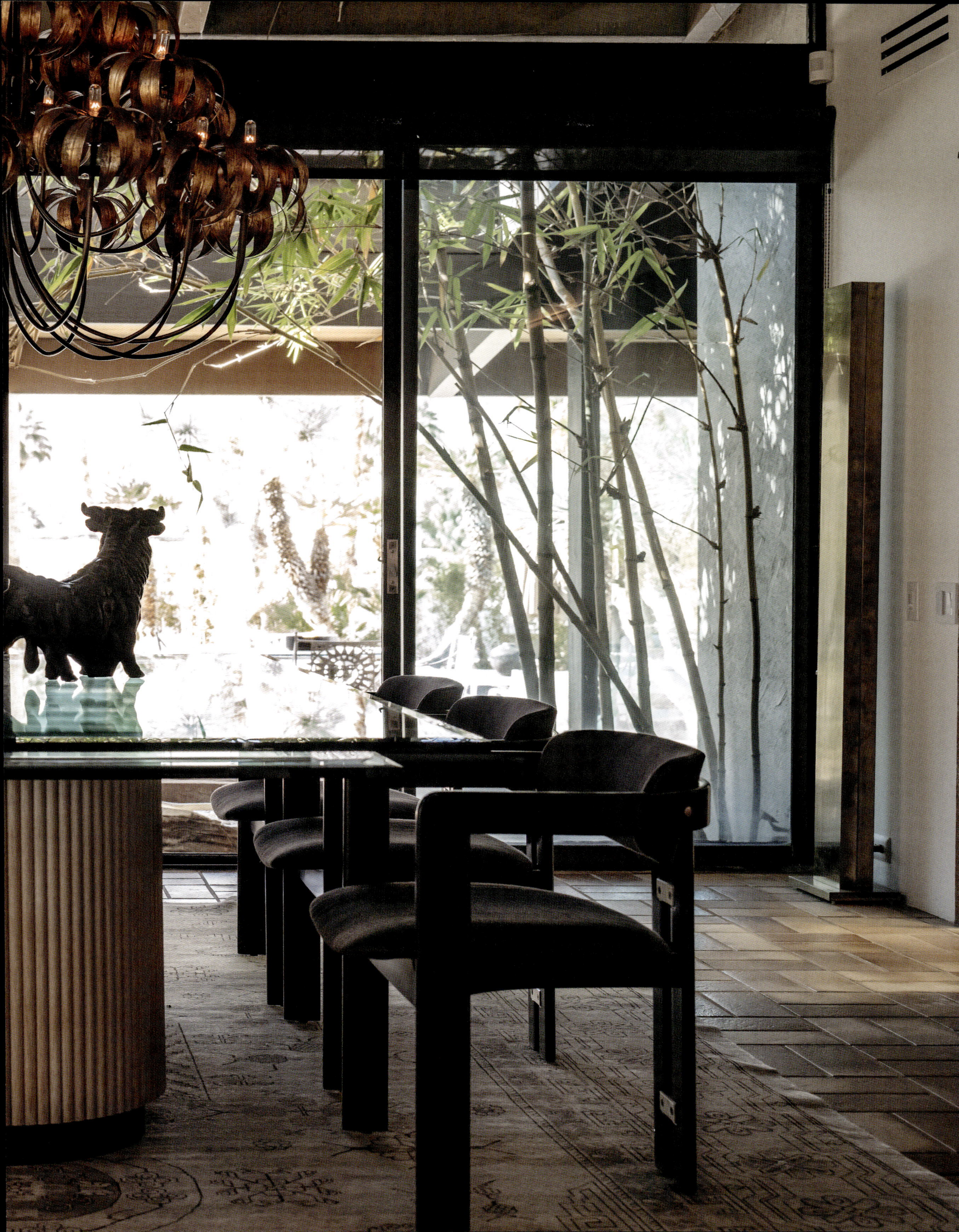

42

43

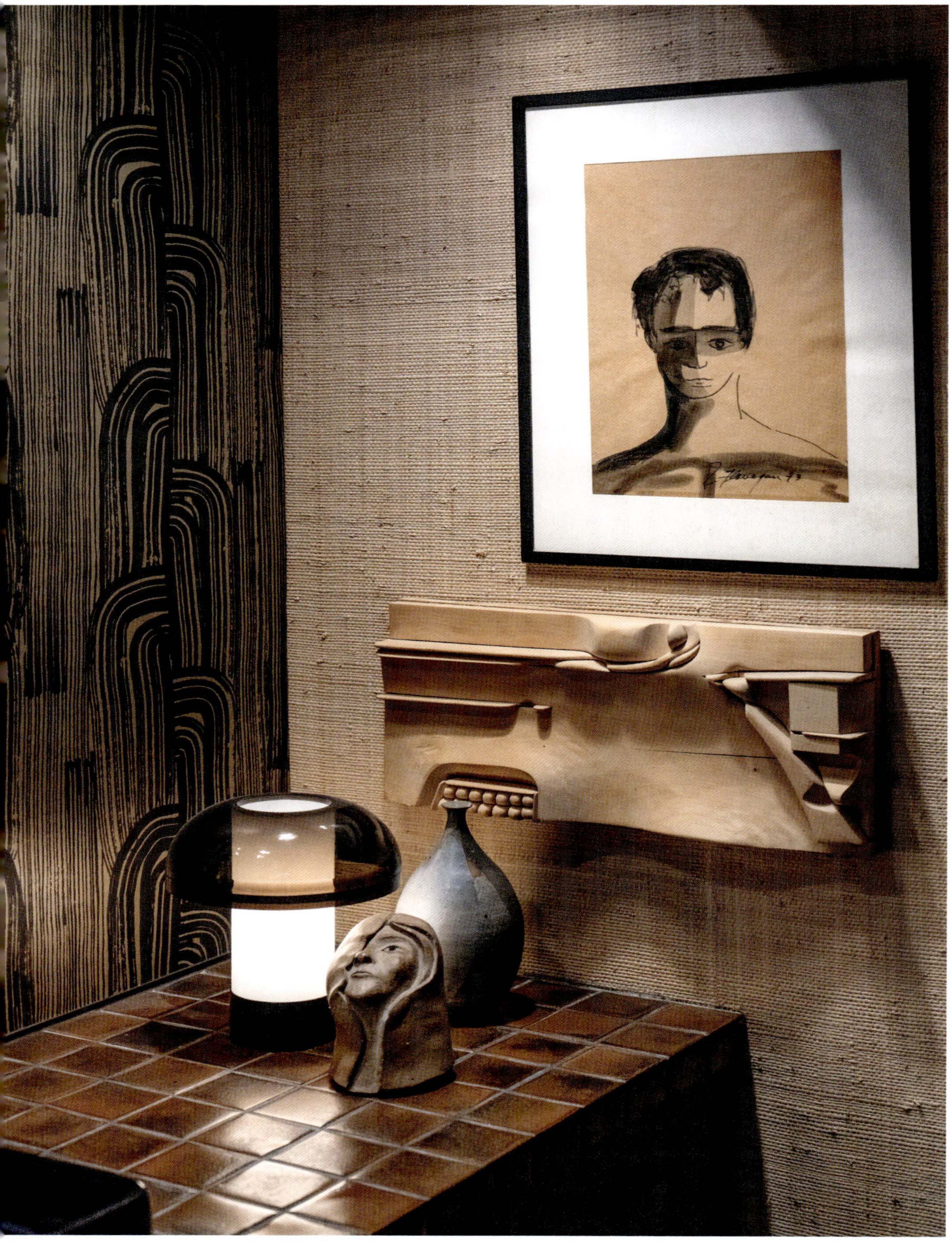

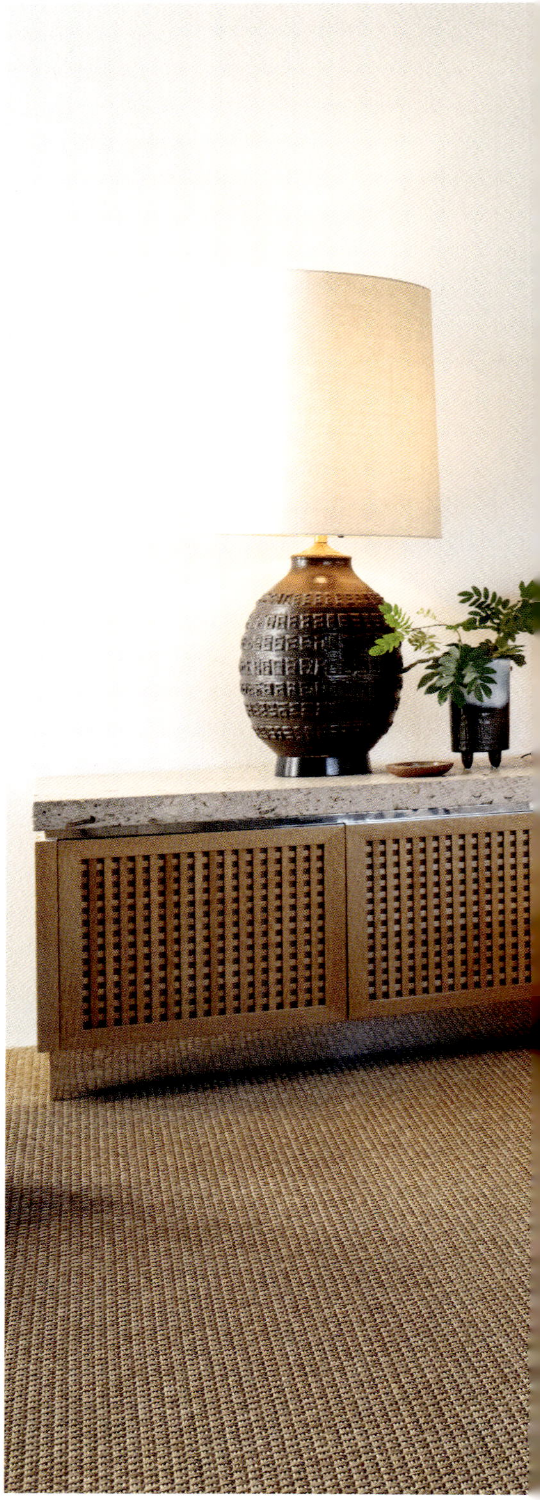

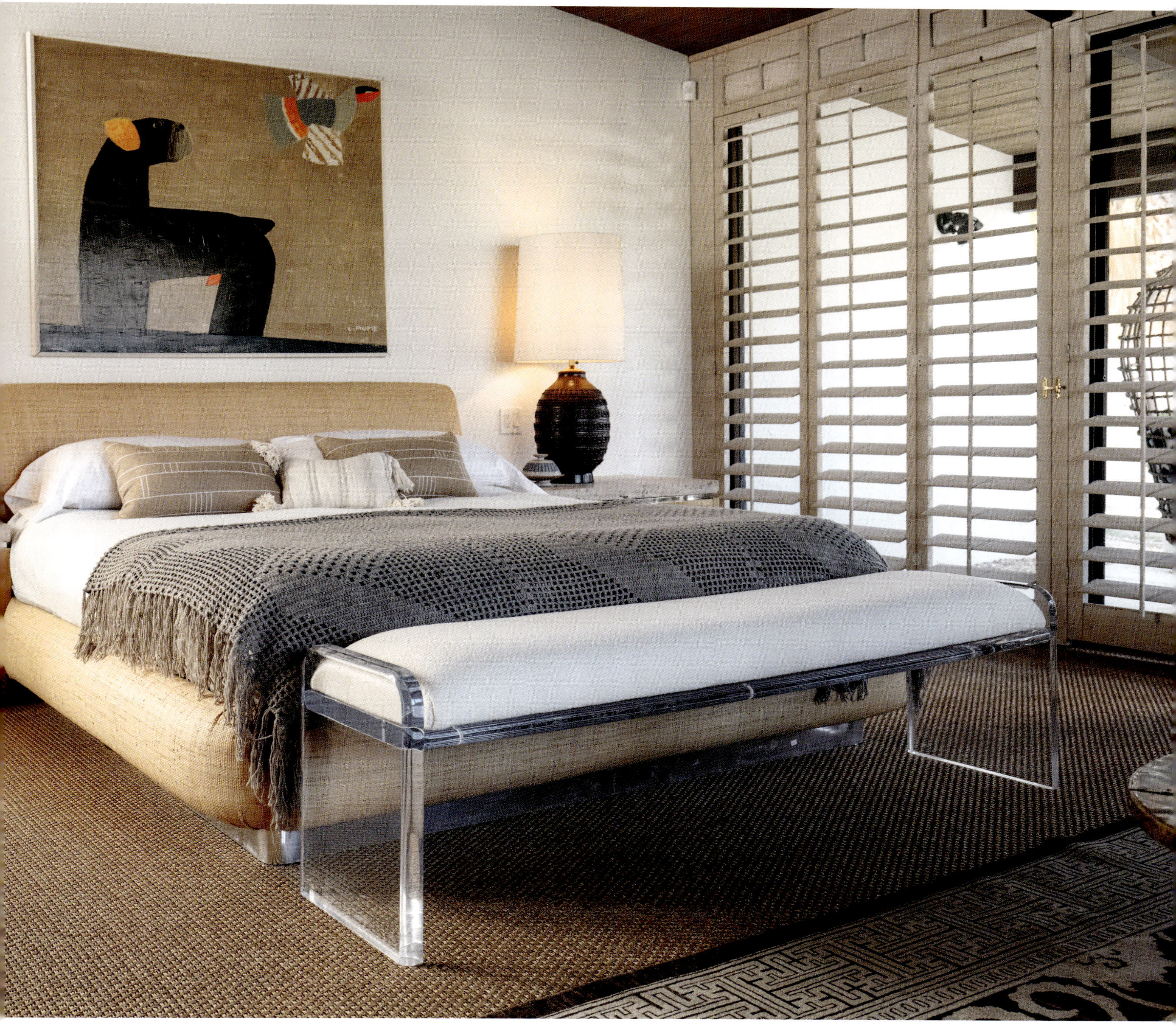

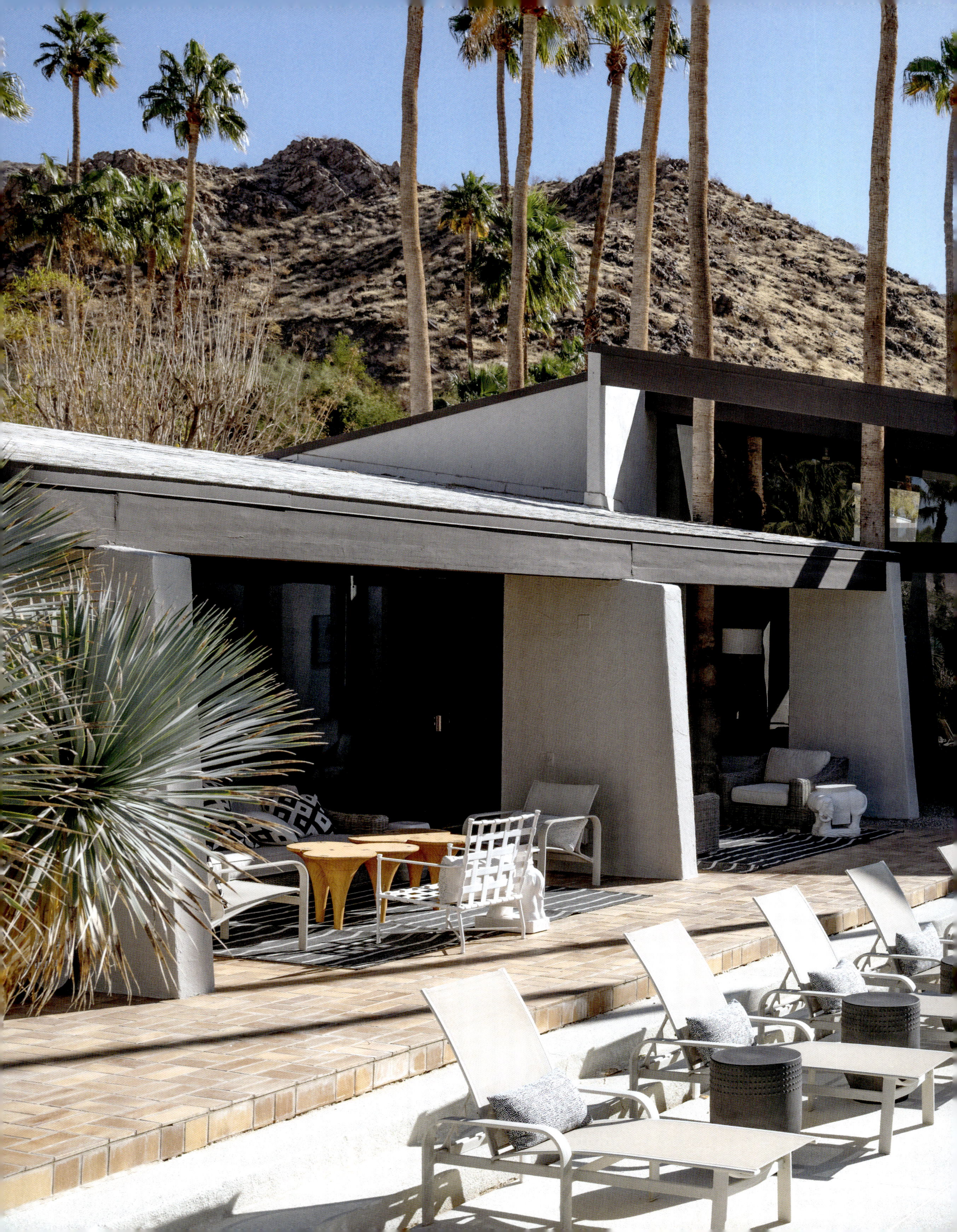

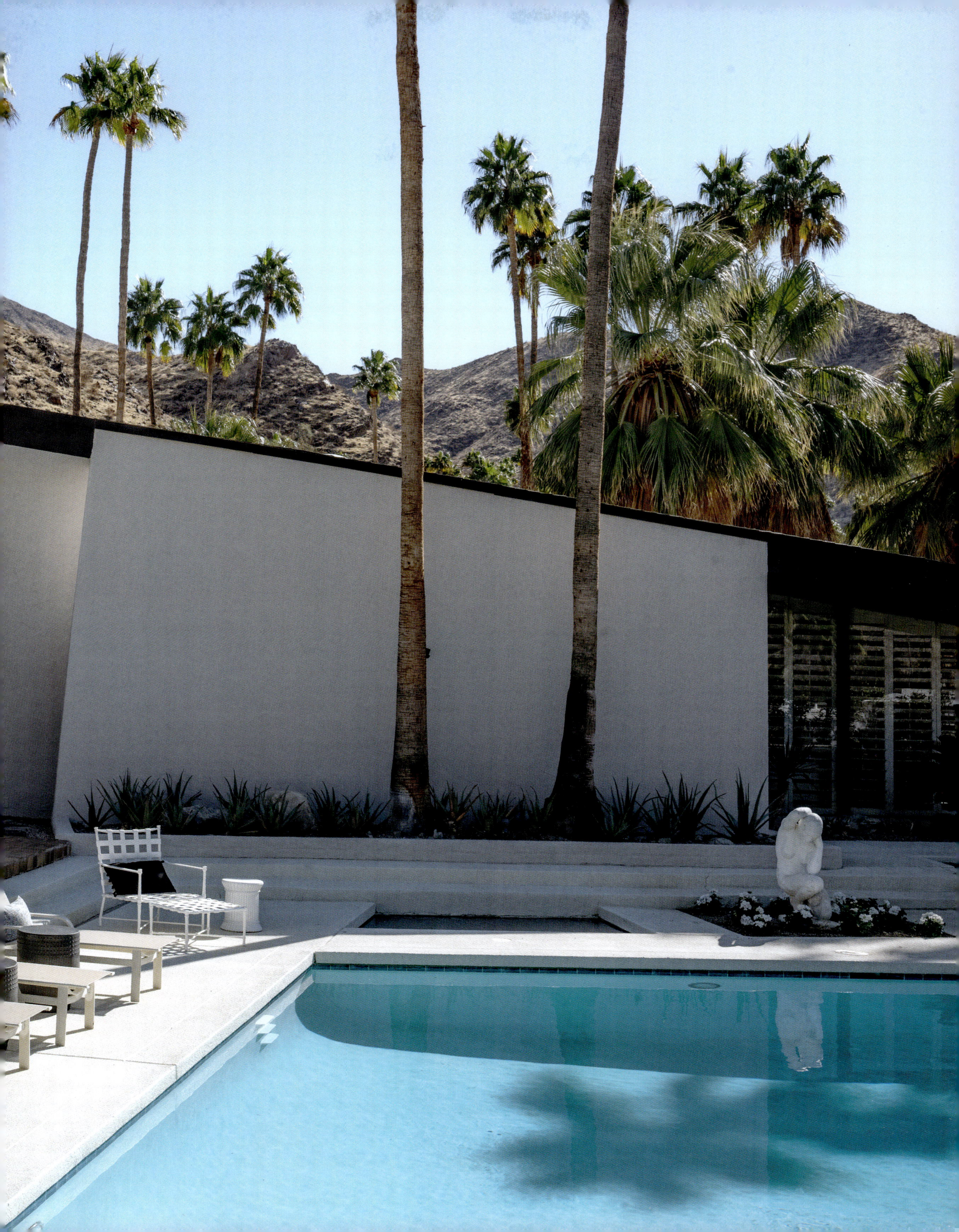

LITTLE TUSCANY

IN 1986 JIM GAUDINEER AND TONY PADILLA were visiting Palm Springs from Chicago, looking after Gaudineer's father, who was recovering from hip surgery, when Gaudineer *pere* noticed an ad in the paper for the house of Raymond Loewy, the noted industrial designer (the Shell logo, the Coca-Cola bottle). Built in 1946, the apparently simple, L-shaped structure featured two bedrooms and a living area framing a boulder-studded swimming pool. "We called up the realtor, and he said, 'Oh, yeah, it's been on the market for two years,'" recalls Gaudineer. "'Nobody wants it because the pool comes inside the house and everyone thinks that burglars will swim under the sliding glass doors.'"

Gaudineer and Padilla wanted it. It was only after they'd bought the place, however, that Gaudineer picked up a book on Loewy at the MoMA bookstore and learned about Albert Frey, the architect who built this radically organic house twelve years after he designed the first modernist building in Palm Springs. In the late '90s, after the architects Leo Marmol and Ron Radziner had begun a comprehensive rehabilitation of Richard Neutra's Kaufmann House next door, Gaudineer and Padilla hired the firm to restore the Loewy House. They added a primary bedroom suite while they were at it, infuriating Frey, who was still alive then. The couple have lived here thirty-nine years now, and the house is filled with artwork by Padilla and others, rocks collected from the Salton Sea, midcentury pieces by Florence Knoll, Hans Wegner, Serge Mouille. (Gaudineer runs the Palm Canyon Galleria.) Over the decades they've watched Palm Springs grow into an international destination for design fans, and they're "big on sharing" the Loewy House. Padilla laments that "we can't leave our doors open anymore"—but to date no one has tried to break in via the pool.

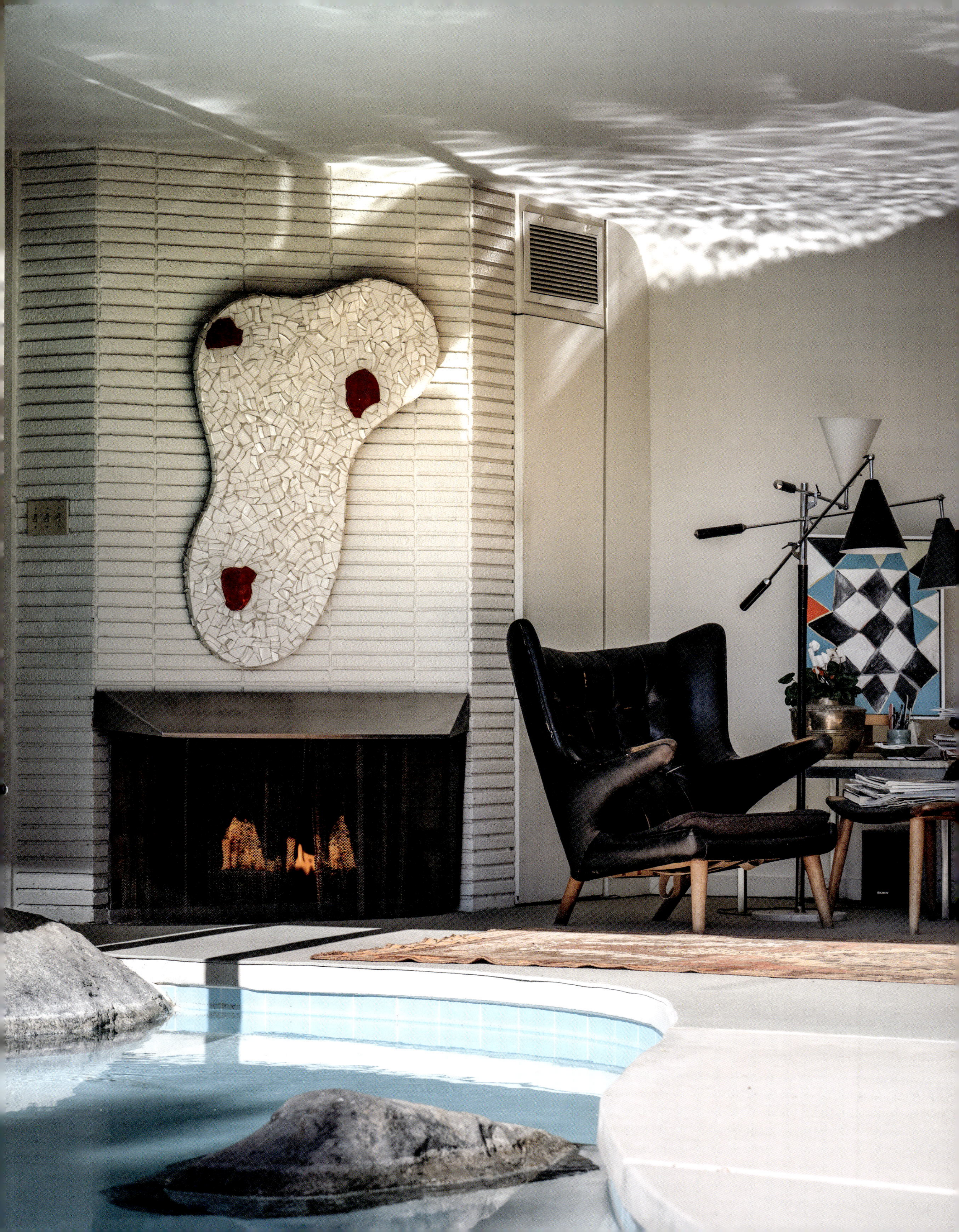

50

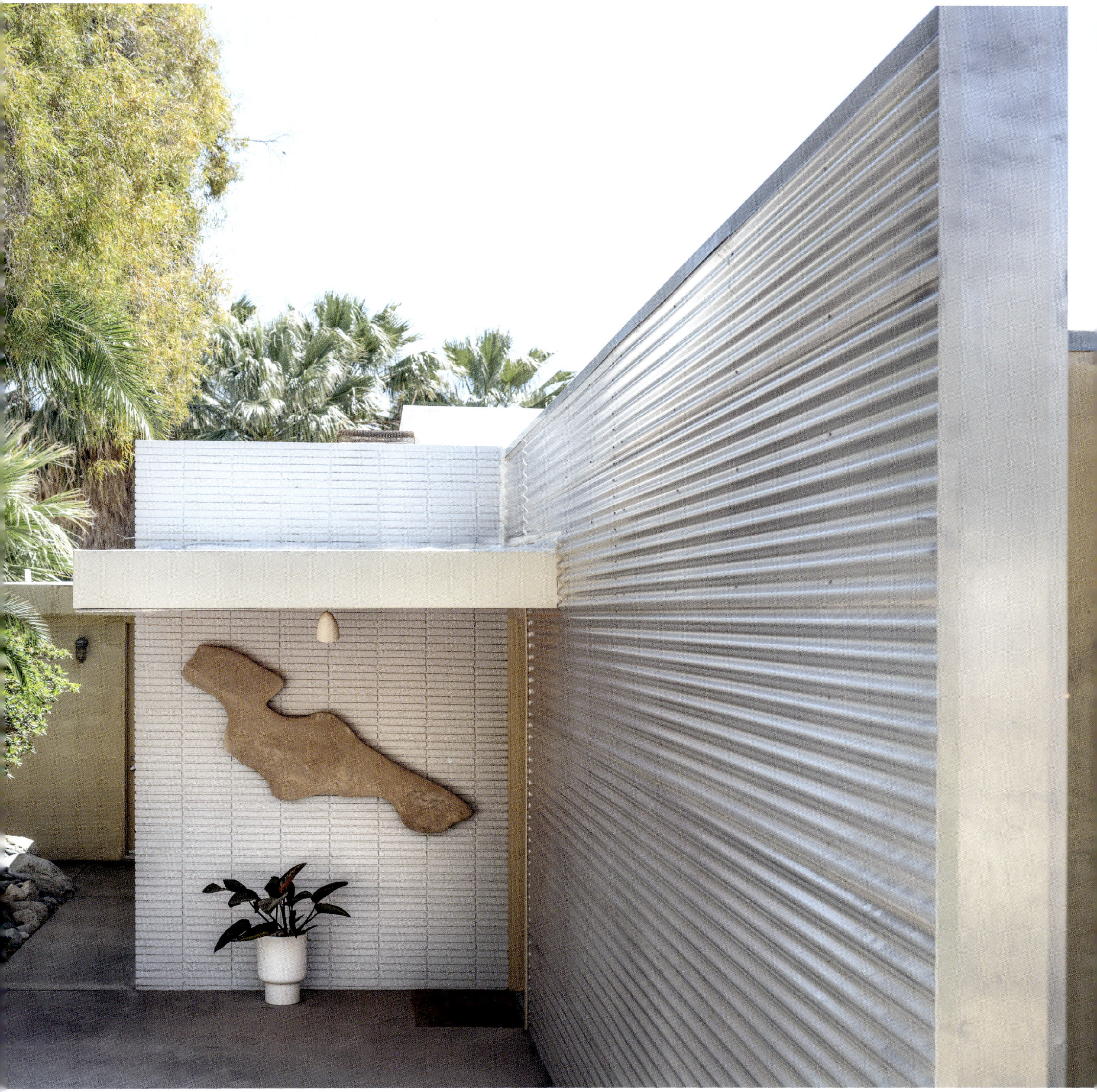

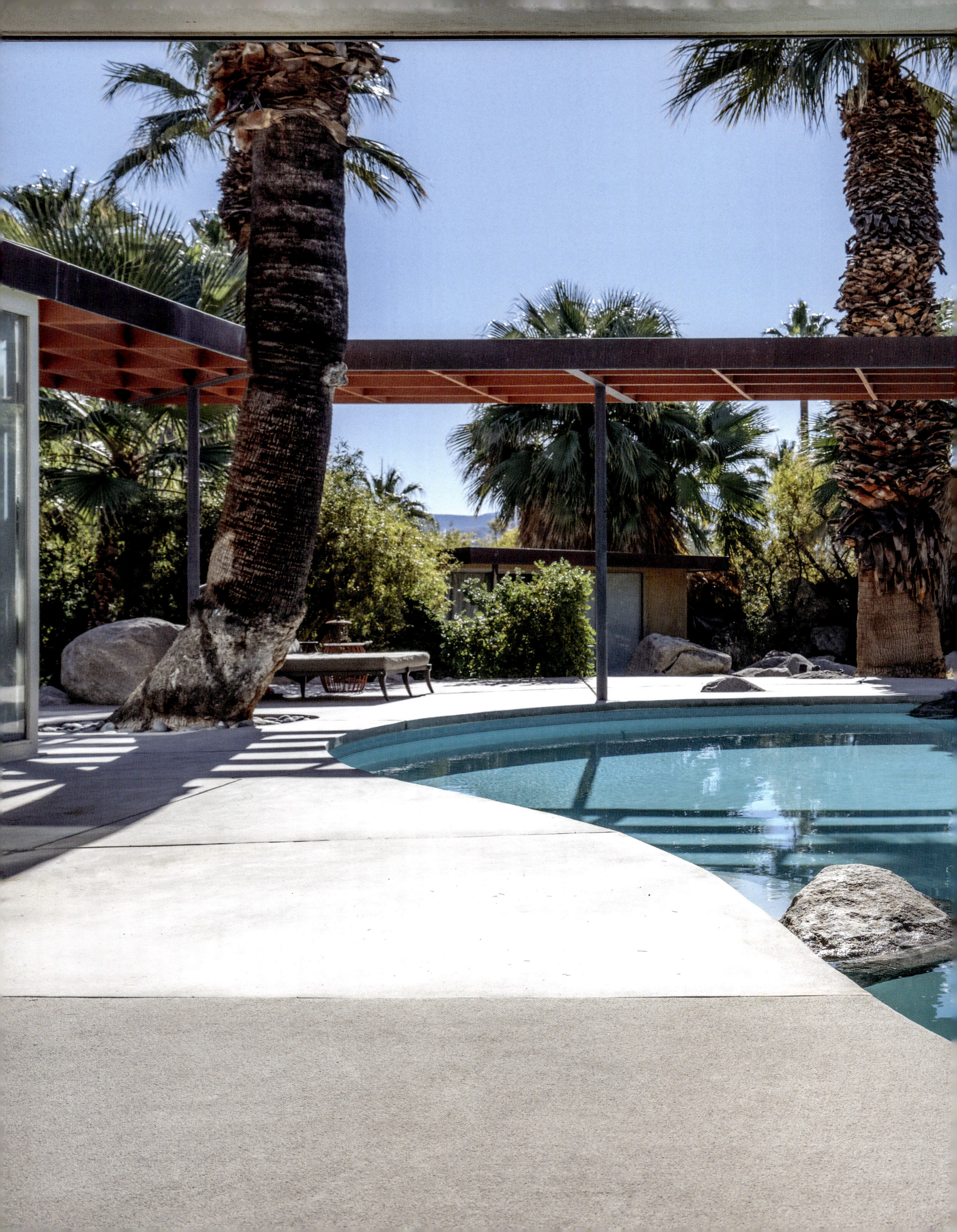

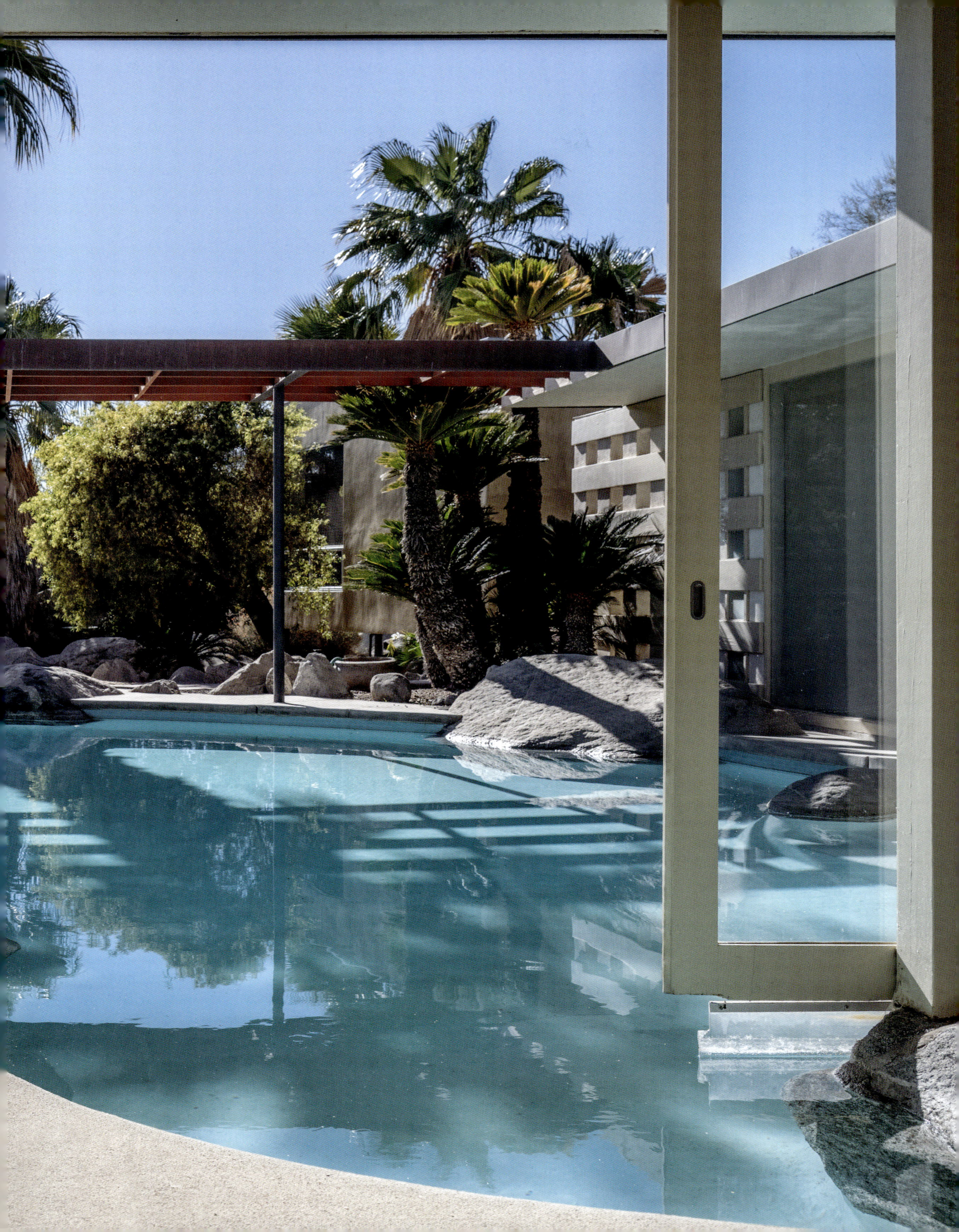

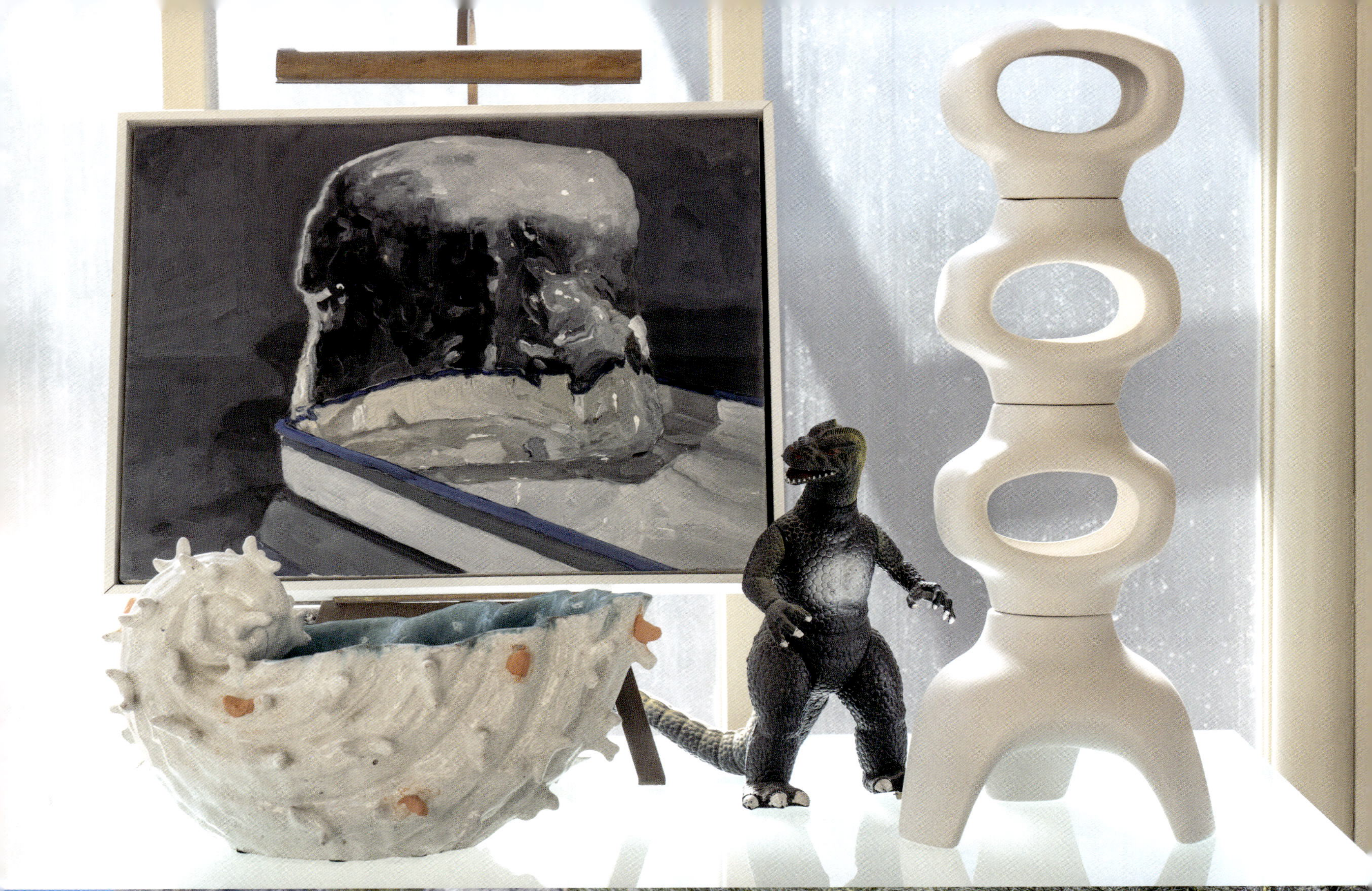
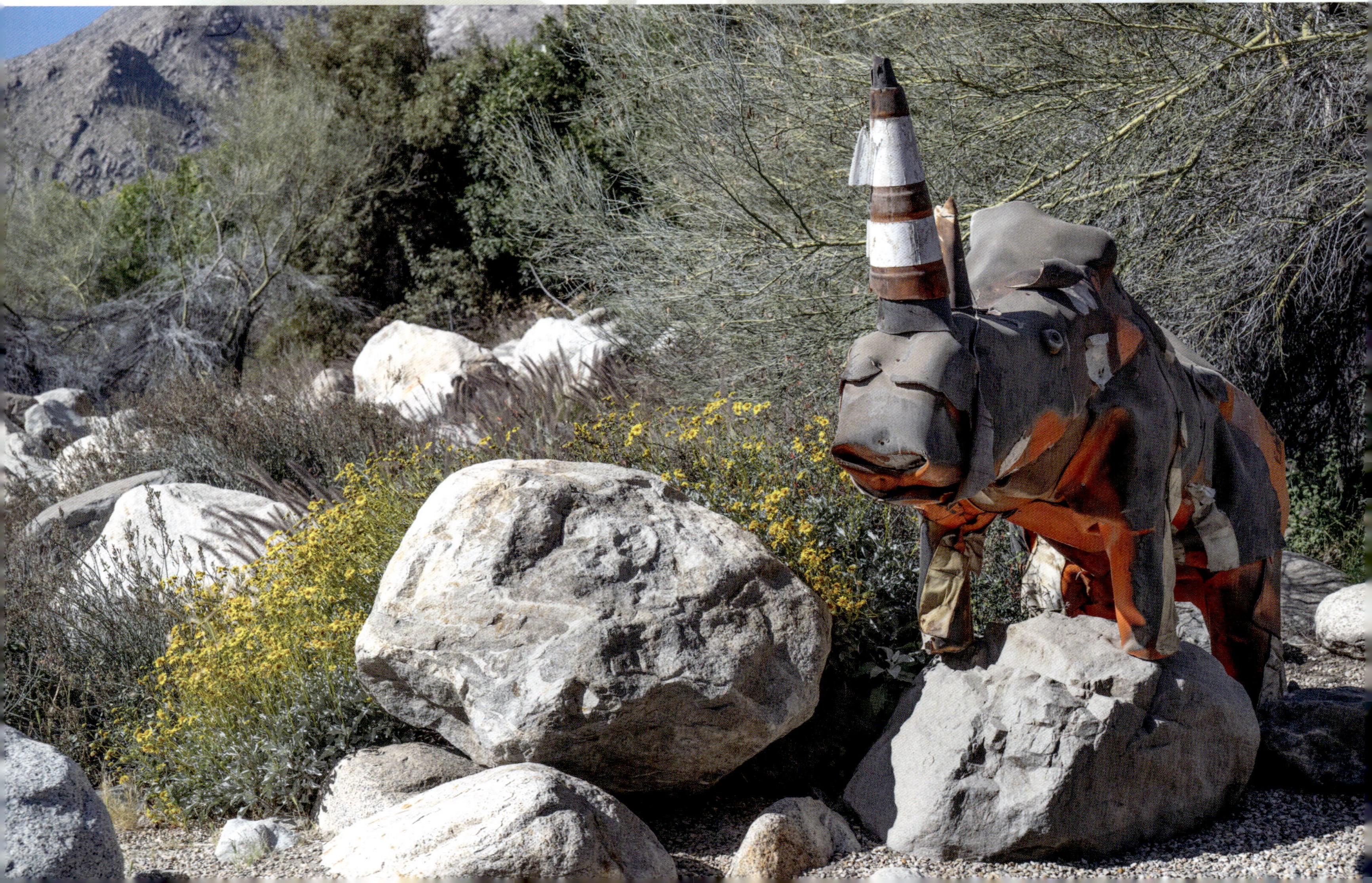

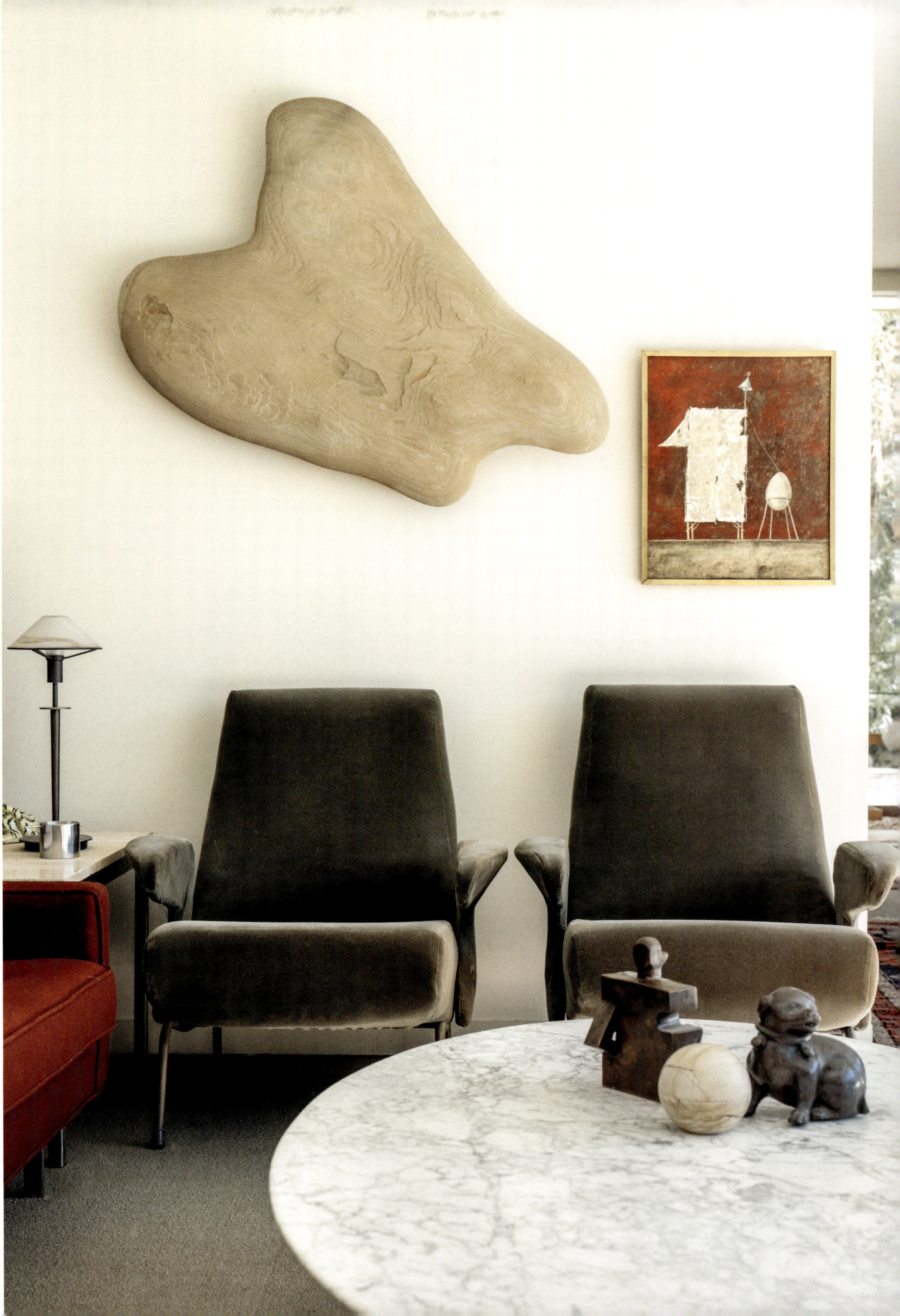

56

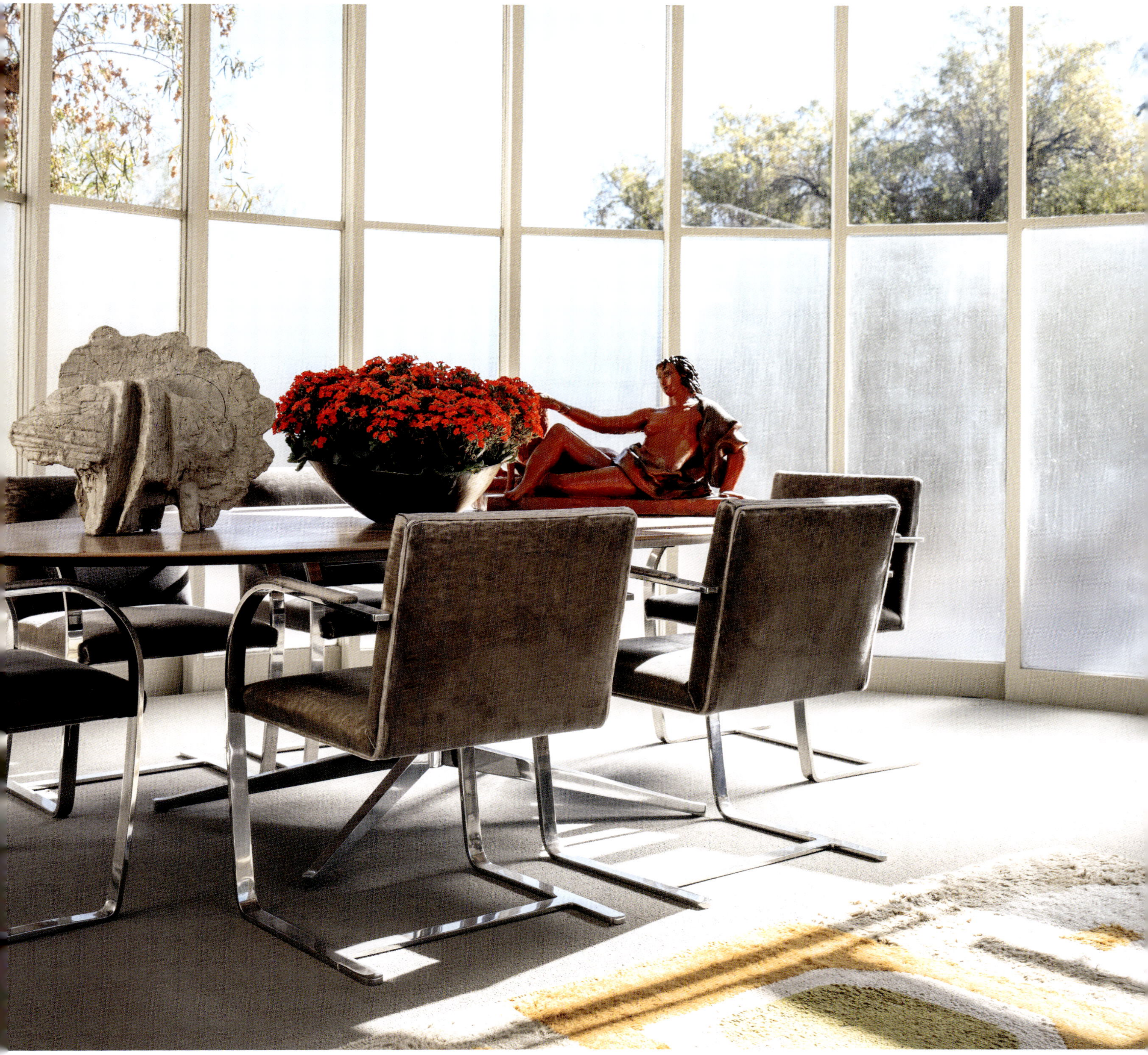

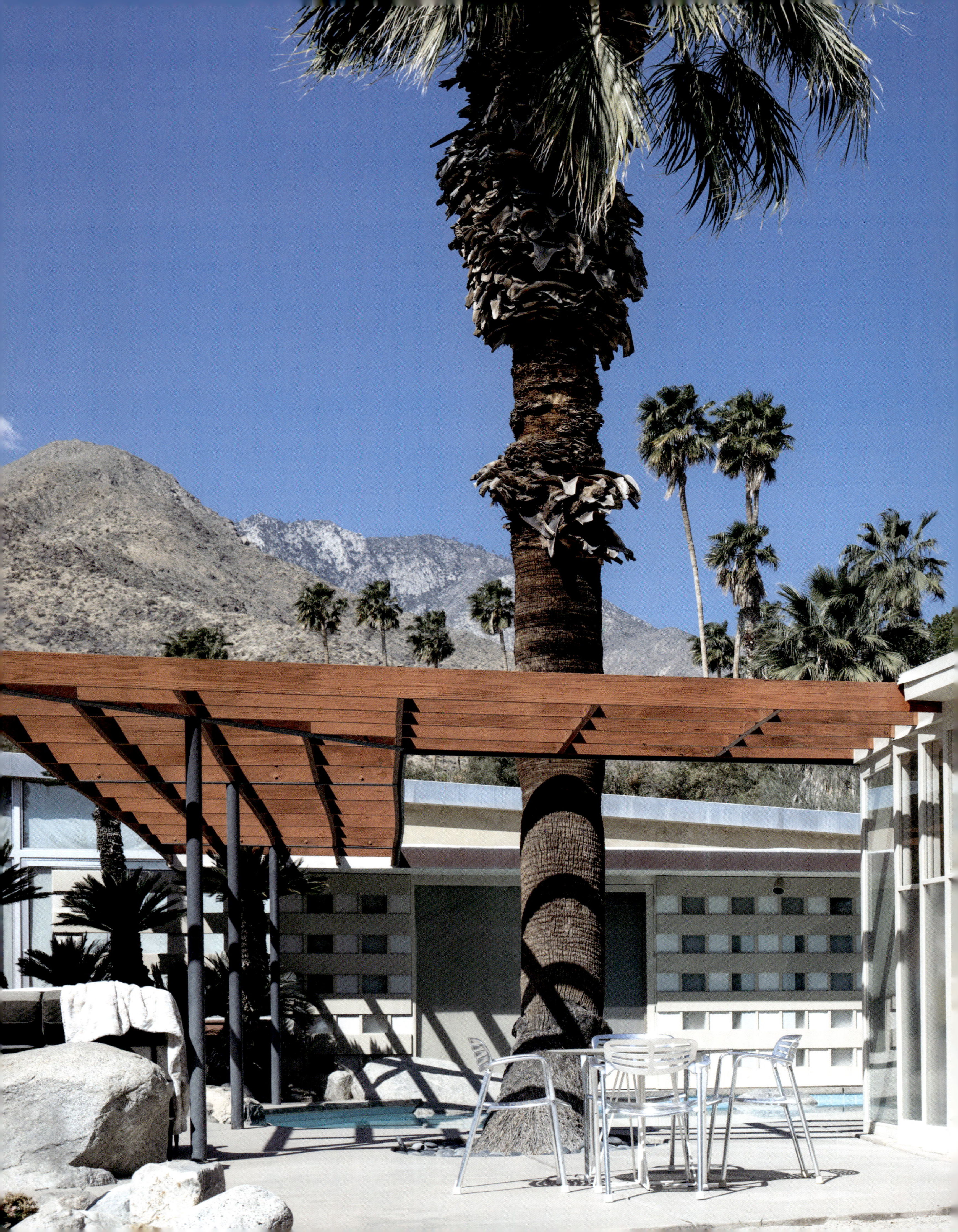

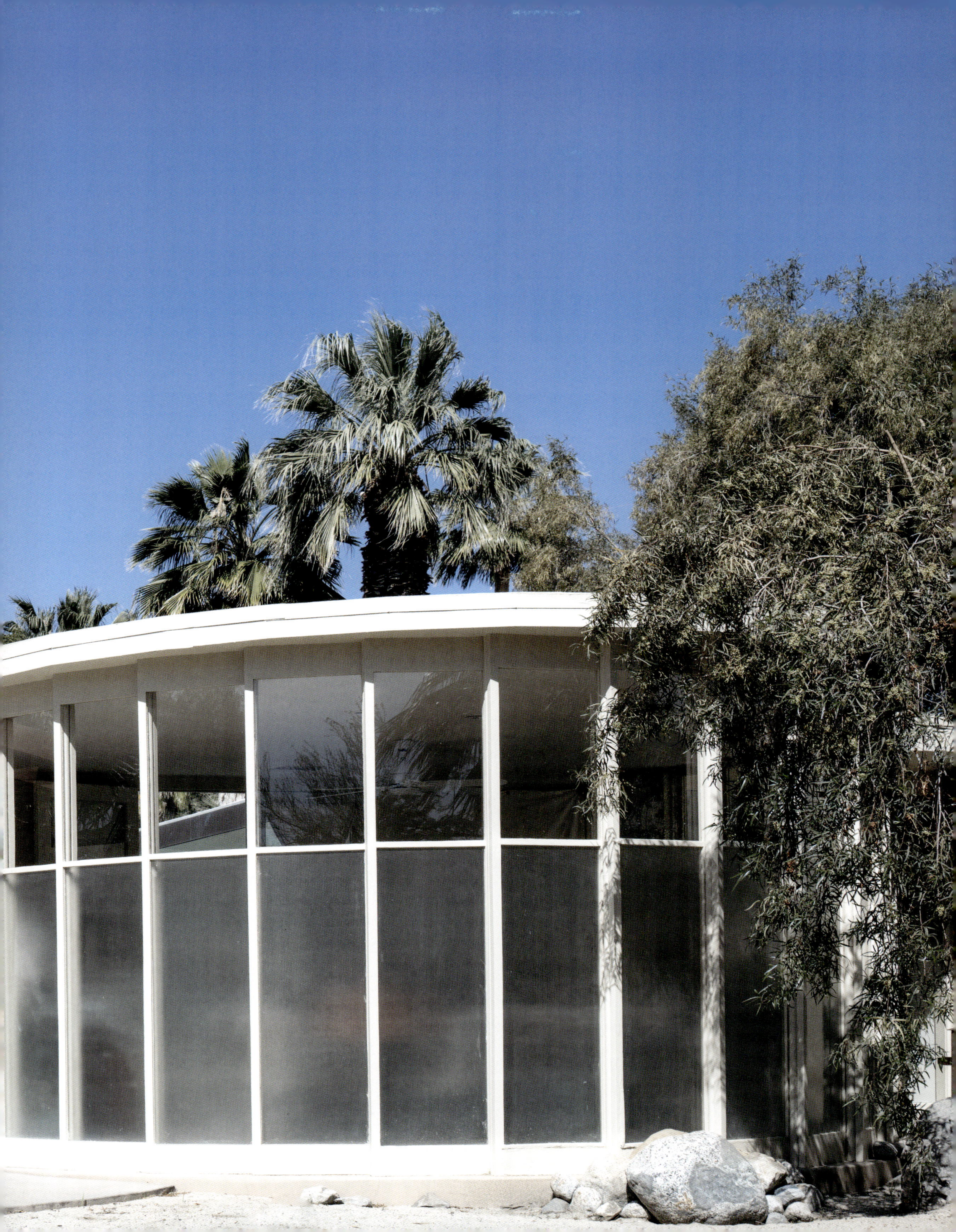

TWIN PALMS

THE NEW YORK FASHION DESIGNER Helene Verin was visiting her son in Los Angeles during the Covid pandemic when a friend offered them the keys to his house in Palm Springs. Verin had never been to the desert before and had only heard one thing about it: In 1959, an architect named Donald Wexler had built a place in Twin Palms called Royal Hawaiian Estates for his mother and her friends, who as Jews were excluded from other neighborhoods in the area. After settling into their borrowed house, Verin and her son decided to go take a look at Wexler's tiki-themed development. "There happened to be a For Sale sign in front," she fondly recalls.

None of her friends believed that Verin could leave New York. "I've been into fashion, design, and art my whole life, and everyone said I'd come running back. But I very easily got into the art world here, which is incredibly vibrant." In her sunny apartment, art and furniture that Verin has acquired since she moved to Palm Springs mingle with personal trophies from New York. In the living room a 1979 portrait of her by Andy Warhol, a friend, hangs above a stuffed lobster-covered bench by Oscar Velasquez. A giant pair of woven wool "lungs" by local artist Adriana Lopez-Ospina separates the living and dining areas. The coffee table is by Yves Klein. Two more portraits of the designer by Philip Pearlstein counterbalance the Warhol. Verin explains: "Andy made everyone beautiful, and Philip made them ugly."

Other ephemera from her New York years include a powder compact in the shape of a telephone dial by Salvador Dalí for Elsa Schiaparelli and a pair of Studio 54 VIP tickets. Also an "I ♥ New York" coffee mug that the designer altered slightly after relocating to the desert: "I added a *D* after the heart."

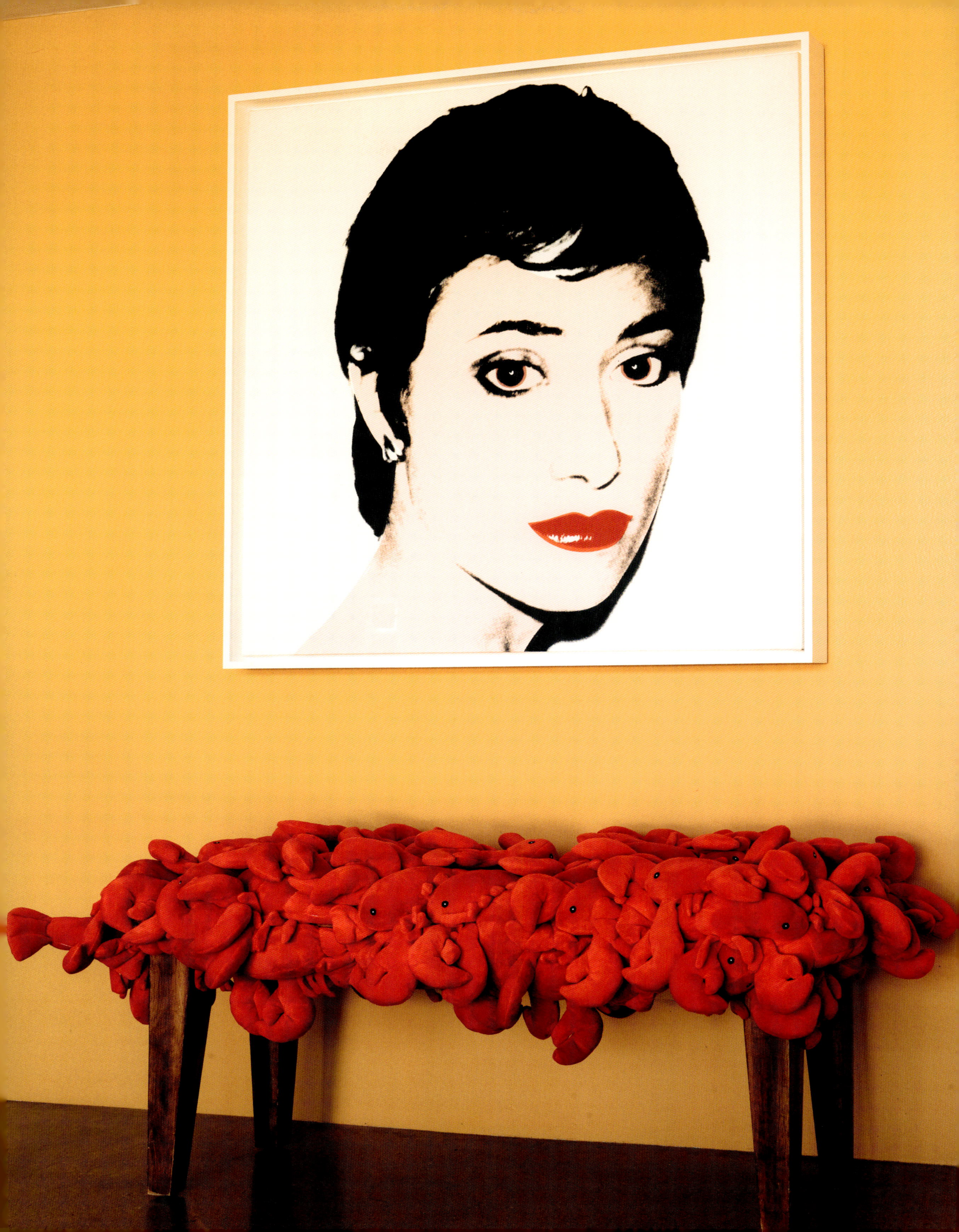

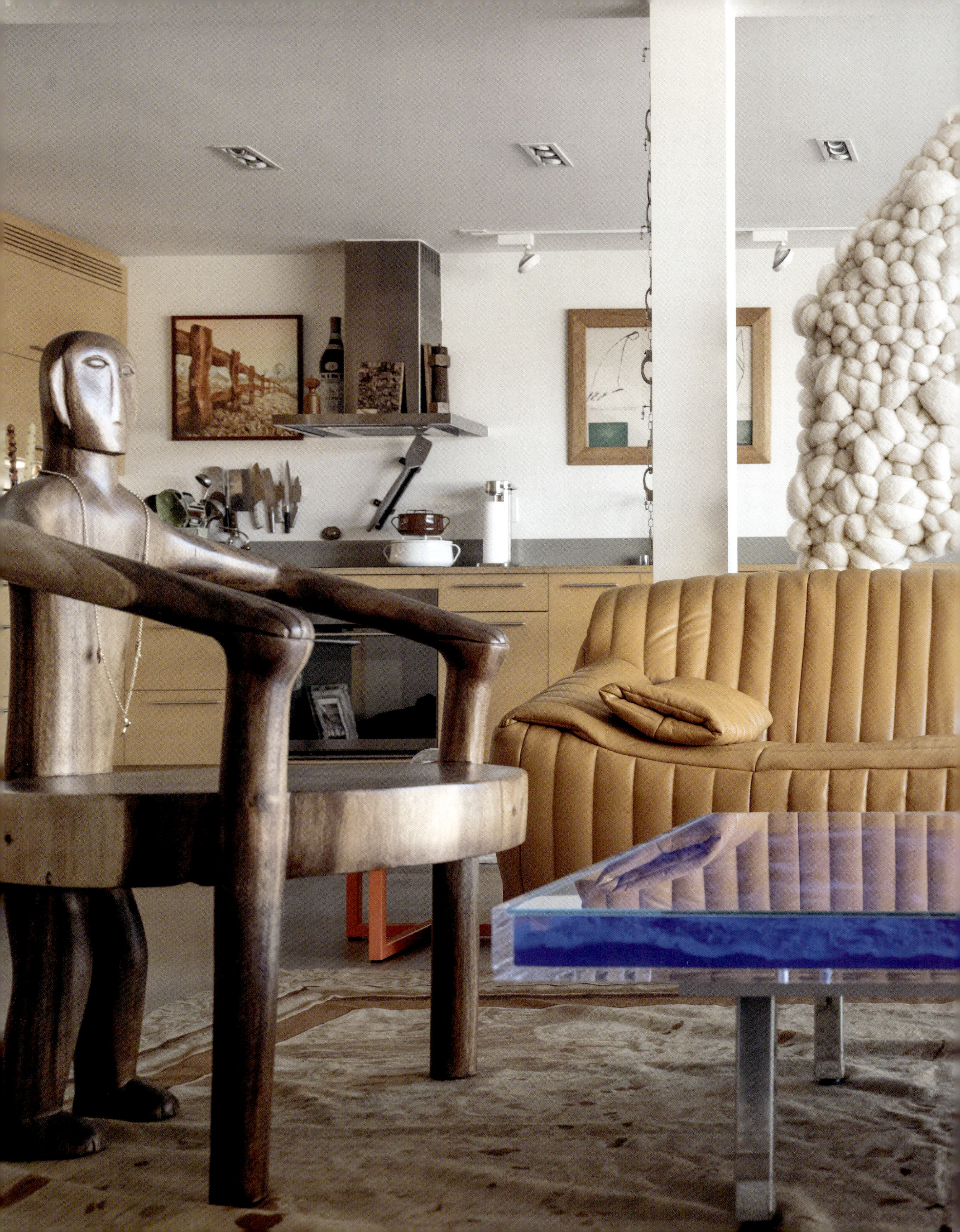

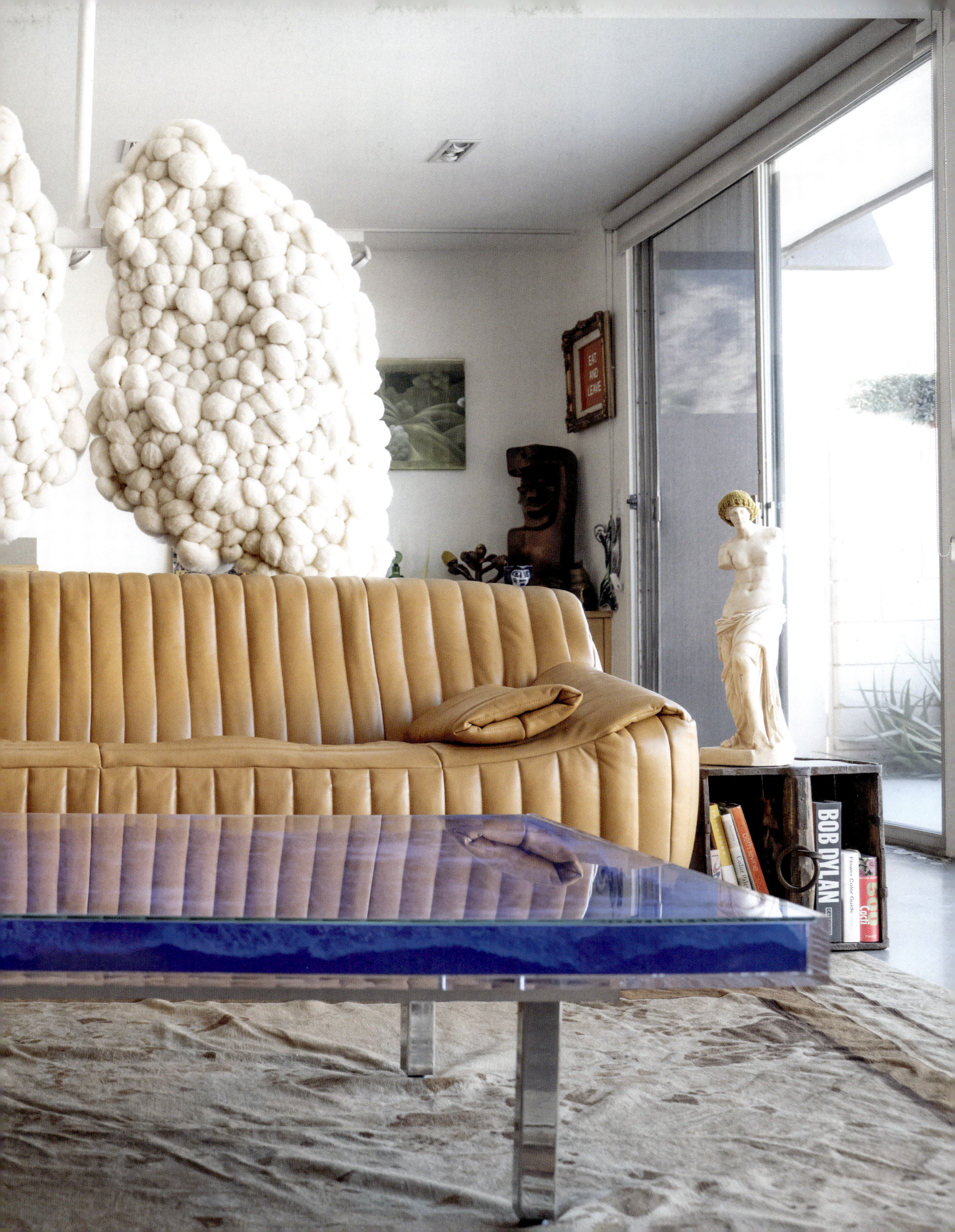
EAT AND LEAVE
BOB DYLAN

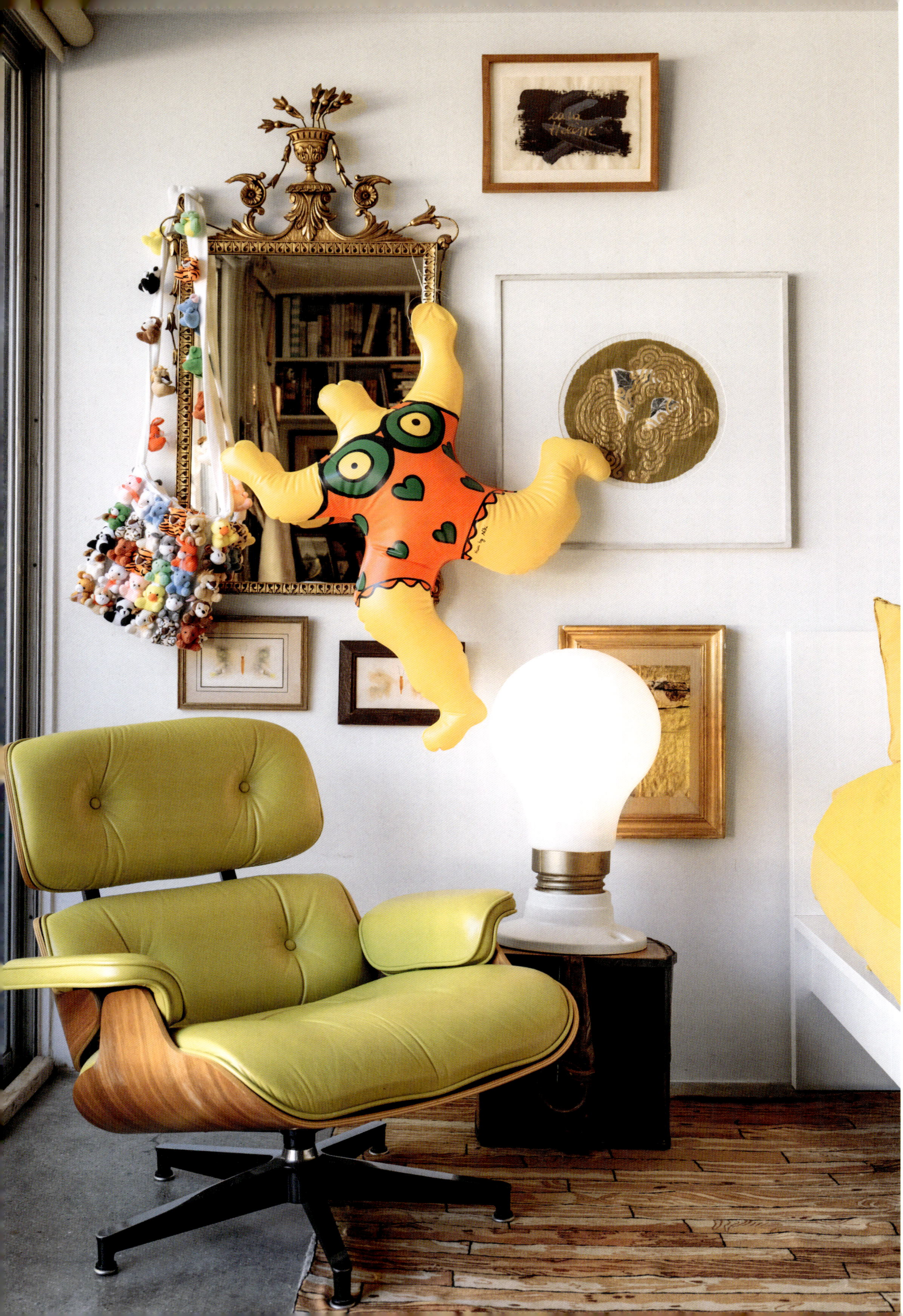

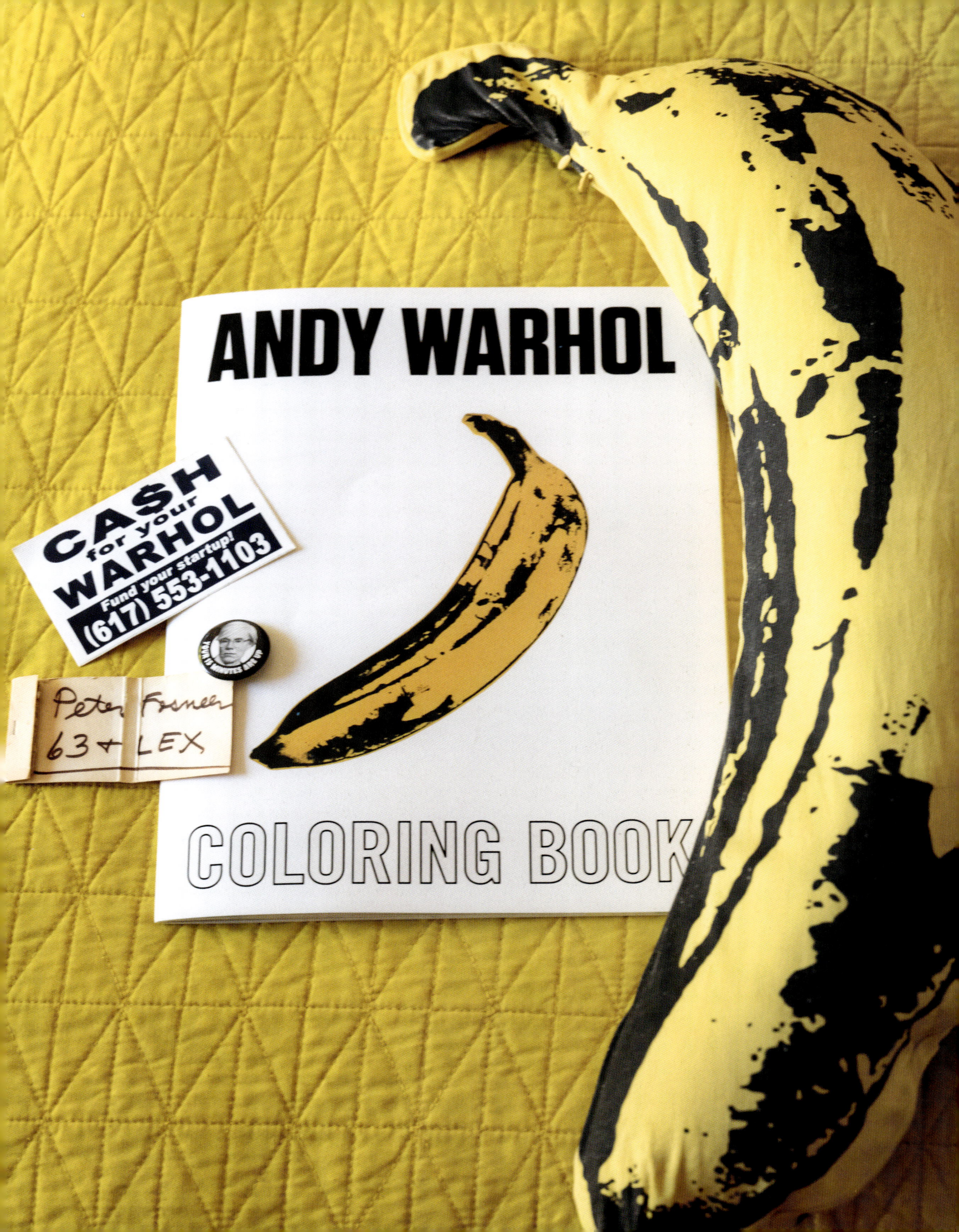

ANDY WARHOL
COLORING BOOK

CA$H for your WARHOL
Fund your startup!
(617) 553-1103

Peter Fraser
63 + LEX

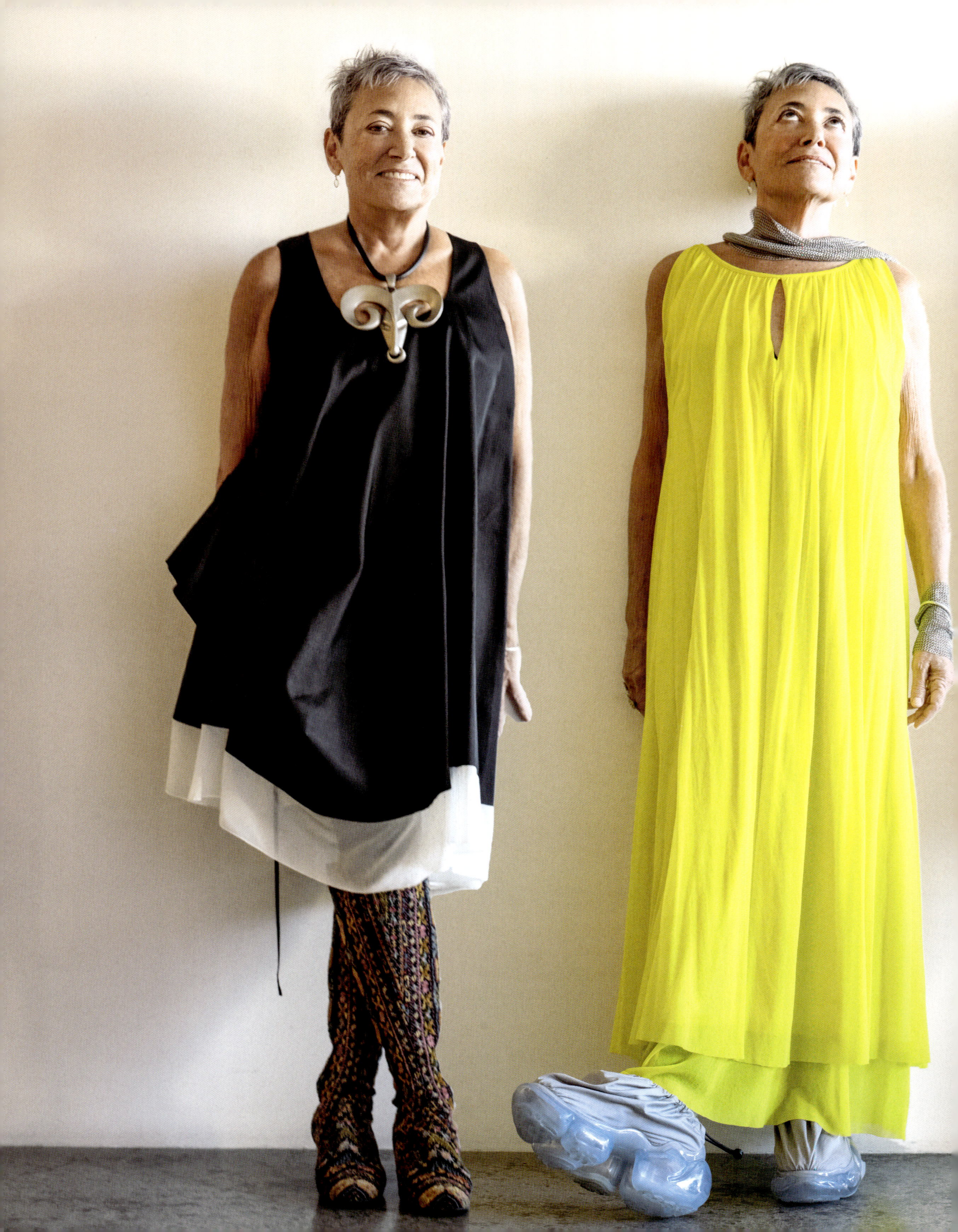

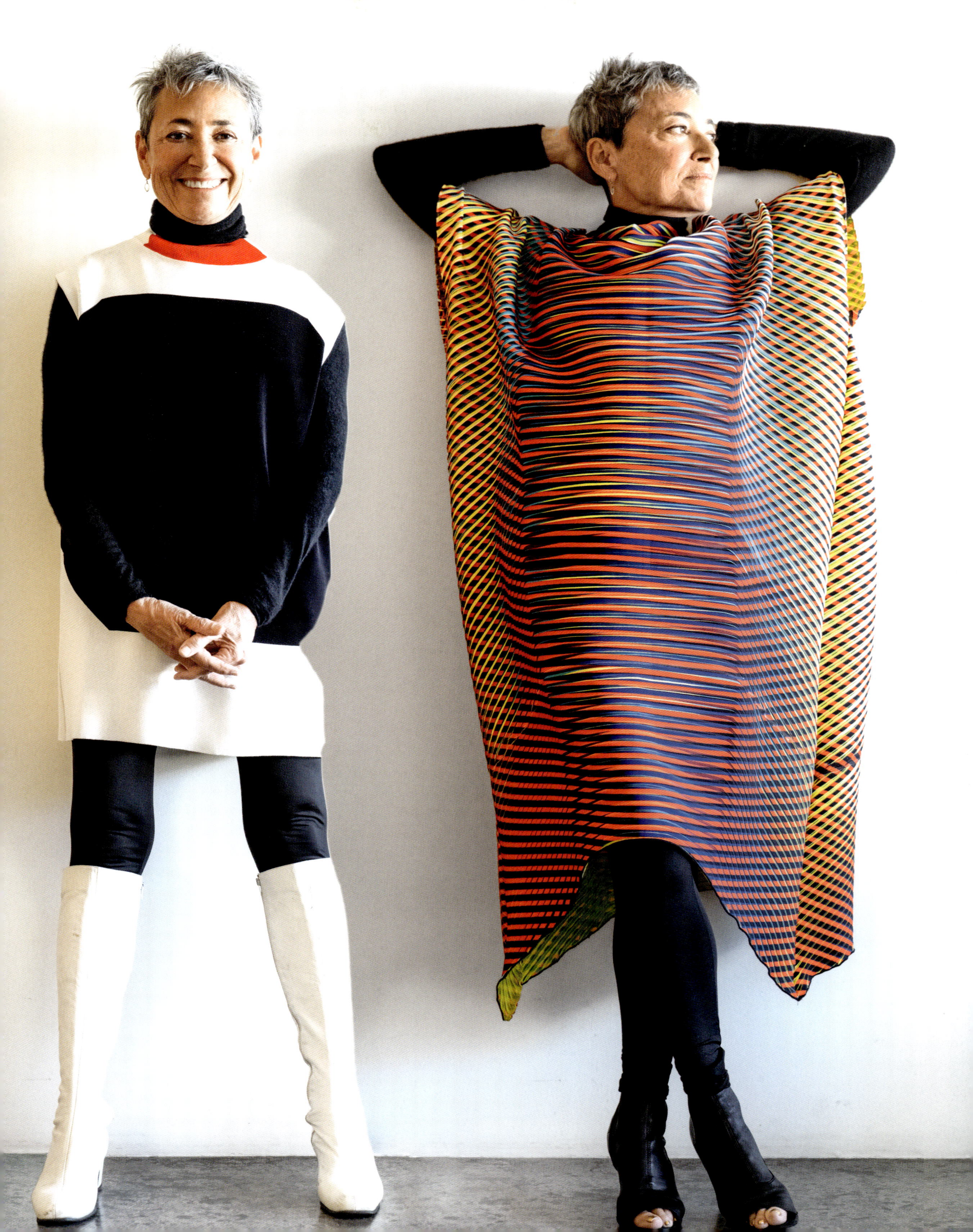

VIKTOR&ROLF for shu uemura

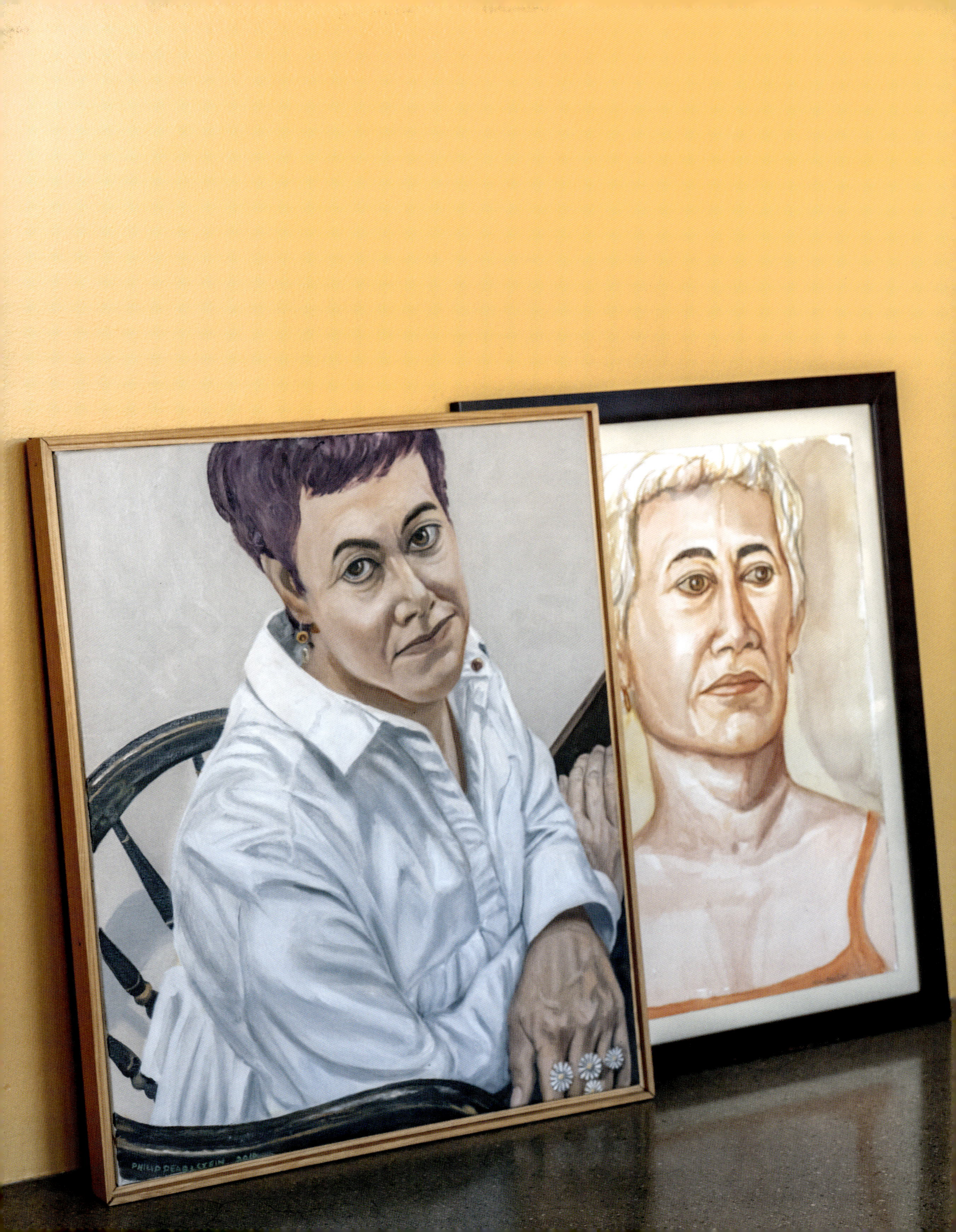
PHILIP PEARLSTEIN

MUSEUM WAY

O F ALL THE ARCHITECTS WHO HELPED turn Palm Springs into a modernist mecca, none is more indelibly associated with the city than Albert Frey. Swiss-born Frey codesigned the first modern structure in Palm Springs, the Kocher-Samson Building, in 1934, and after moving to the desert five years later spent the rest of his long life producing local landmarks ranging from the Palm Springs Visitors Center to his own home, Frey House II.

After spending a year in the Paris atelier of International Style pioneer Le Corbusier, Frey moved to New York in 1928, where he began working with the American architect A. Lawrence Kocher. In 1931 the pair were commissioned to design a small, cost-efficient residence with prefabricated materials donated by manufacturers. Constructed in ten days, their three-story, 1,200-square-foot Aluminaire House was an all-metal, nearly cubic structure with wide window banks, a third-floor terrace, and airy, sculptural interiors—a prototype for modern American living that was as beautiful as it was efficient. The following year the Museum of Modern Art featured the house in an exhibition introducing the International Style to the United States.

After the show the Aluminaire House was dismantled, and it changed hands and locations over the years. In 2020, the Aluminaire House Foundation, formed to preserve the structure and find a permanent site for it, gifted the house to the Palm Springs Art Museum. Four years later it was rebuilt on a parking lot just south of the museum, where visitors can now view it from the outside; ADA and fire-safety regulations prohibit interior access. "Palm Springs is the perfect place for this incredibly important icon," says Adam Lerner, who was the director of the museum during its reconstruction. "Frey was the most prominent architect in Palm Springs, and as a haven for modern architecture, we can now point to where that tradition began."

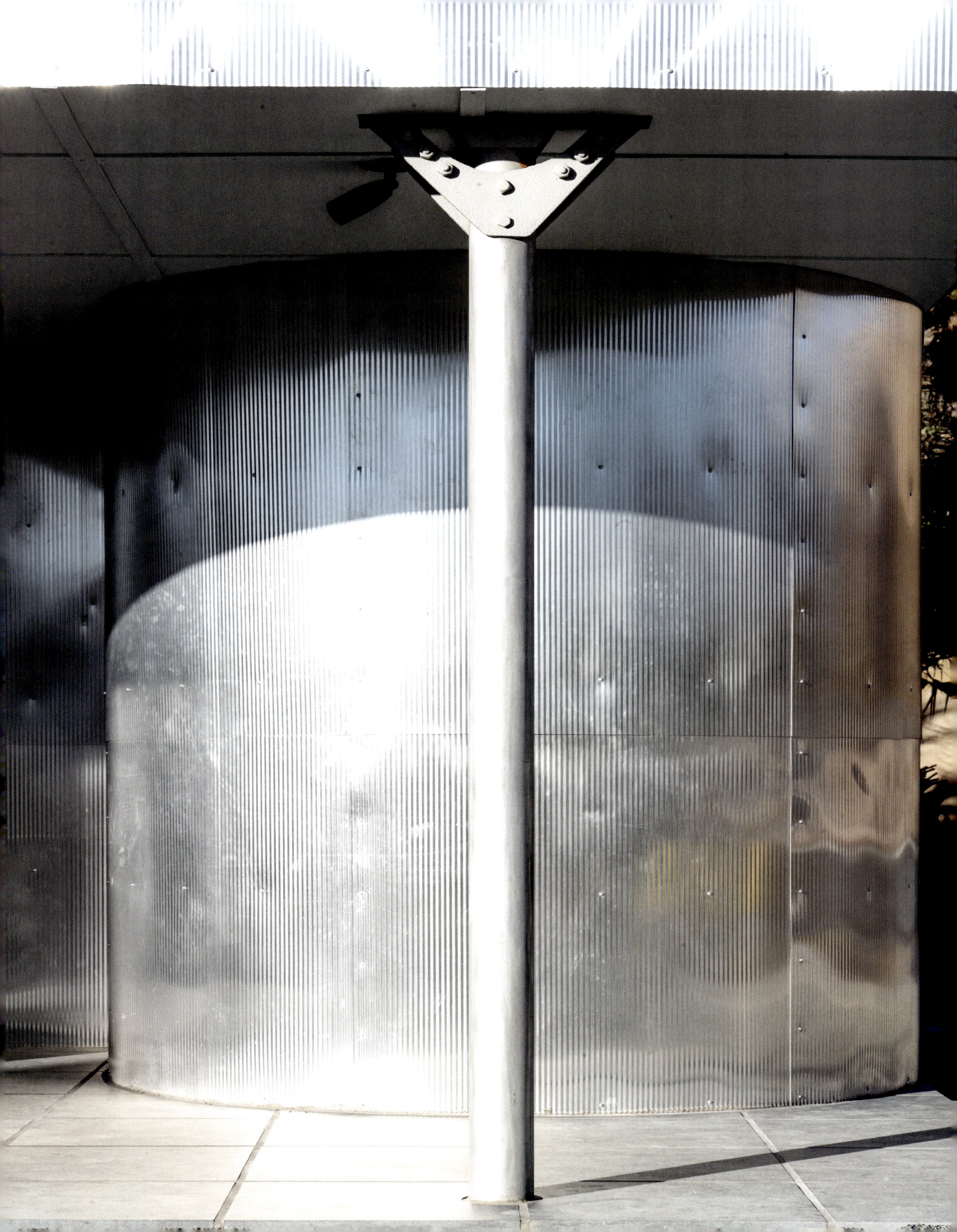

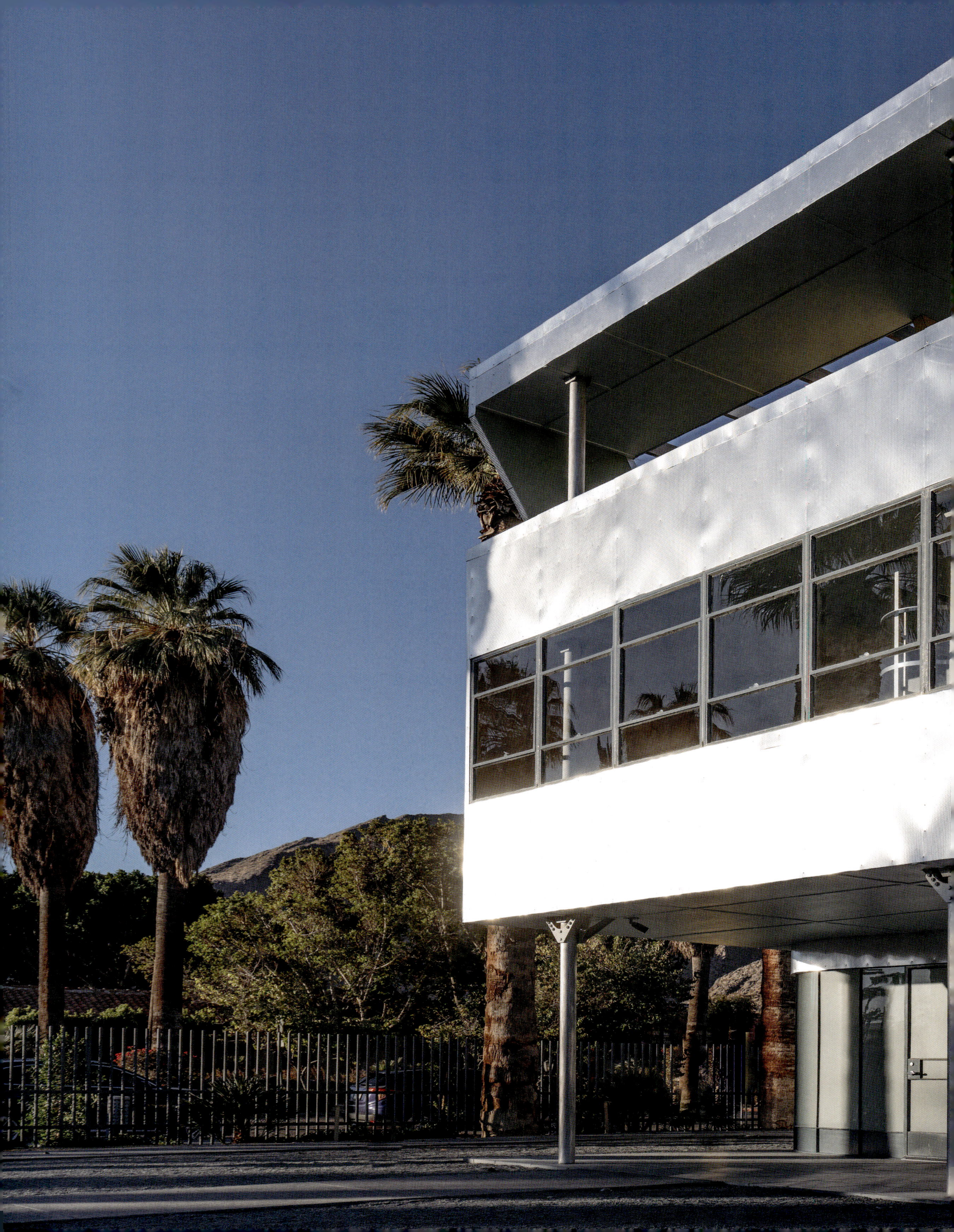

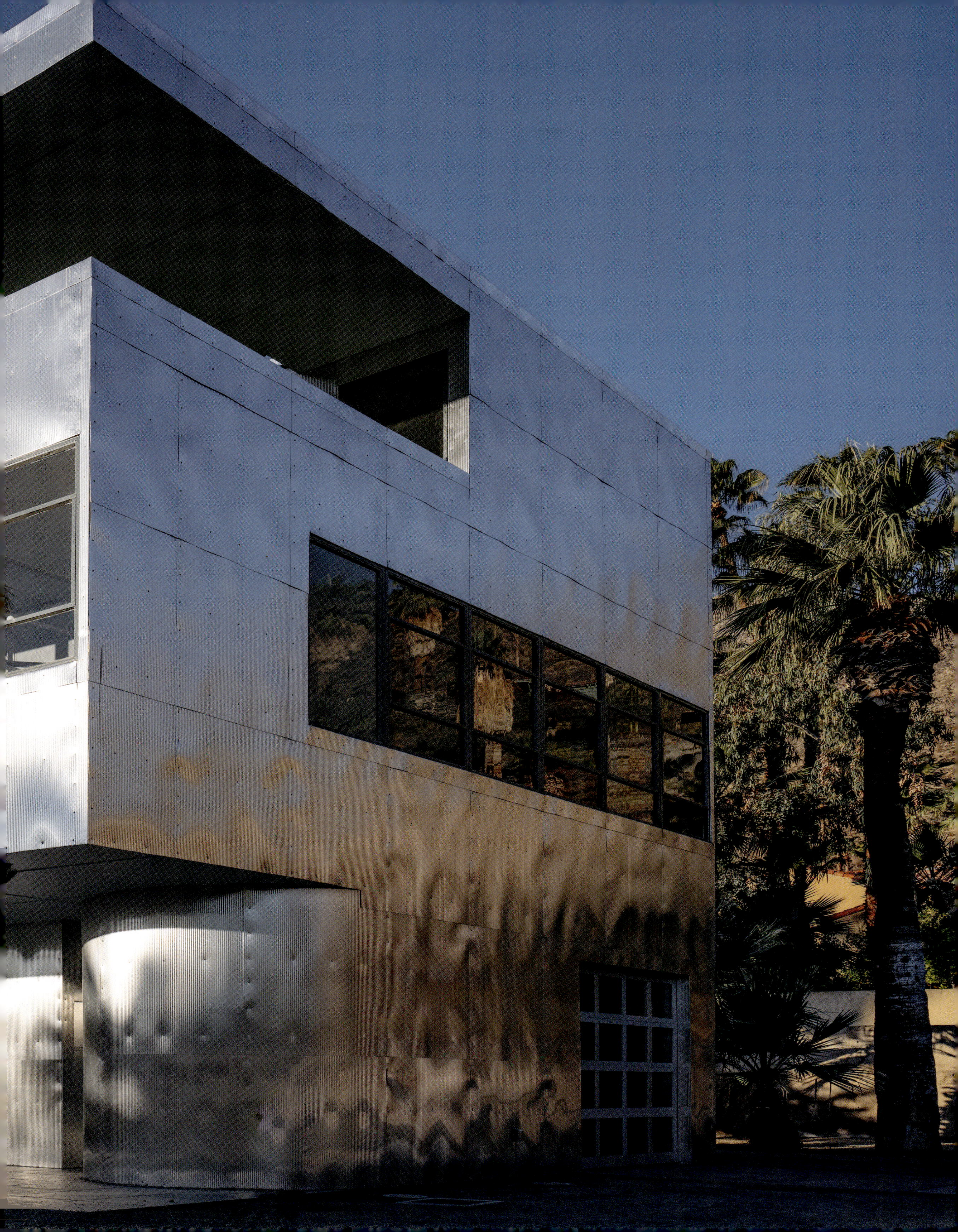

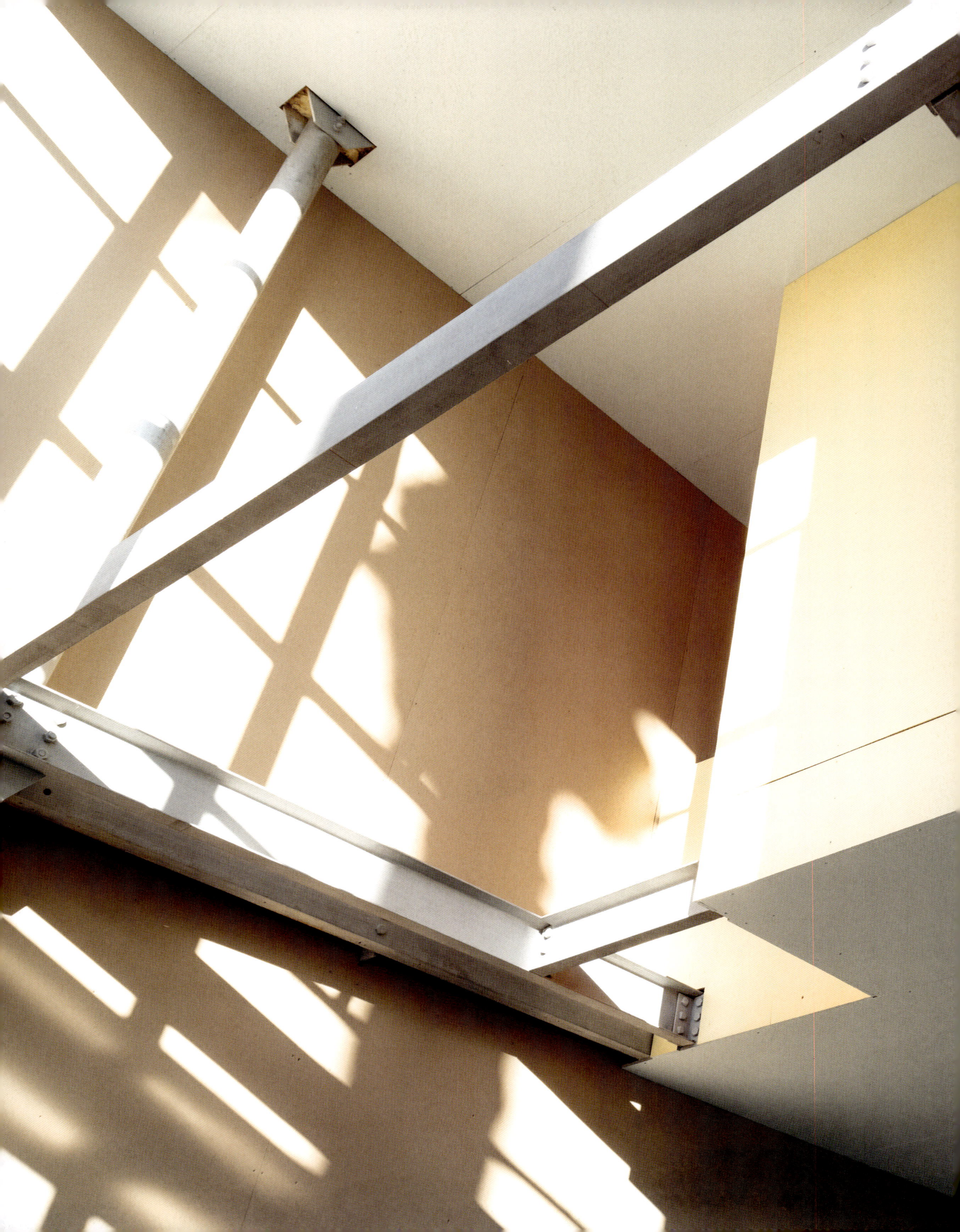

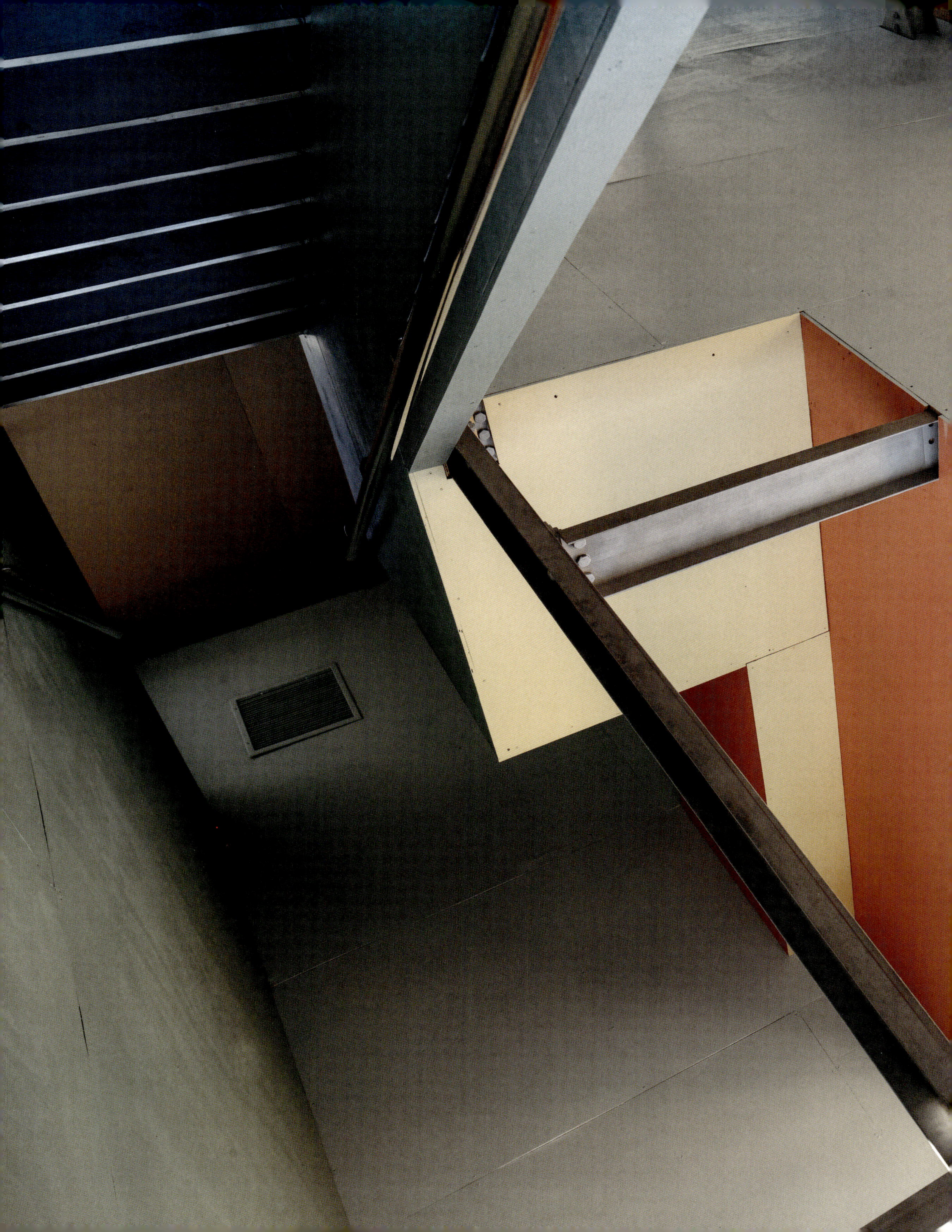

76

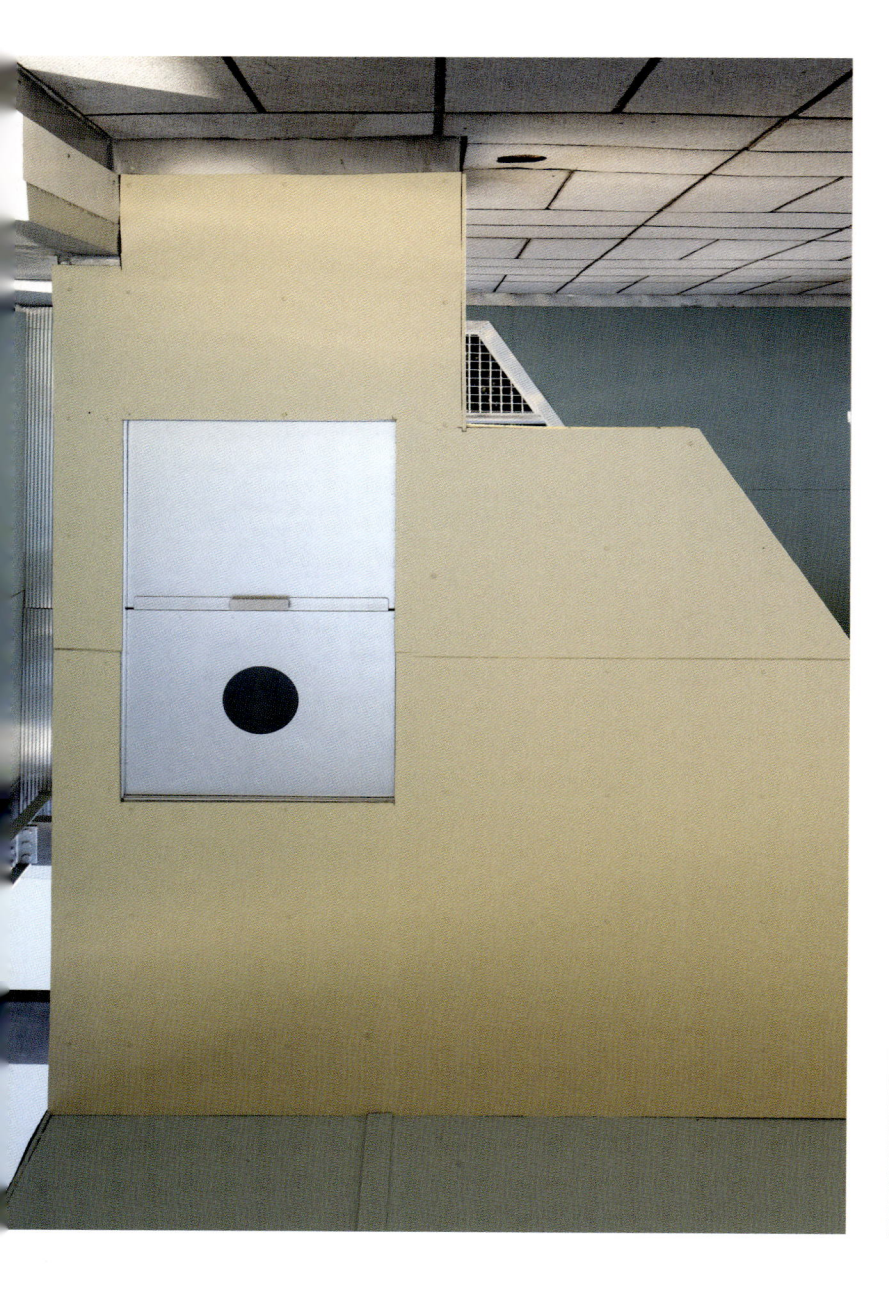

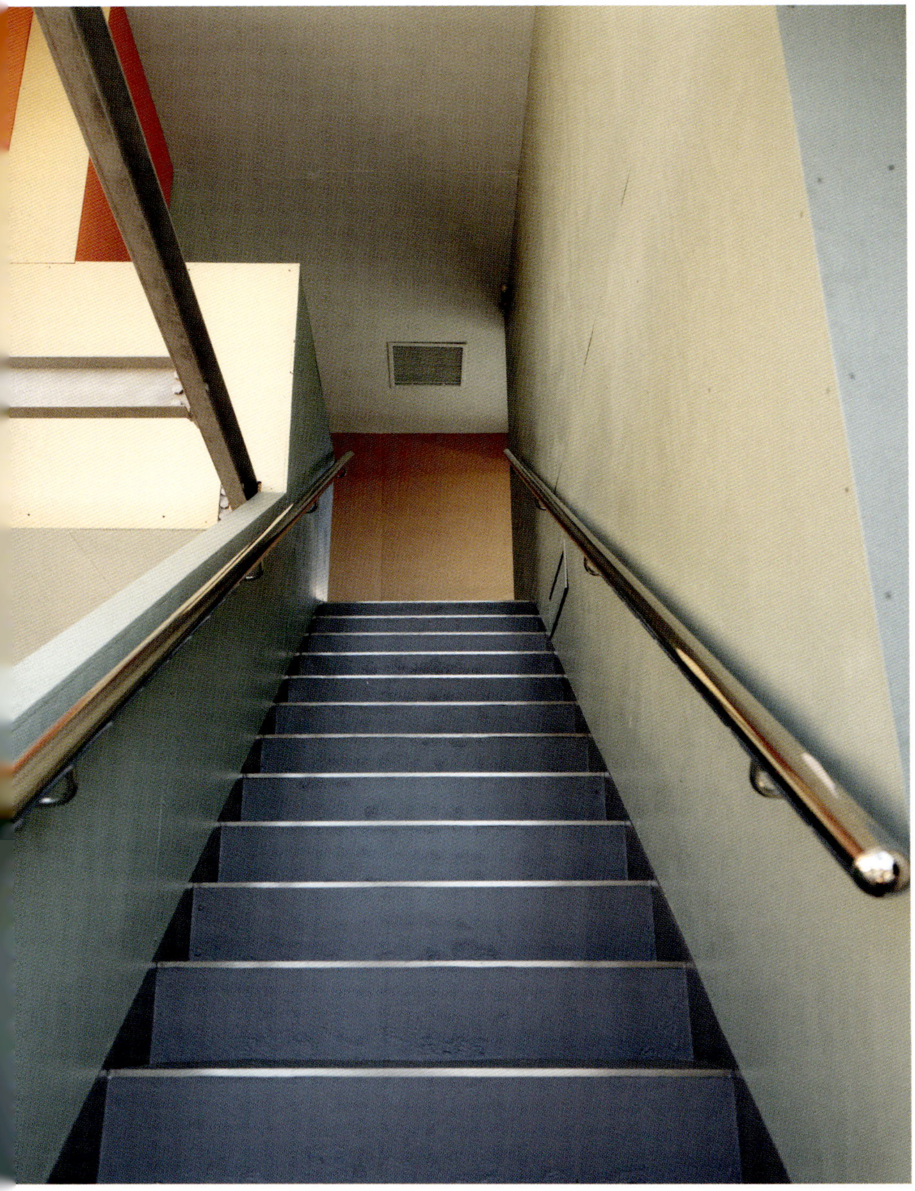

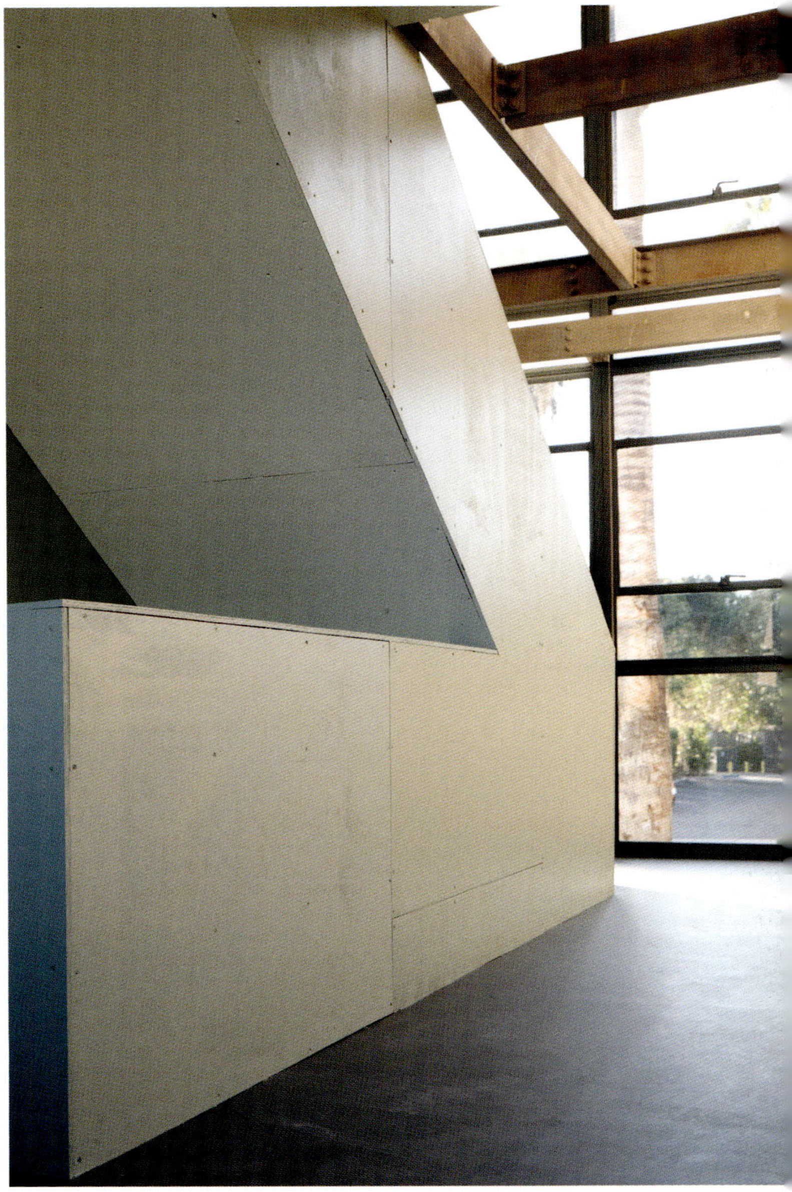

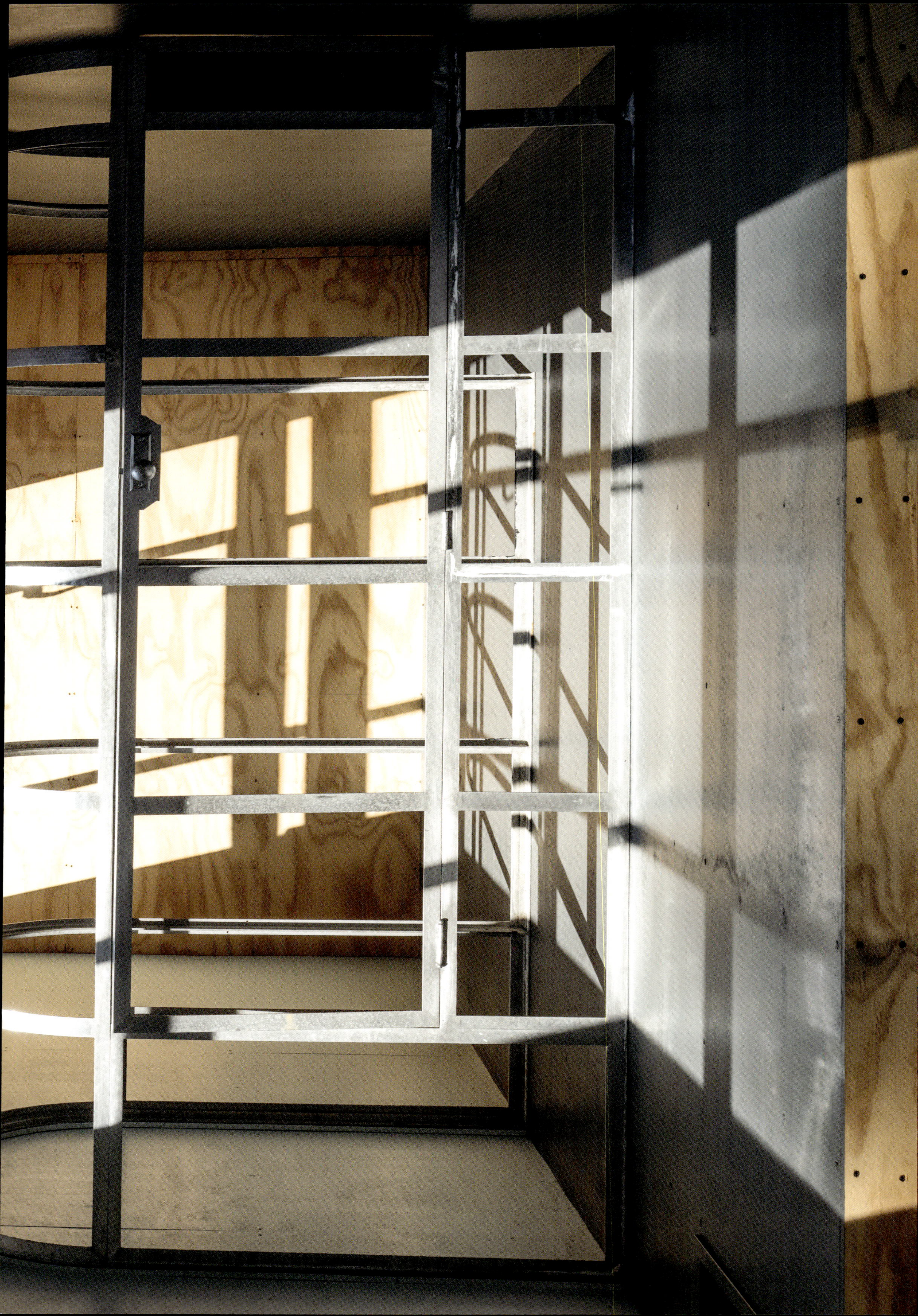

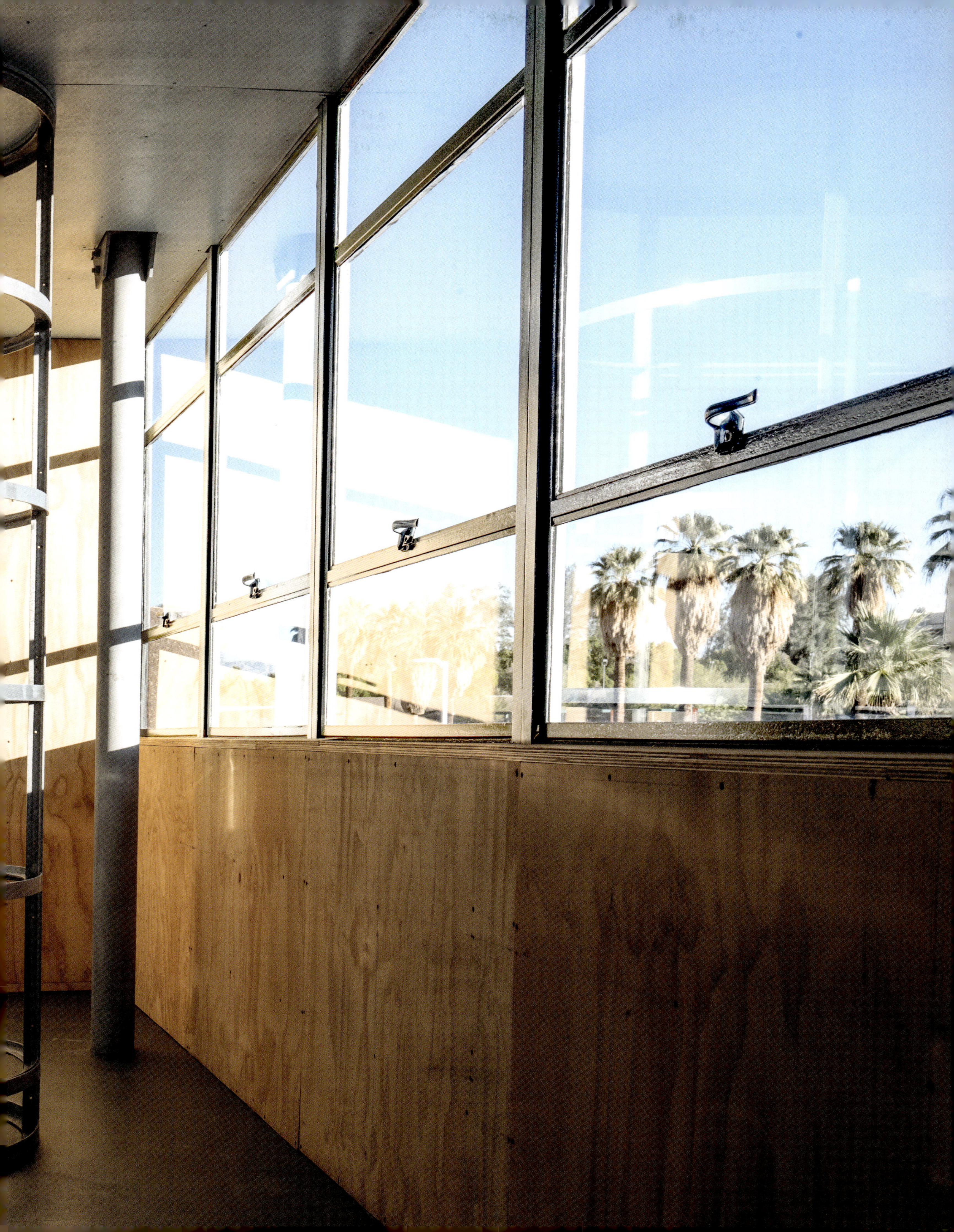

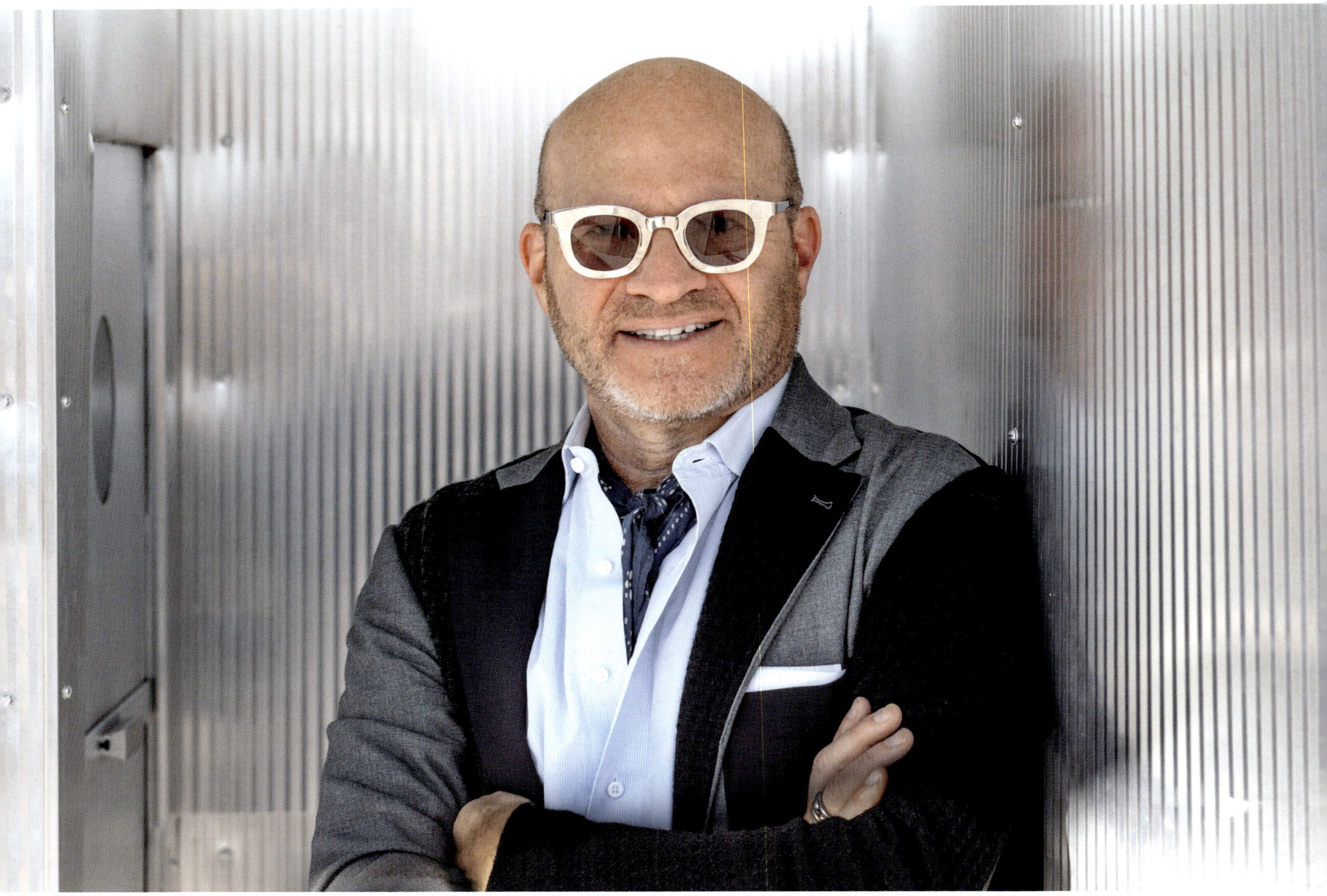

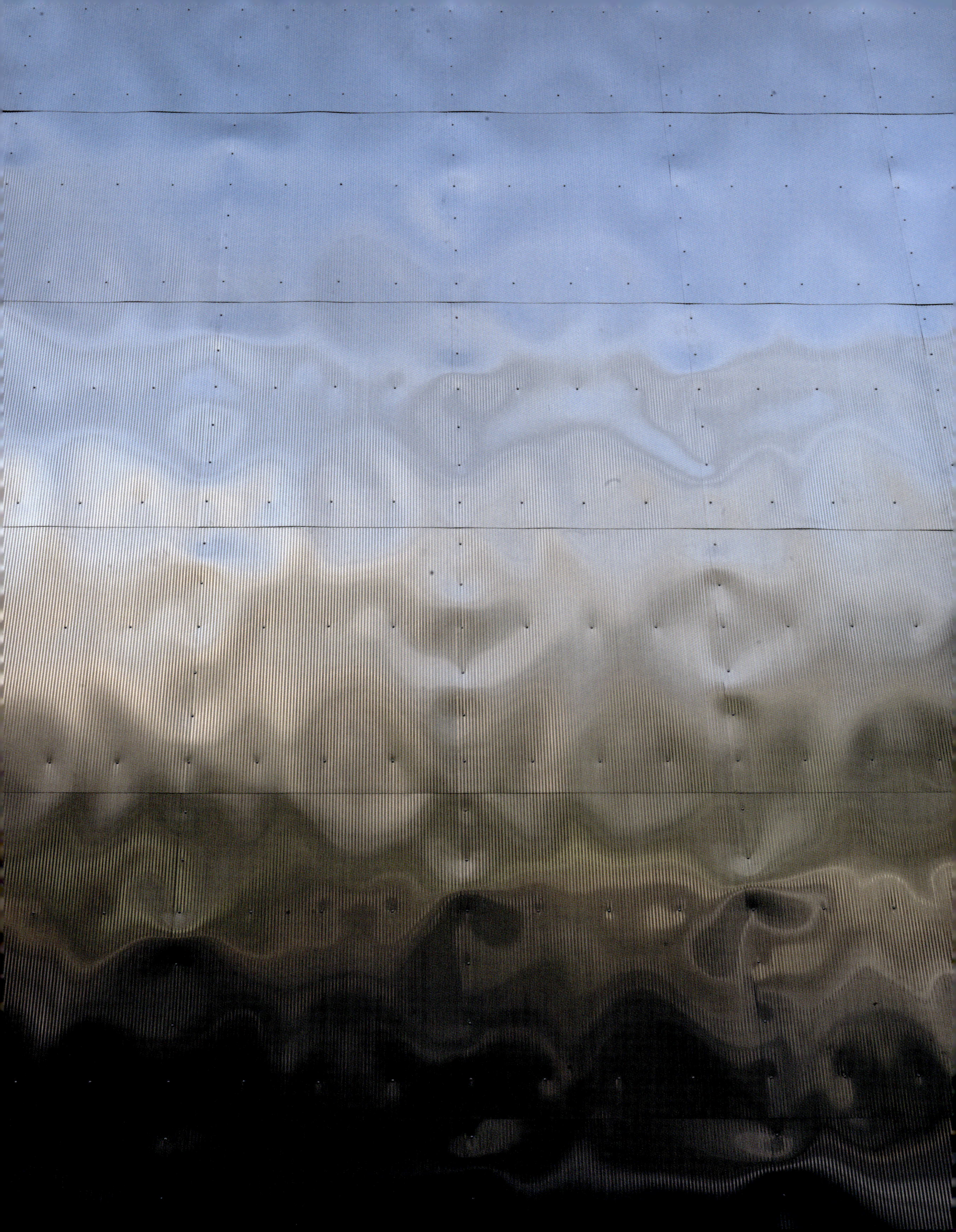

TAMARISK I

PEOPLE STILL JOIN THE TAMARISK Country Club for its eighteen-hole golf course, but today the club is as popular among architecture buffs as golf fanatics, the former lured by the many modernist gems scattered around the emerald-green fairways. In 2017 Steven Harris, himself a celebrated architect, and his husband, interior designer and painter Lucien Rees Roberts, restored one of the first homes built on the golf course, Donald Wexler's 1957 Charney House. Realizing they were spending more time there than they'd anticipated—they have several residences—the couple recently built a second, roomier house on the lot across the street.

"Knowing that it would be a bit larger to accommodate a bigger garage for my cars and a better studio for Lucien, we effectively had to build a main house for which the Wexler would be plausible as a guesthouse," says Harris. In other words: the new place echoes the low profile and the rigorous proportions of the old one, but it's clearly the main event. Outside, a 110-foot-long wall sculpture by Mig Perkins offers a dramatic welcome. The house's transparent expanses were achieved using panes of glass 10½ feet high and 20 feet wide. Interior walls are clad in jacaranda wood harvested in Brazil in the 1960s. Rees Roberts furnished the rooms with custom pieces and artwork collected over the years—paintings by his relatives, a sixteenth-century oil attributed to Andrea del Sarto, a tapestry designed by Le Corbusier. The couple's bed once belonged to Gio Ponti; it was purchased at auction years ago. Harris explains: "In some cases you buy something you love and then eventually you build someplace to put it. Hopefully we're not buying any more furniture, because we're not building any more houses."

Are they sure?

Rees Roberts: "Yes."

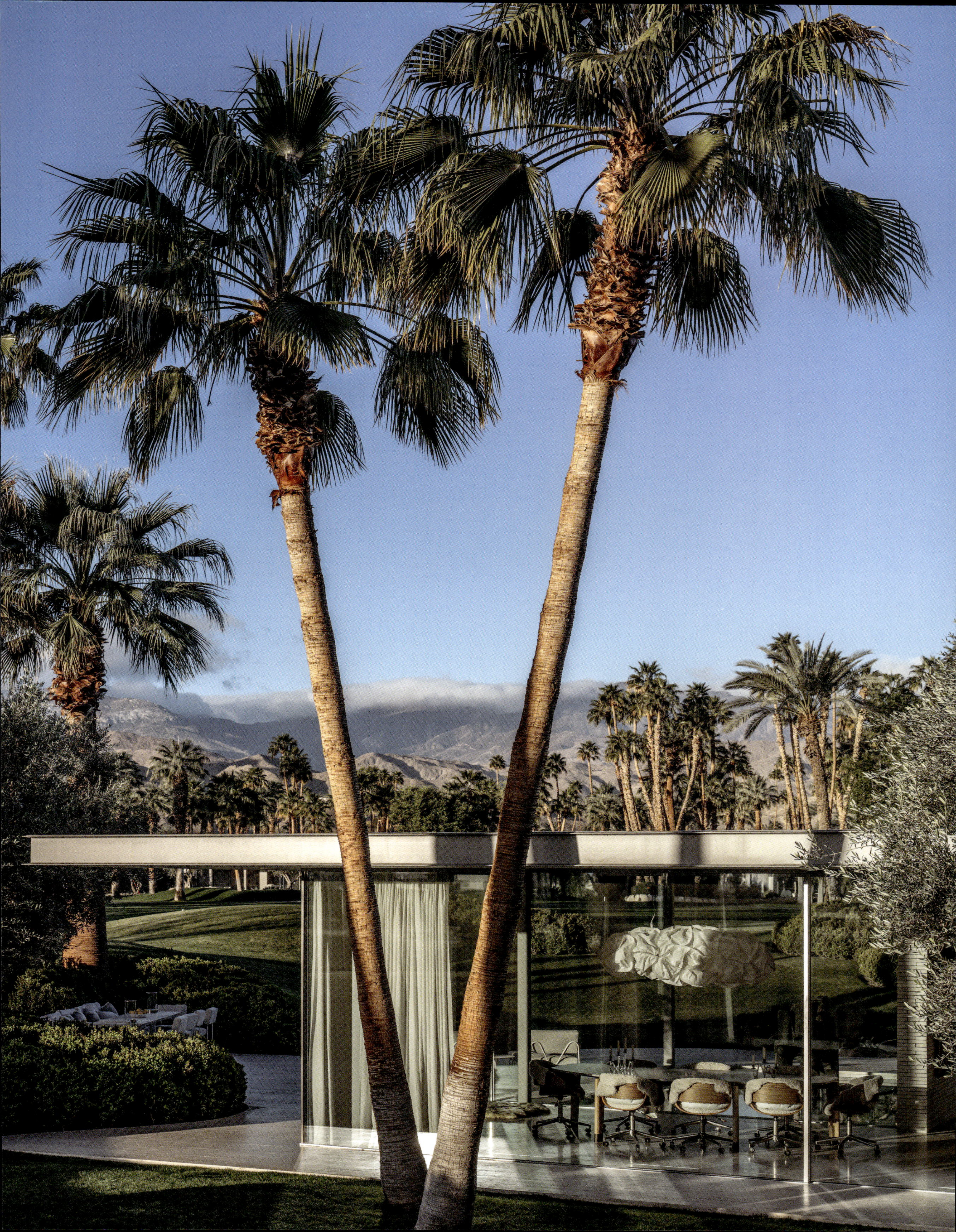

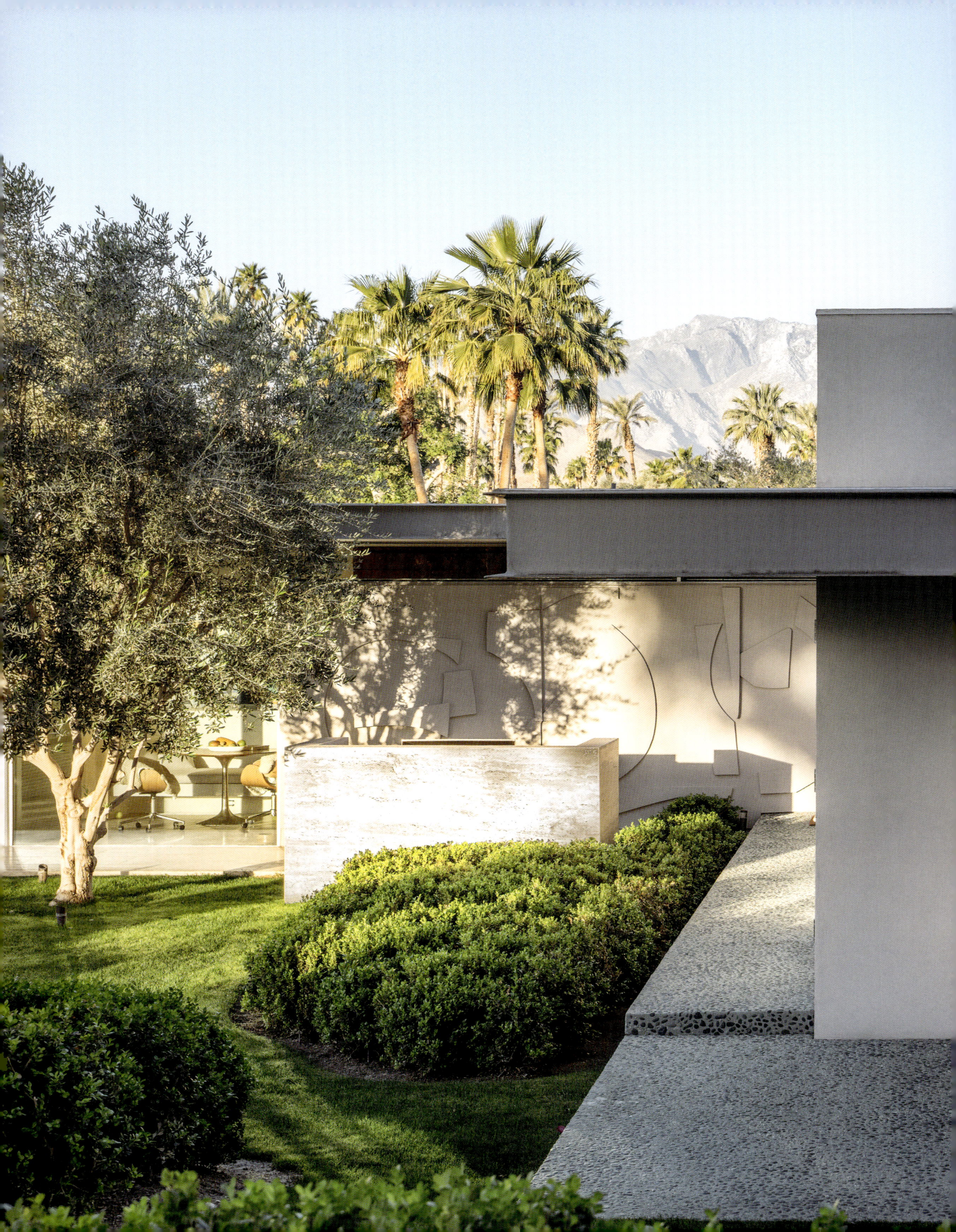

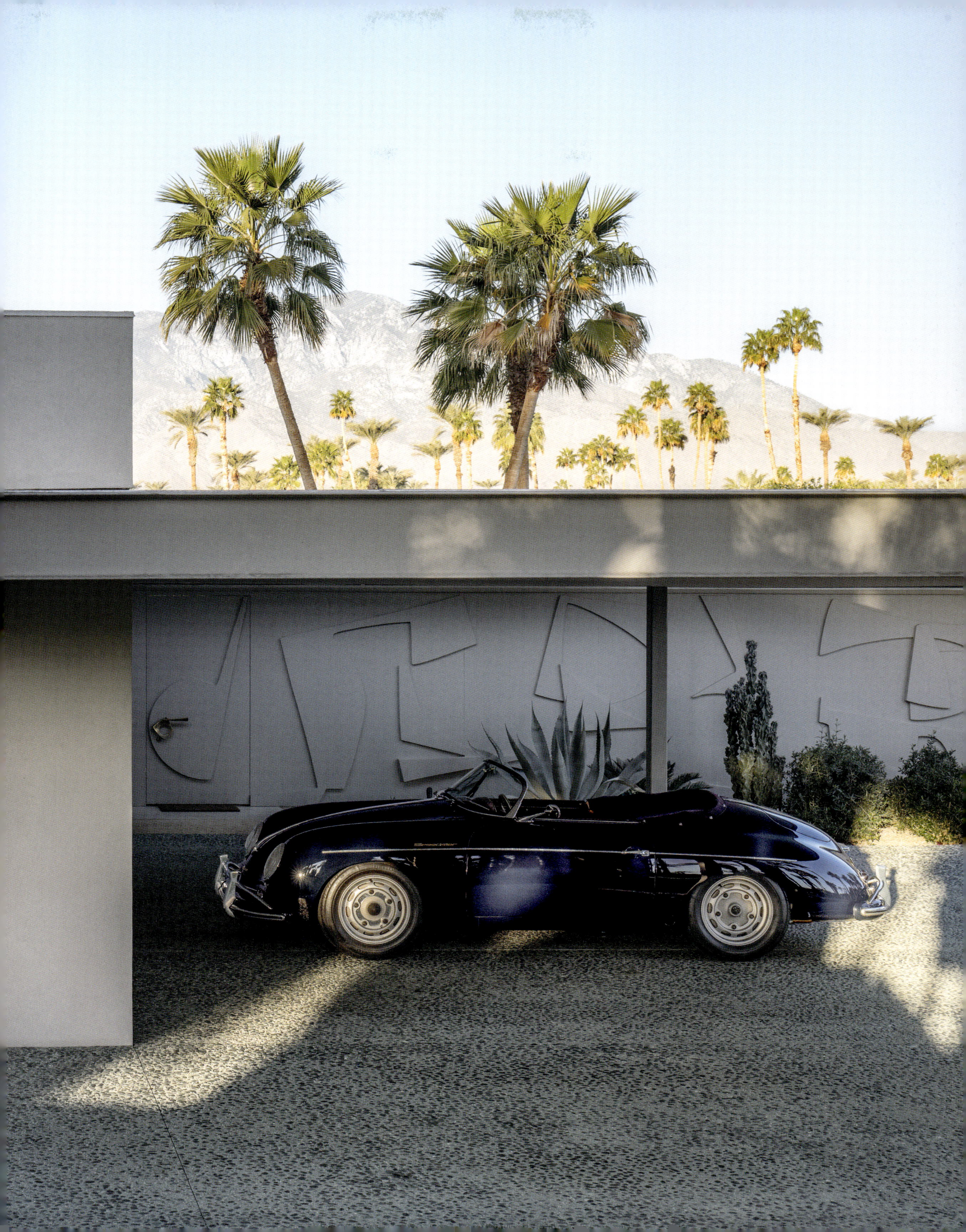

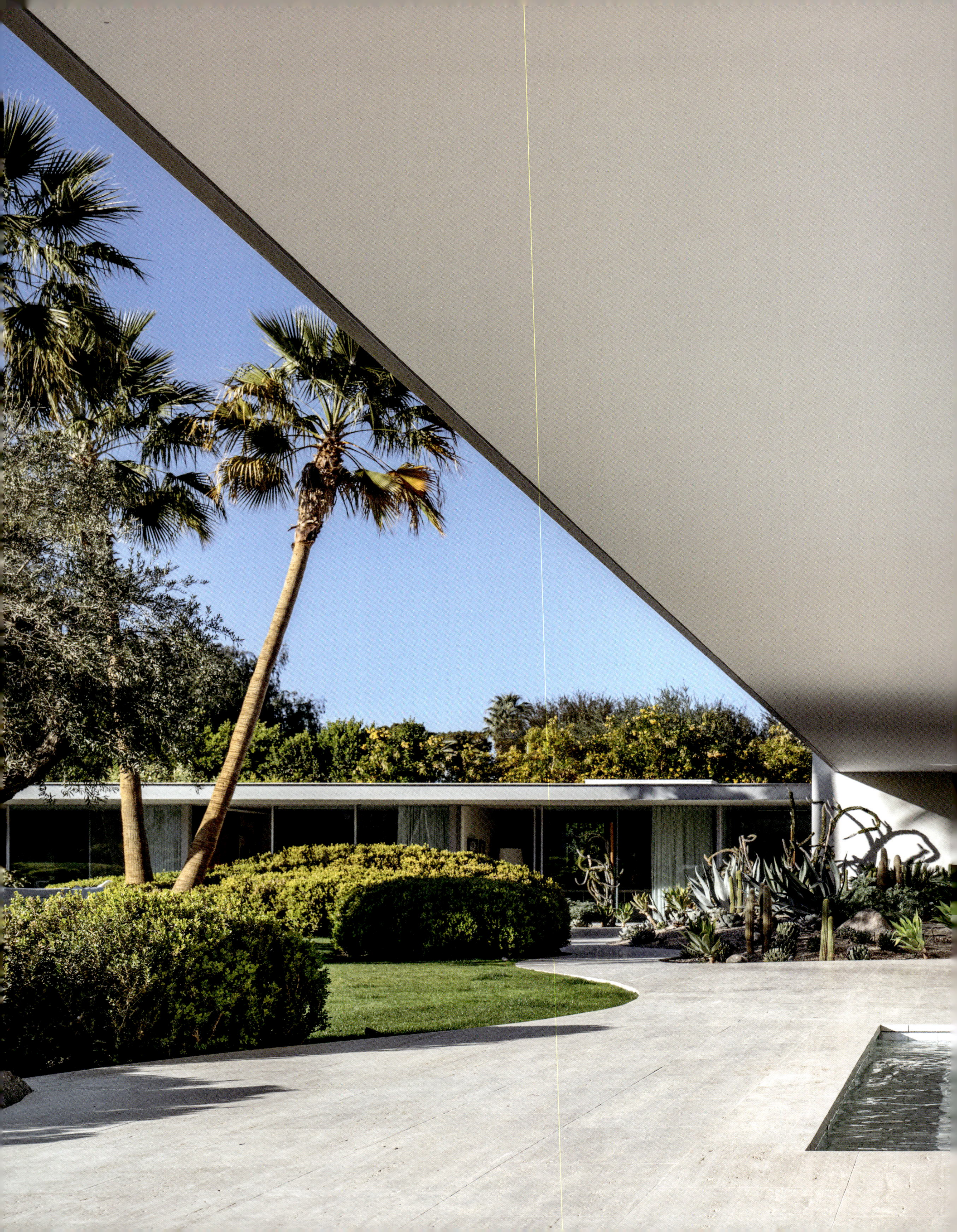

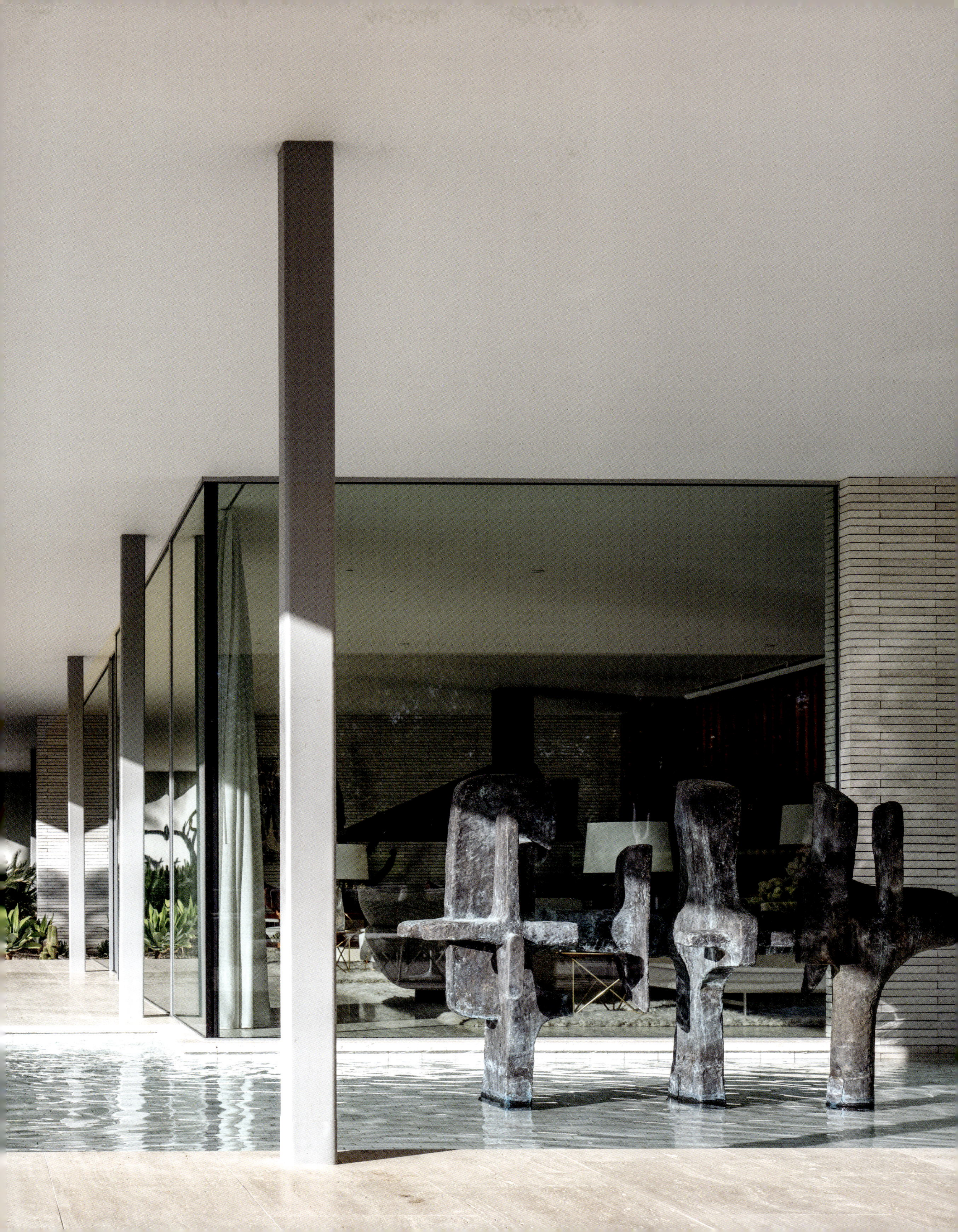

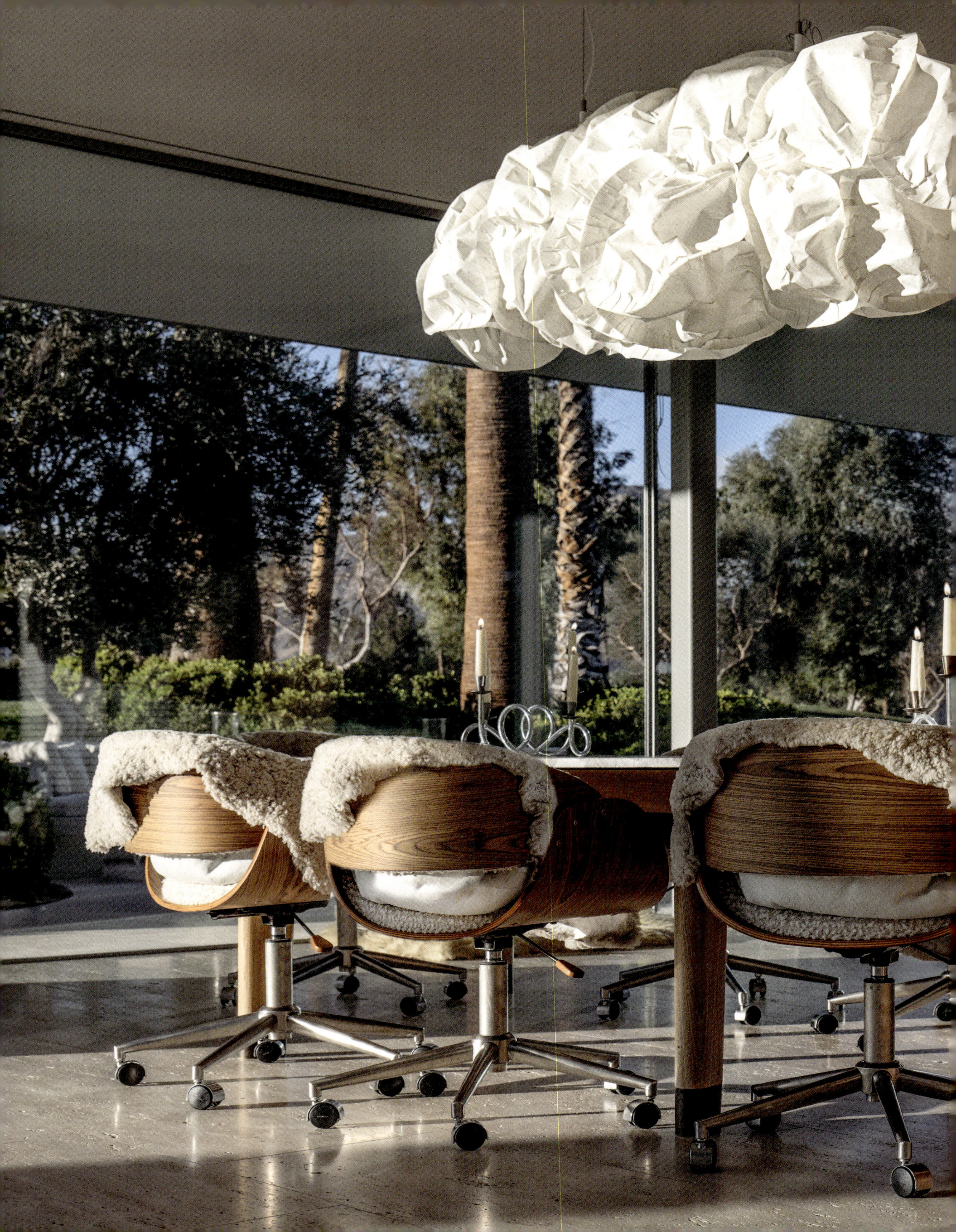

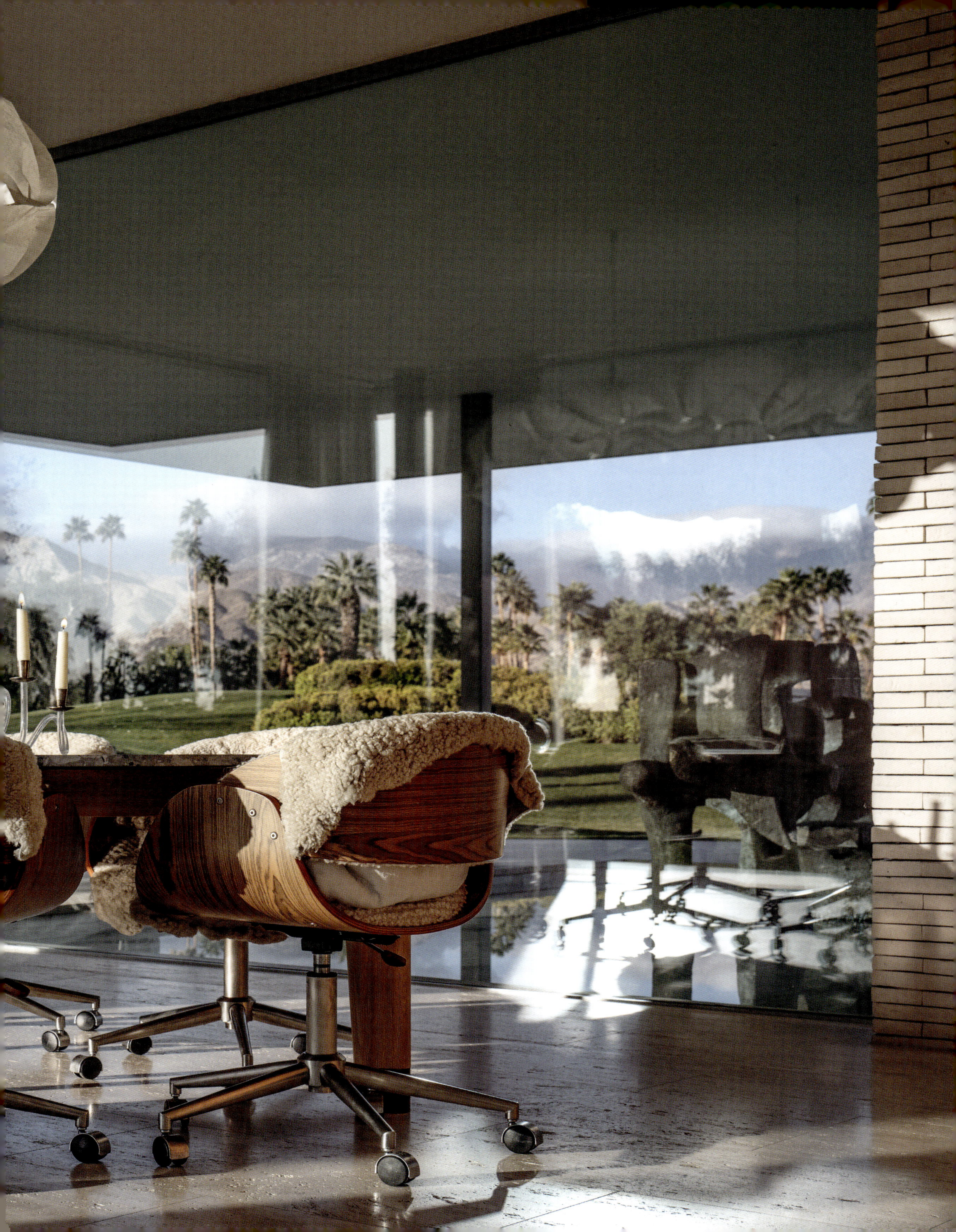

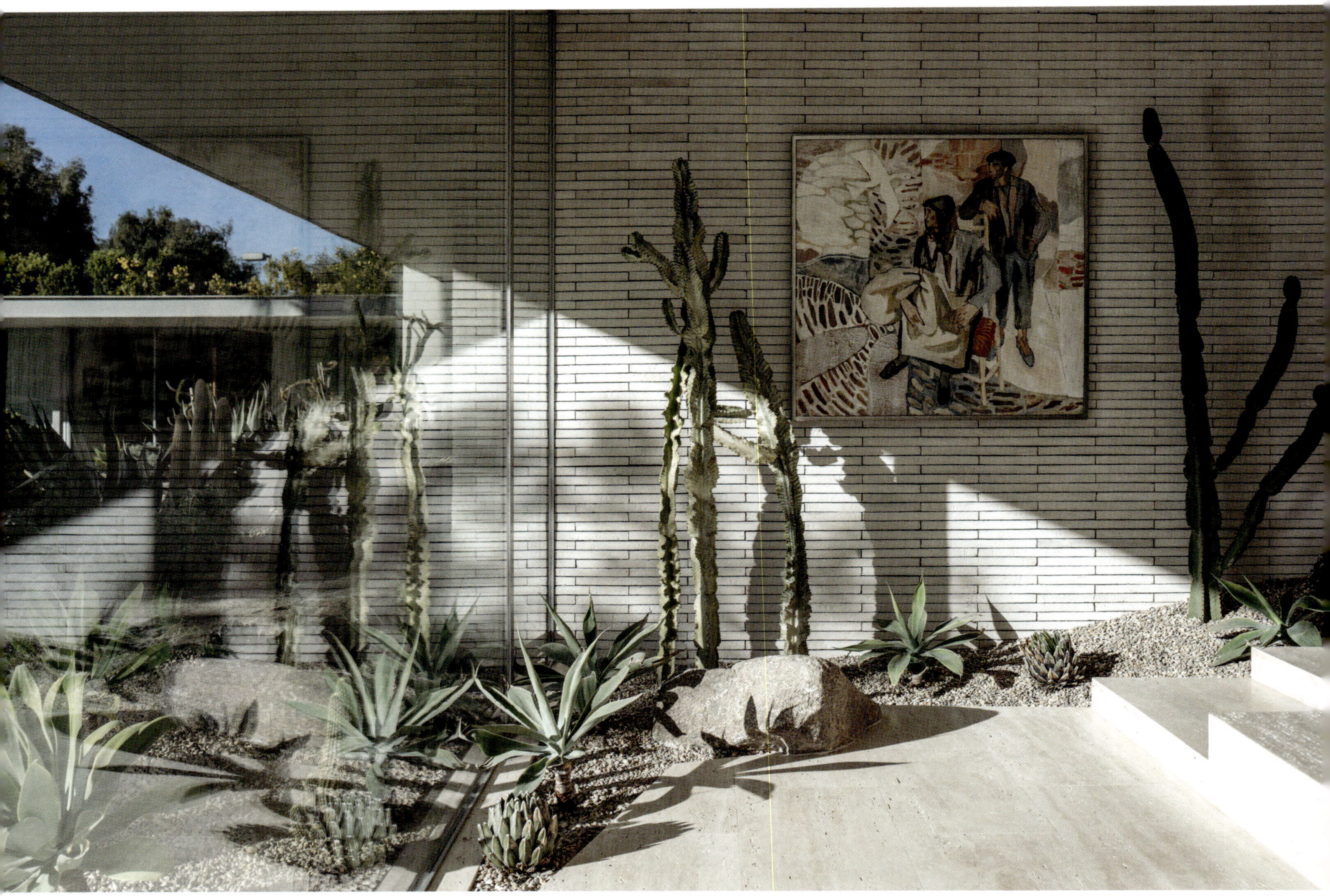

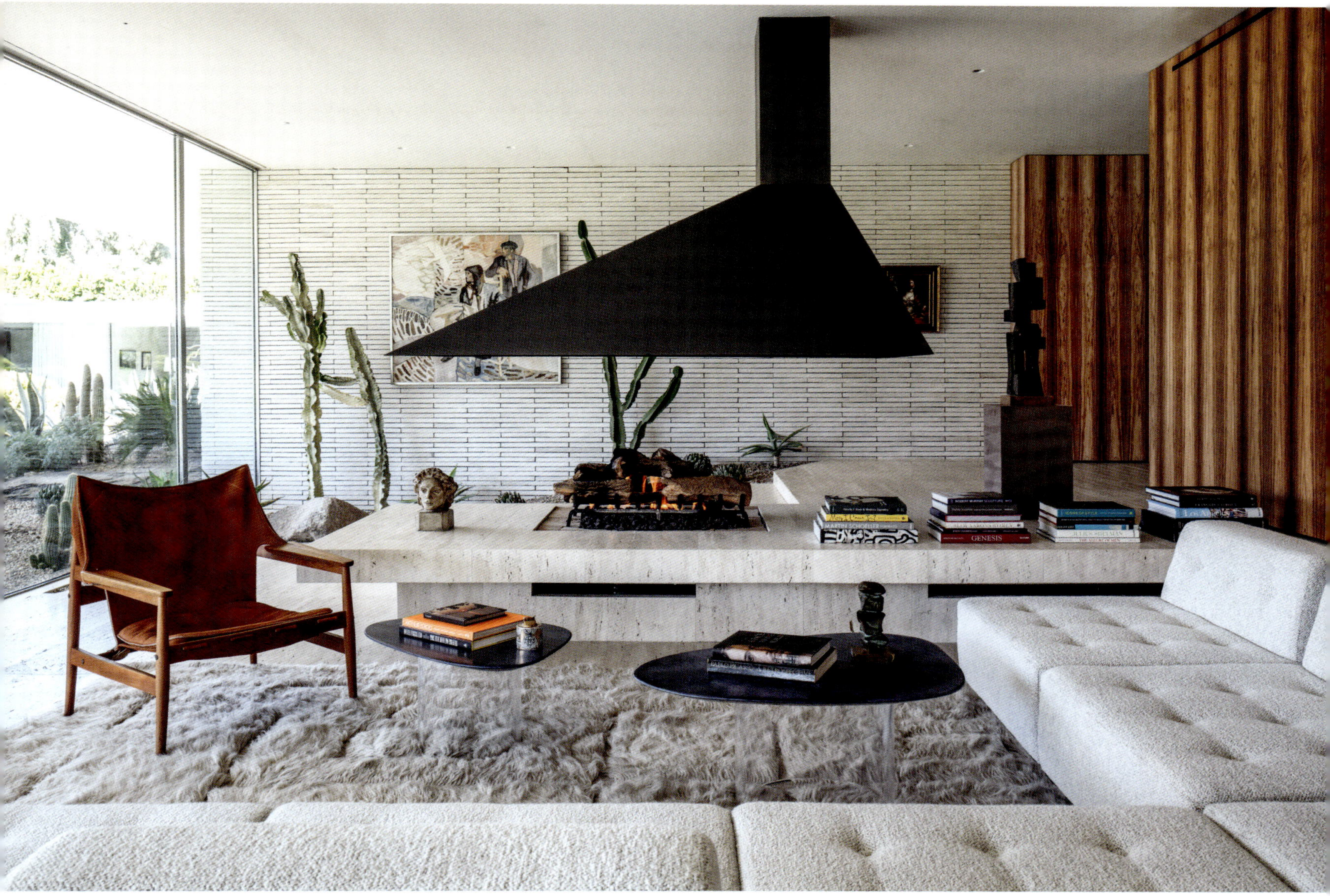
MARTIN SCHOELLER
GENESIS

L-C
PABLO PICASSO: A RETROSPECTIVE
ARTHUR ELROD desert modern design
DIANA VREELAND THE EYE HAS TO TRAVEL

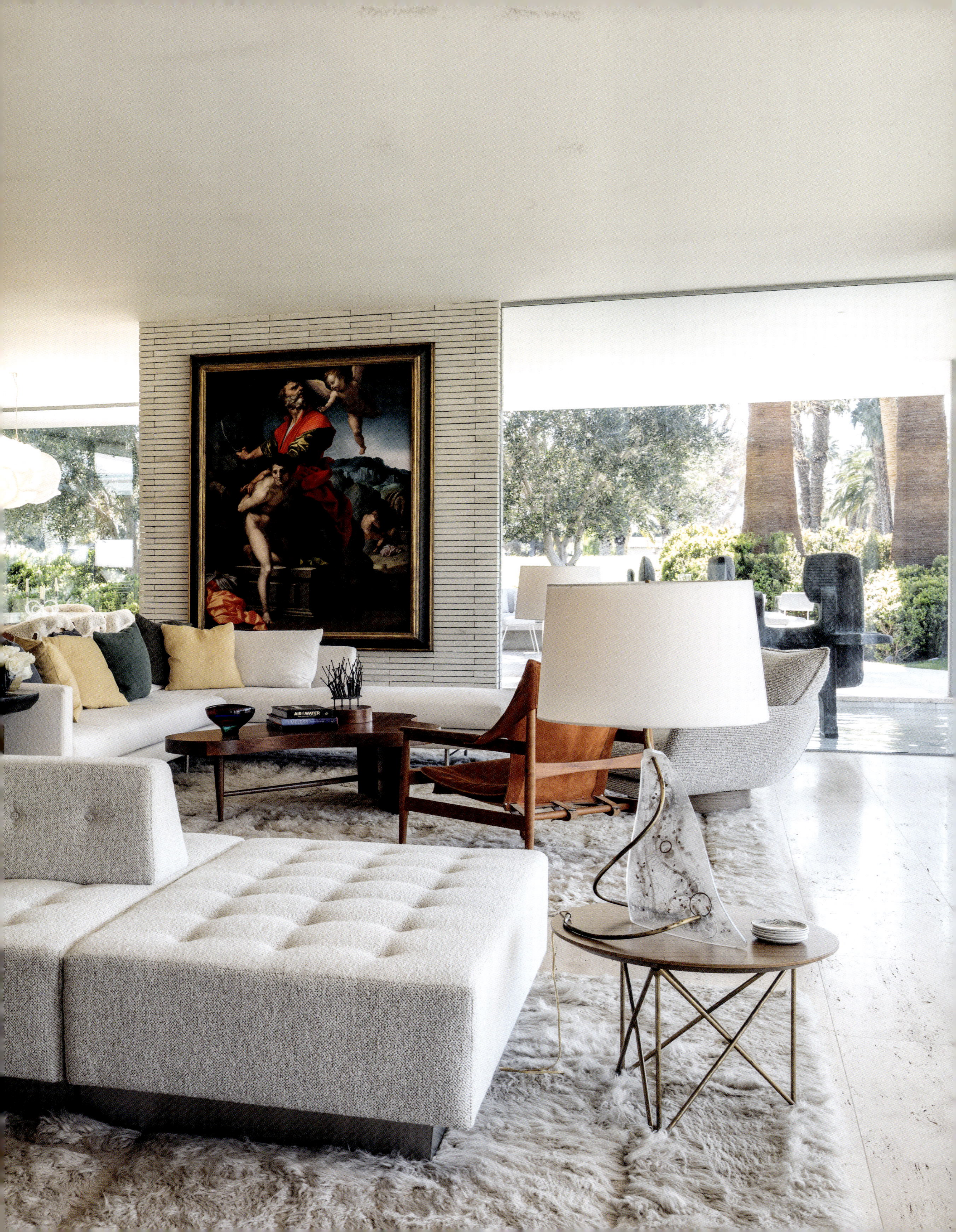

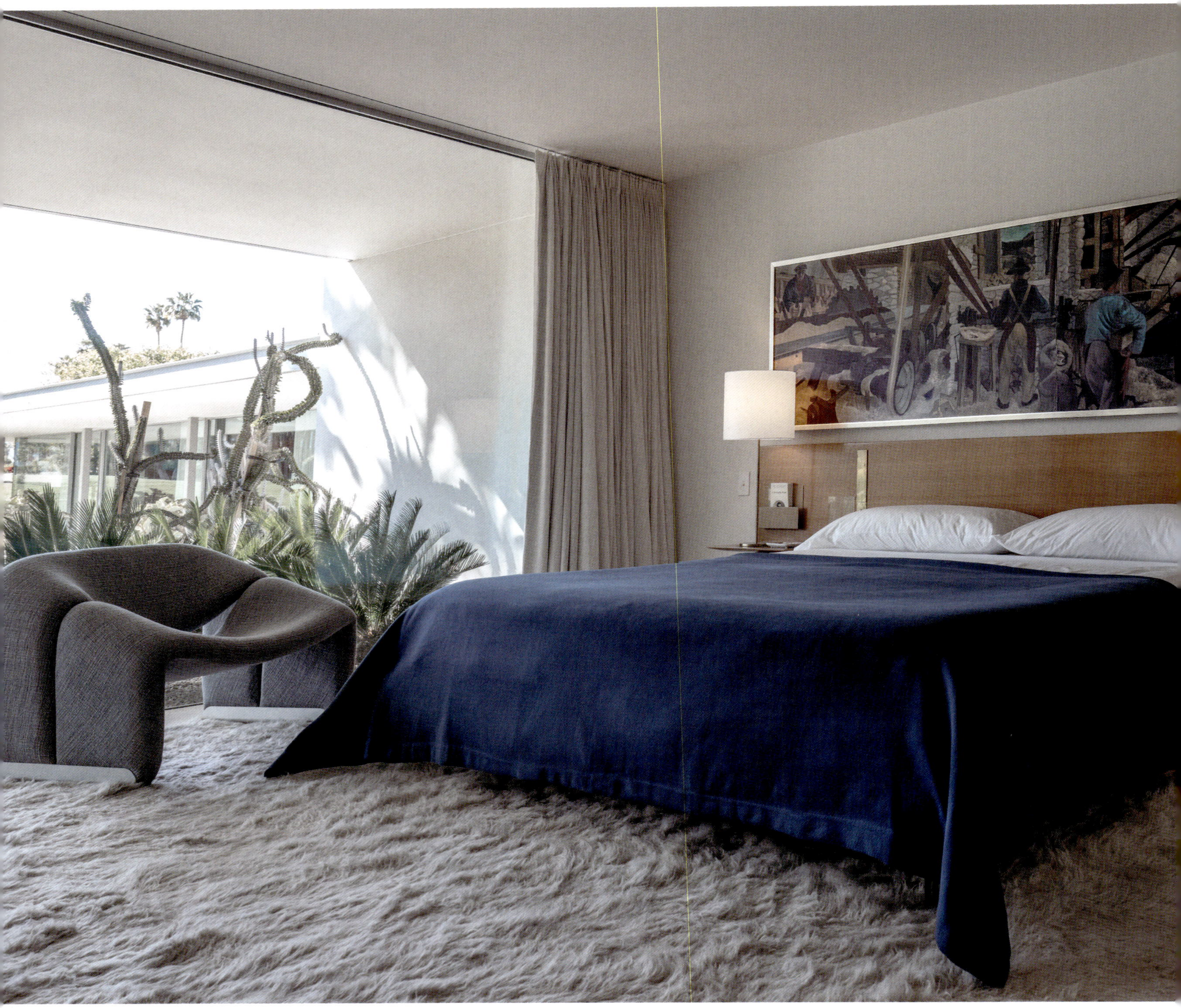

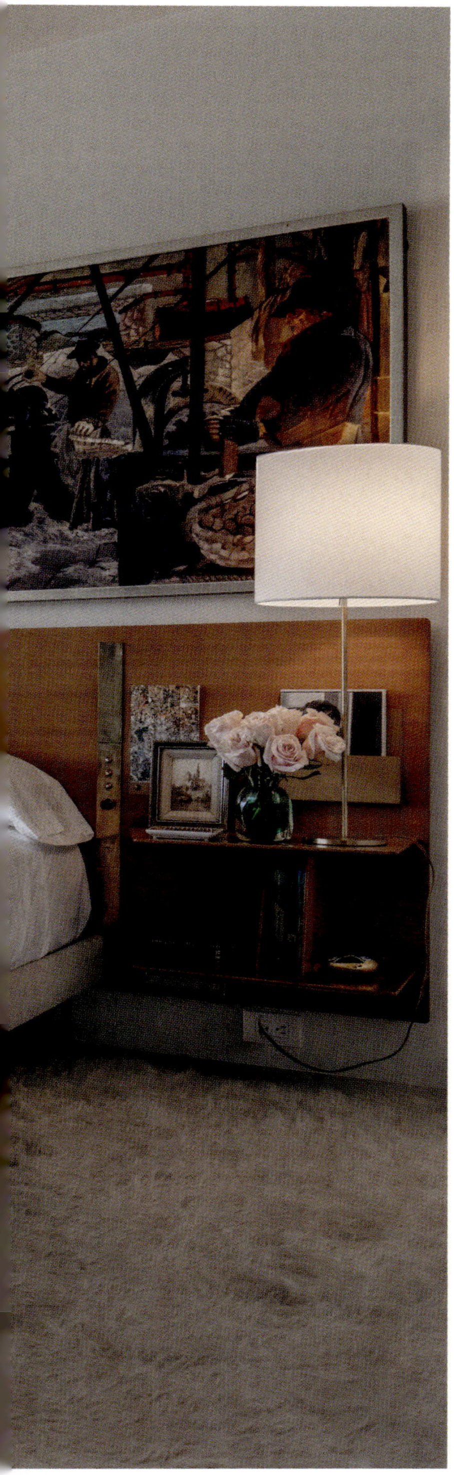

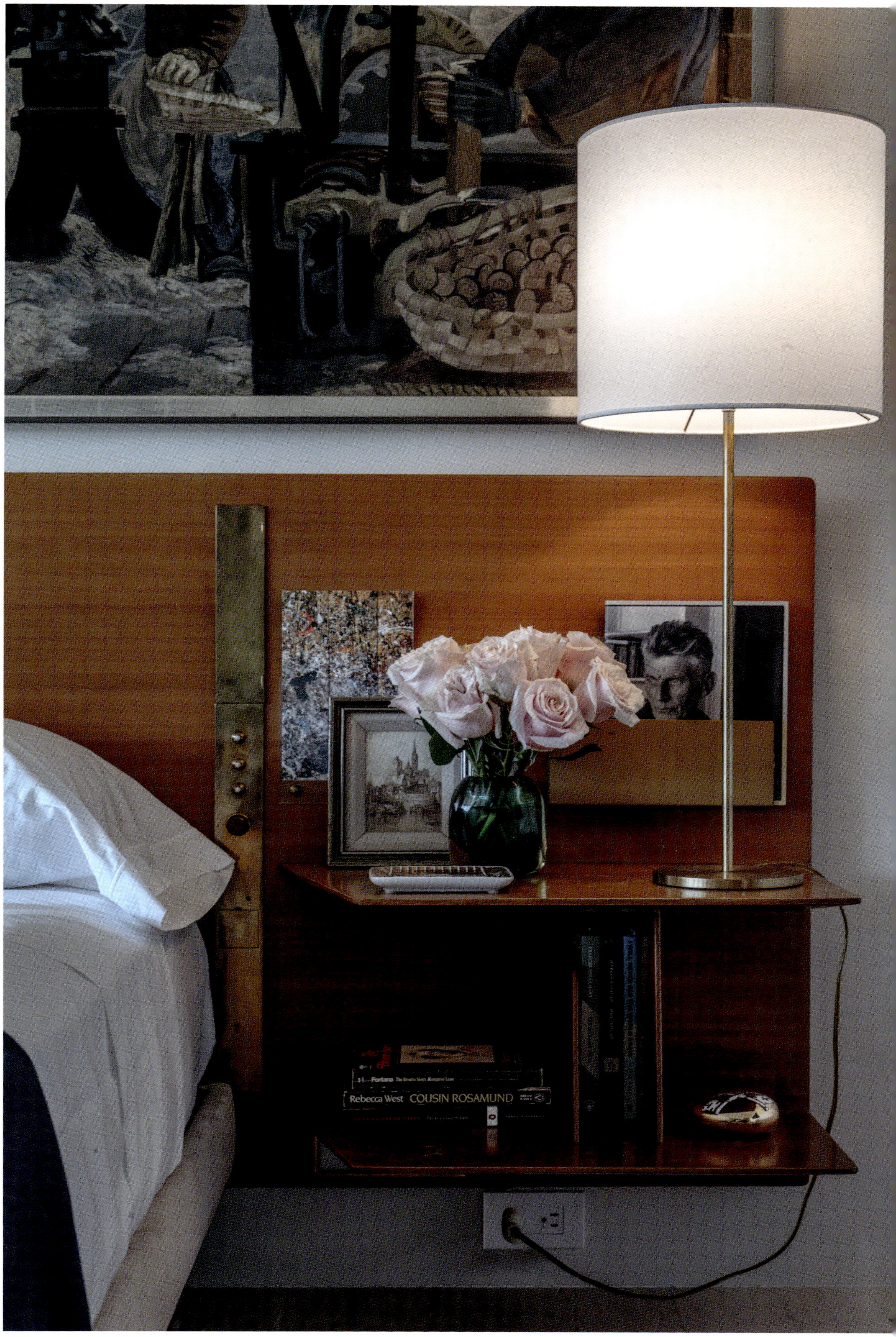
Rebecca West COUSIN ROSAMUND

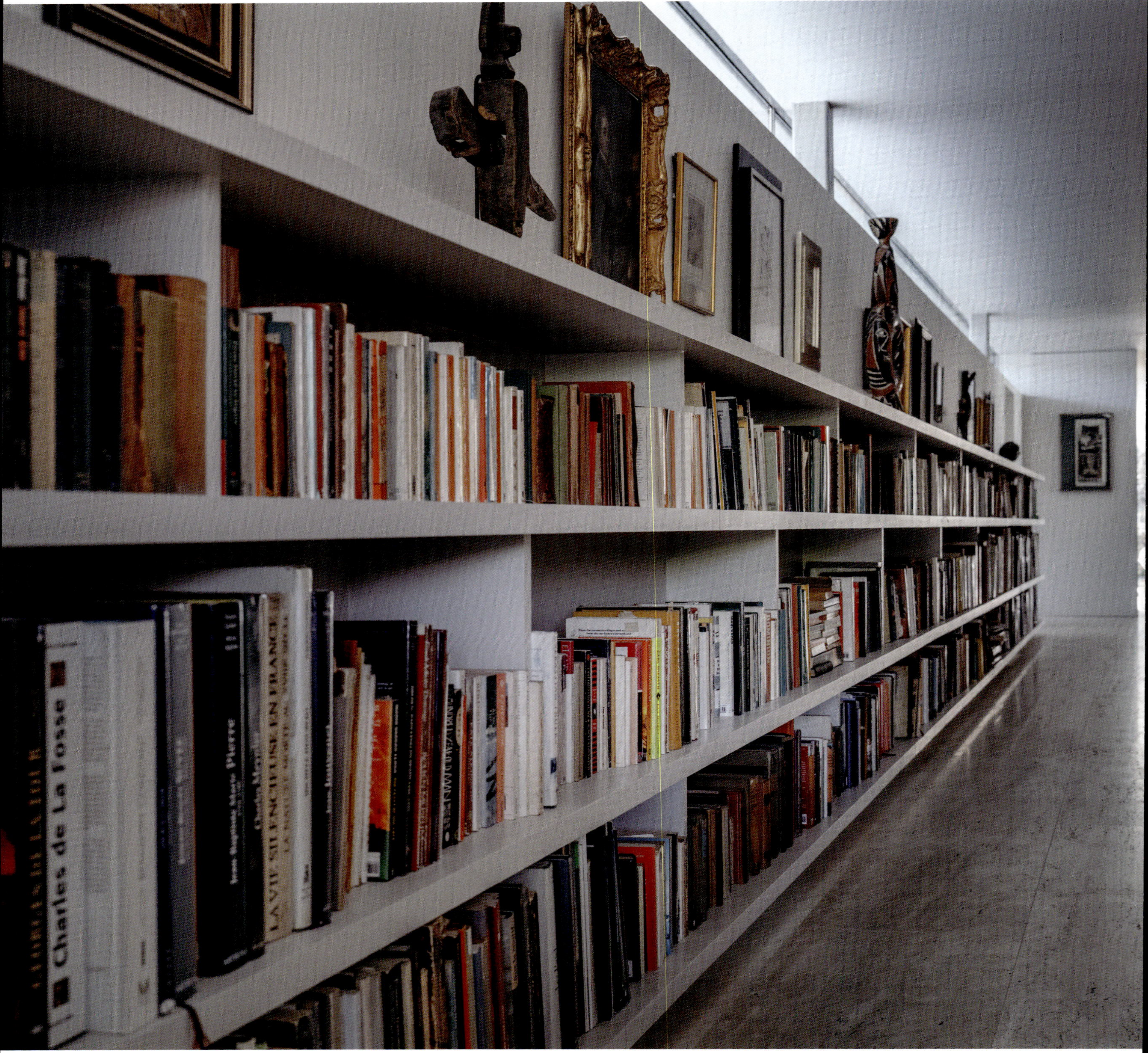
Charles de La Fosse

97

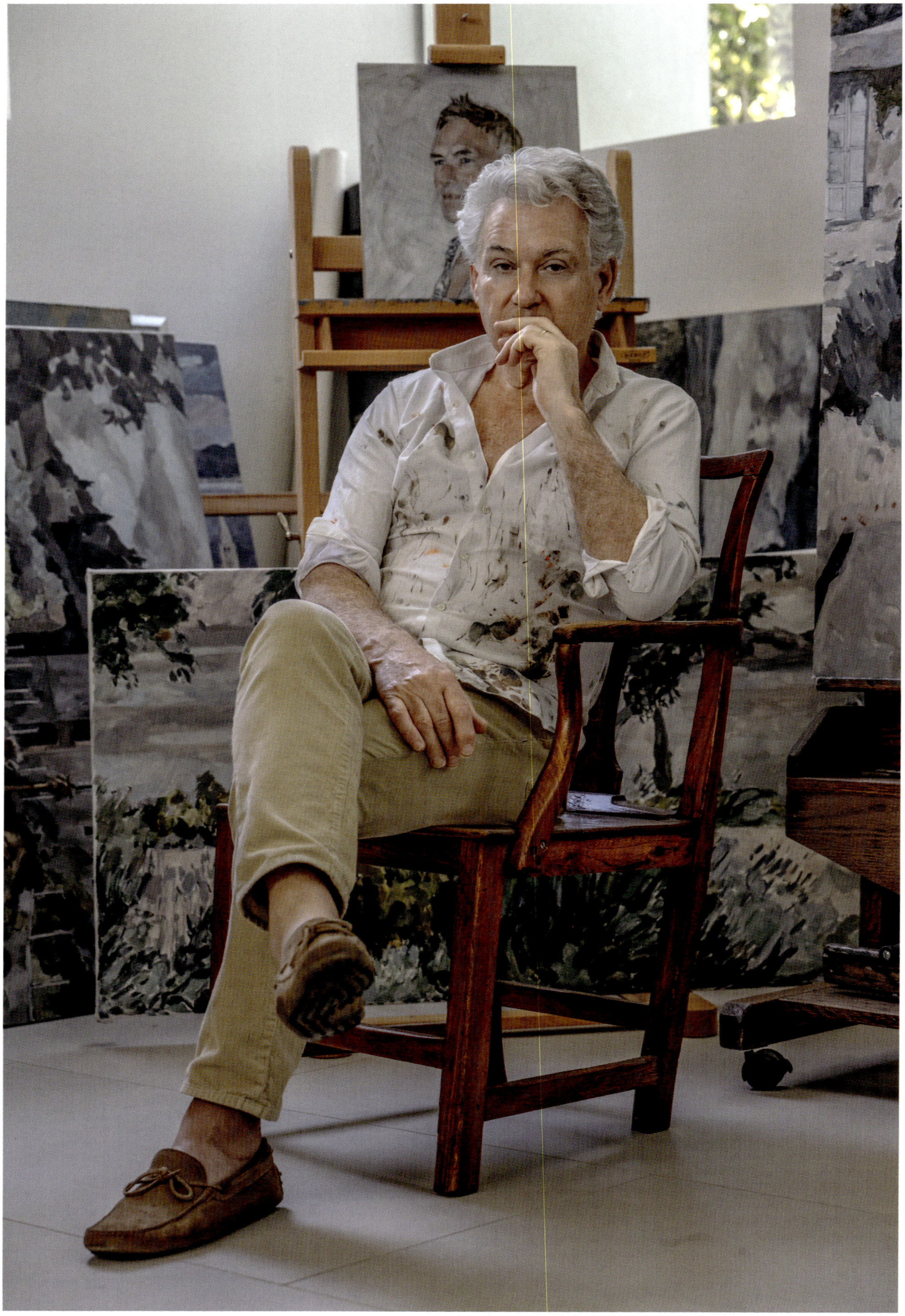

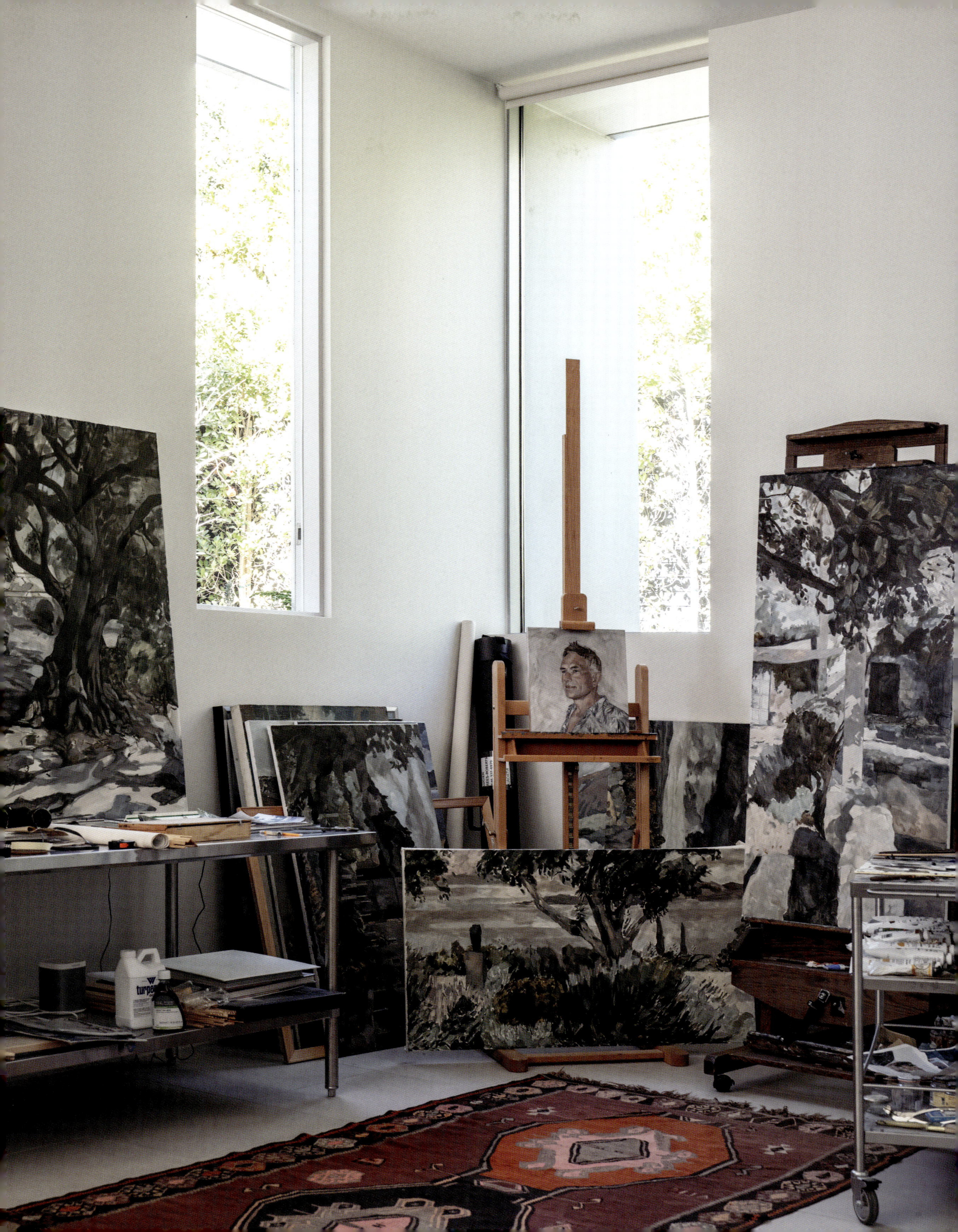

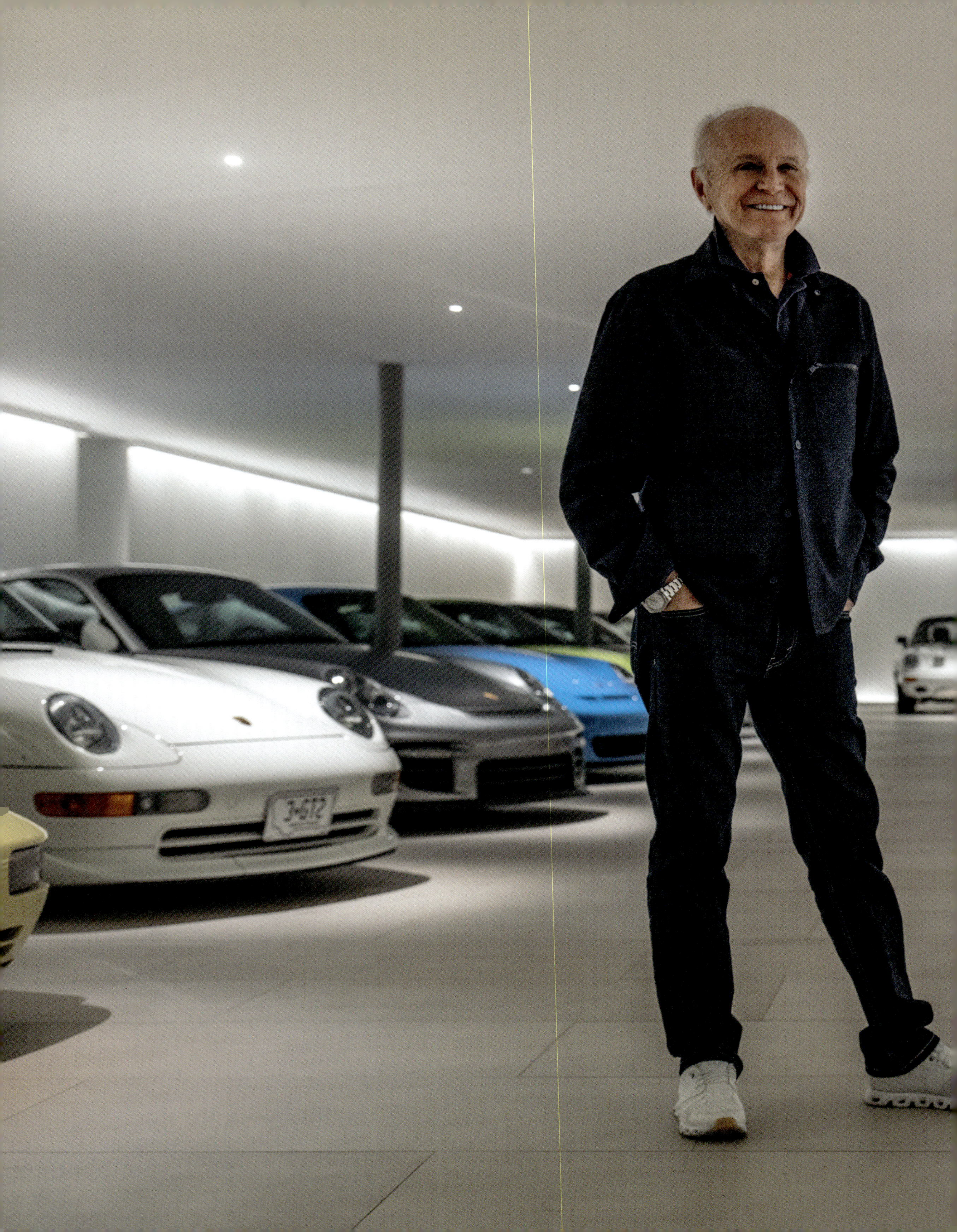

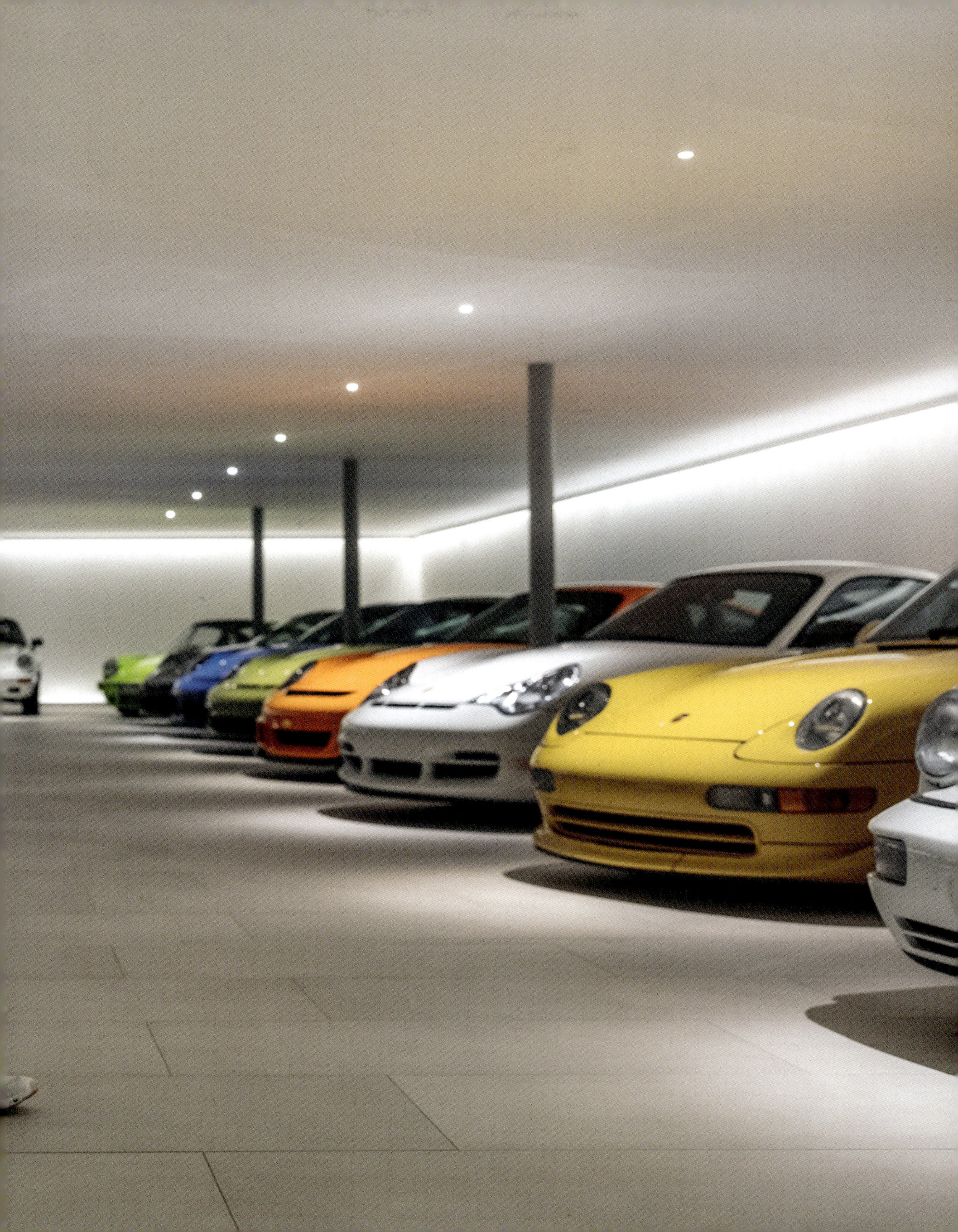

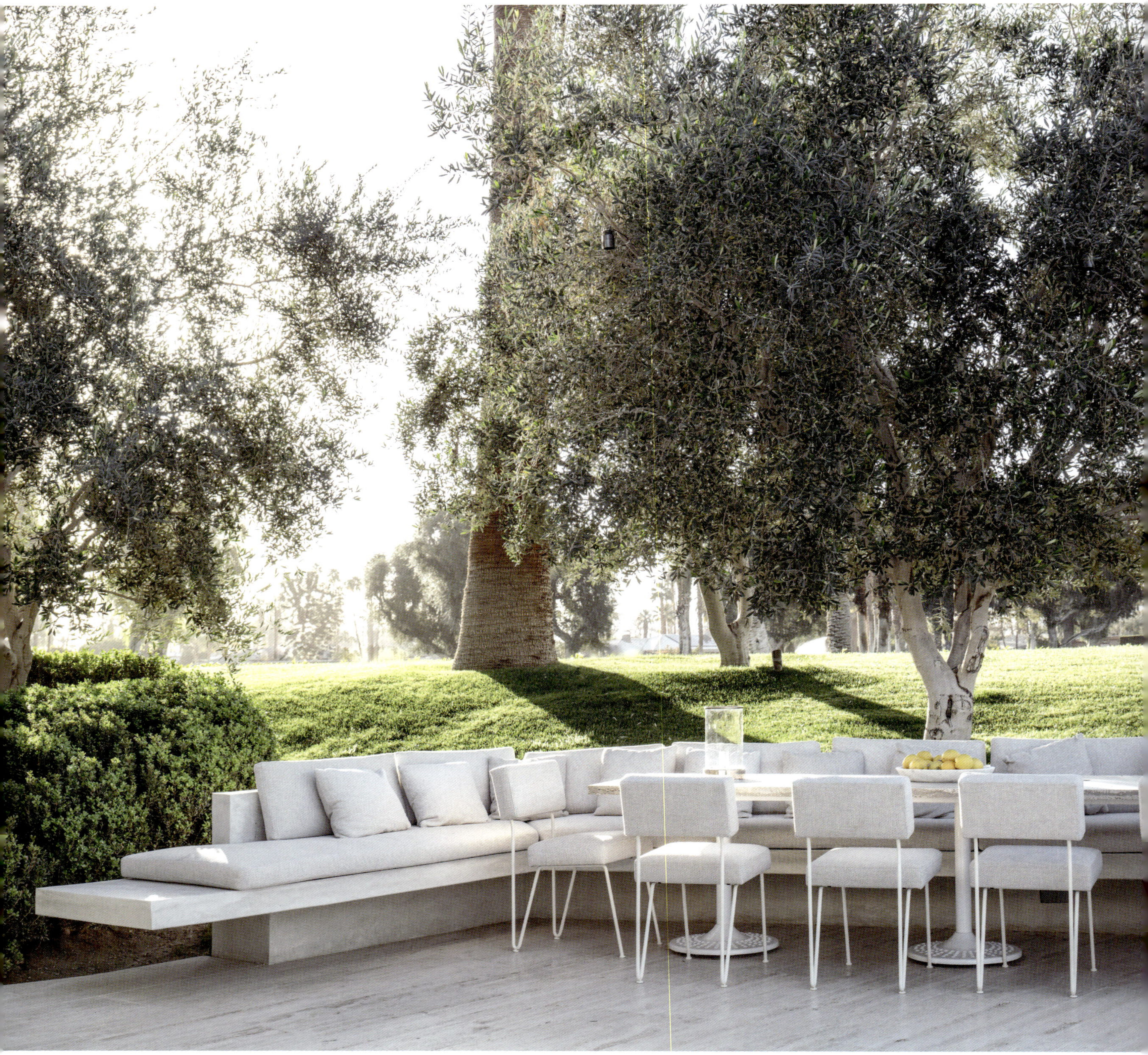

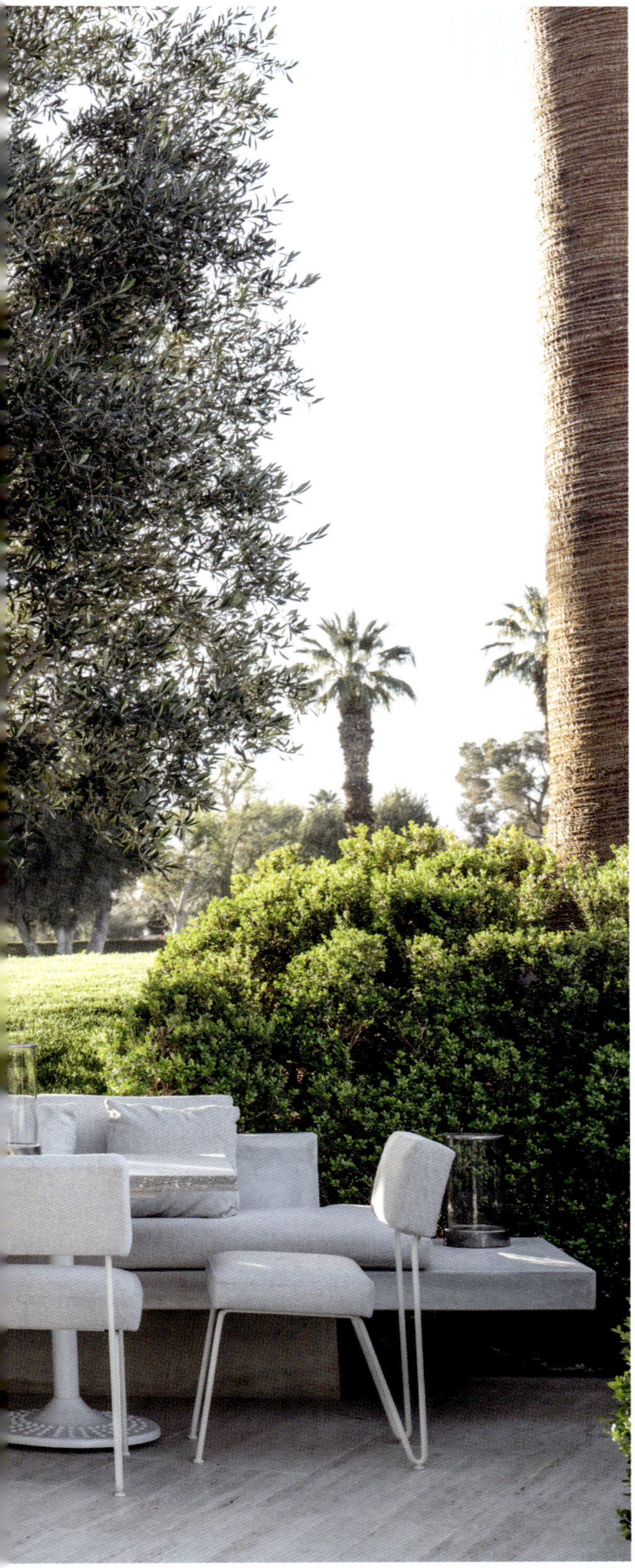

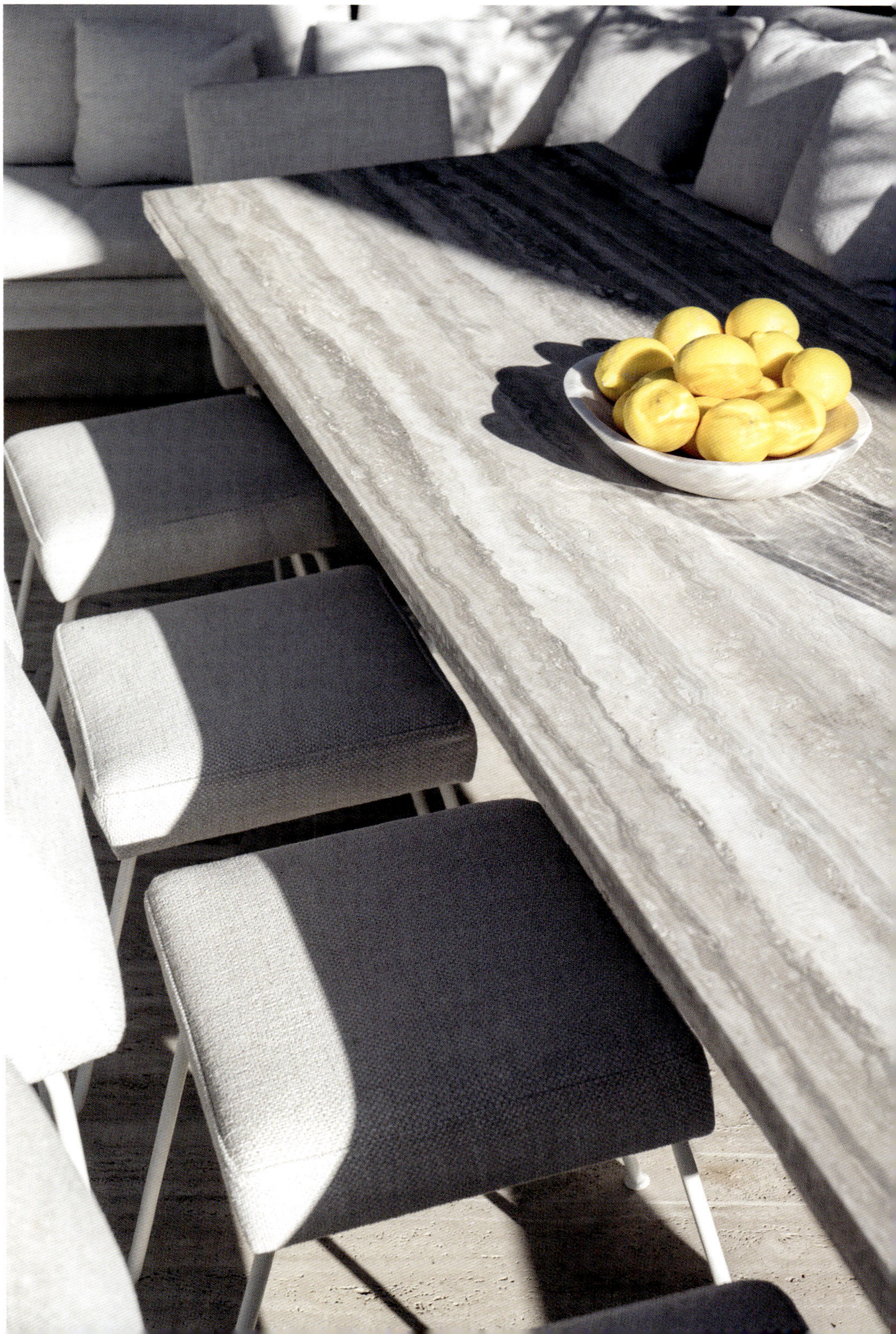

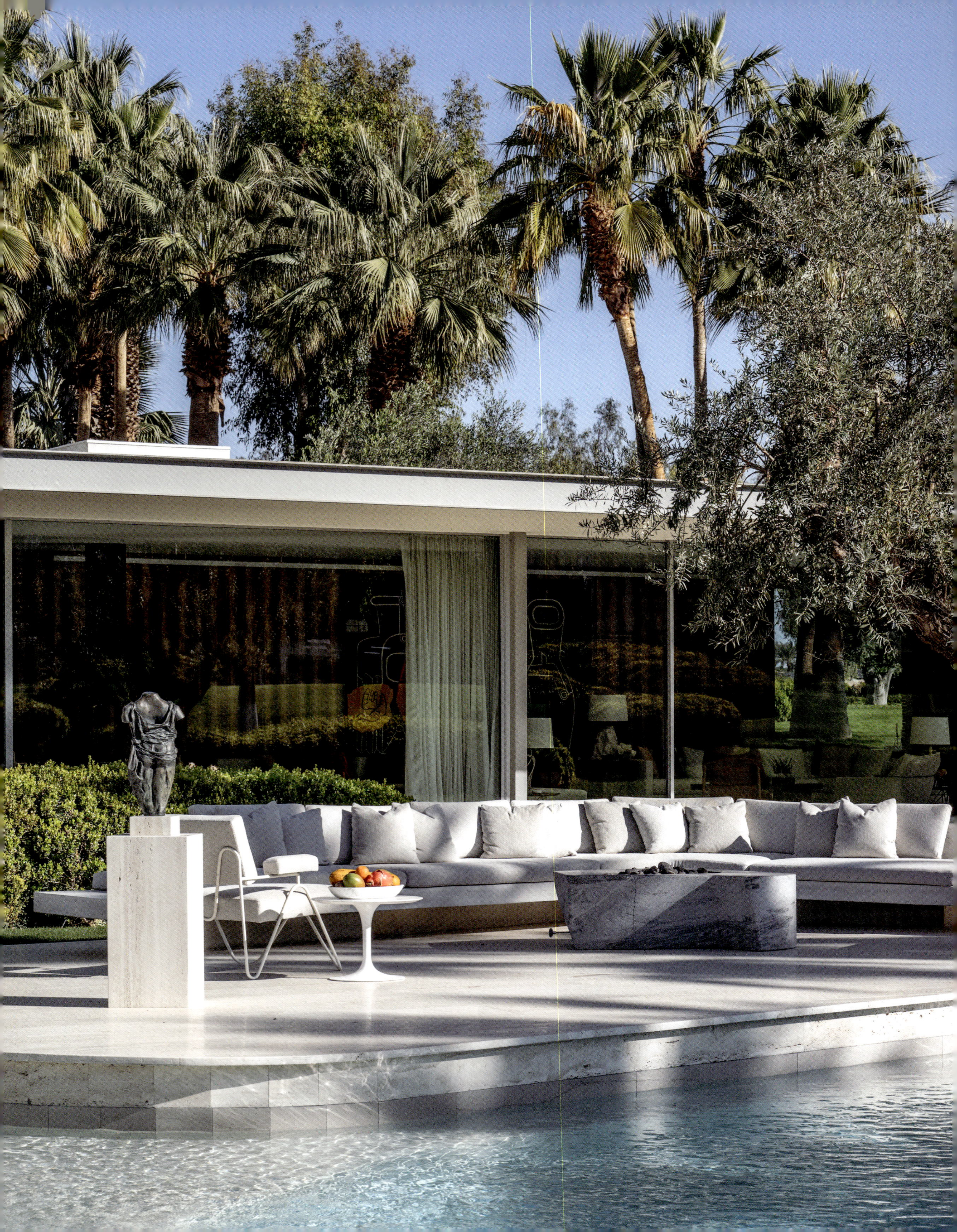

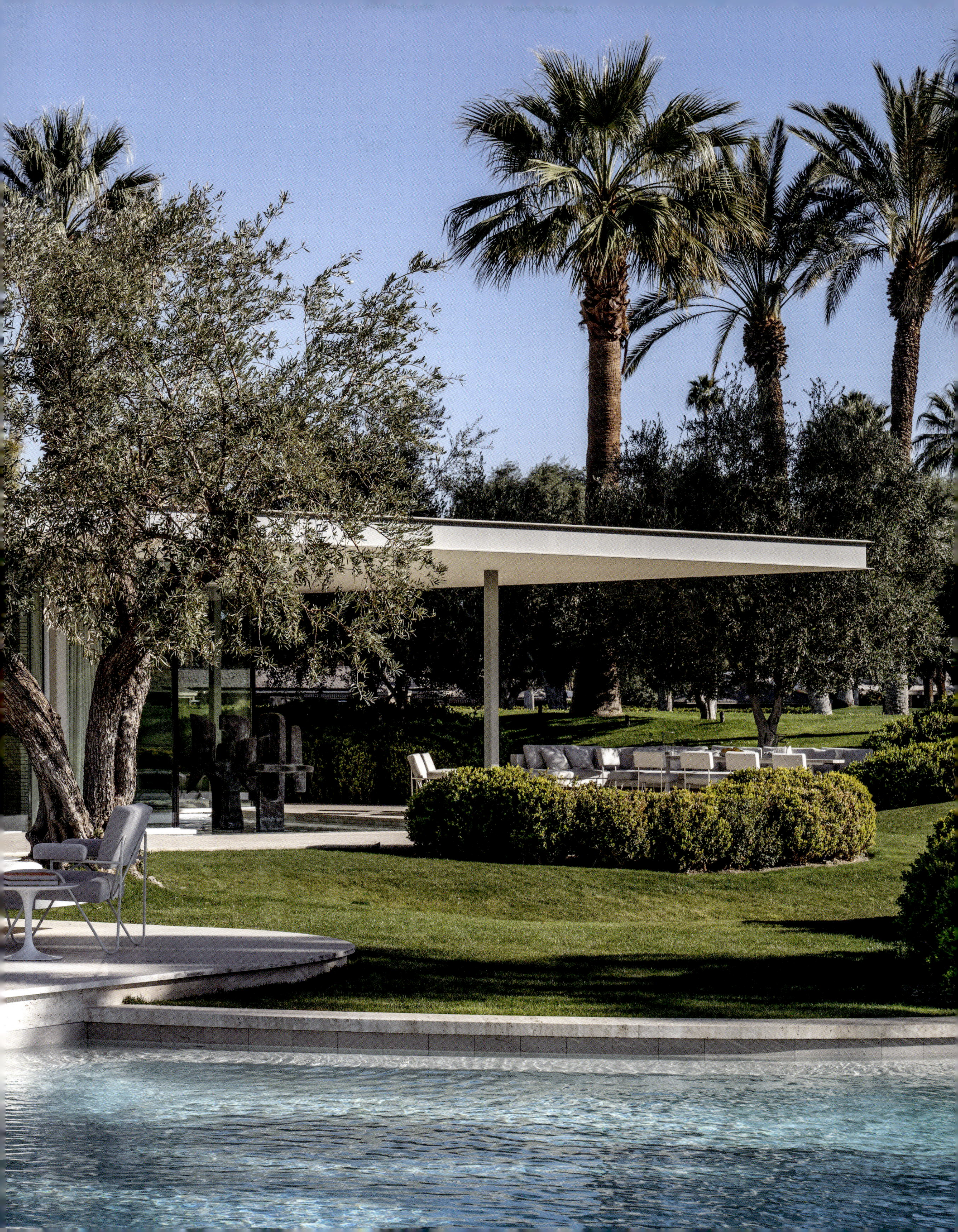

RANCHO MIRAGE II

T'S THE MIDDLE OF MARCH, AND BLIXSETH Mountain in Rancho Mirage is dusted with snow. "Borrowing the view" in the Japanese manner, the path that winds through boulders and palm trees in Jean-Claude Huon's garden appears to lead all the way to the hills. "This is a place where people come to be without other problems," observes the designer, and although he's referring to the desert in general, the description seems particularly apposite to his corner of it.

Huon, who is French, came here somewhat unexpectedly himself. After a twenty-five-year career in the fashion industry in New York, he moved to Palm Springs in 2017 with the intention of preserving both the house and the interior design business of its owners, close friends of his who had recently passed away. The art and furniture that he's collected for decades look remarkably at home in the unpretentious concrete and glass residence, with its sandblasted beamed ceilings and rough concrete floors. "I'm always moving things around," Huon points out. For the moment an early nineteenth-century Japanese screen and an abstract painting by the Russian artist André Lanskoy hang on the living room walls. A de Sede sofa and chairs covered in buffalo skin surround a bronze coffee table, while nearby a classic Eames lounge chair sits under an angular Triennale floor lamp. Modern Japanese and Chinese wood sculptures animate the corners of the room. Everything *feels* moved around—ad hoc and fresh and quietly sophisticated.

One thing Huon won't change is the house's connection to the outdoors. Most of the rooms spill onto the patio and garden, where agaves and grasses grow between the rocks, and the palms have long skirts of dead fronds. "I want to keep a bit of a cocoon around me," Huon says. "Why not, no?"

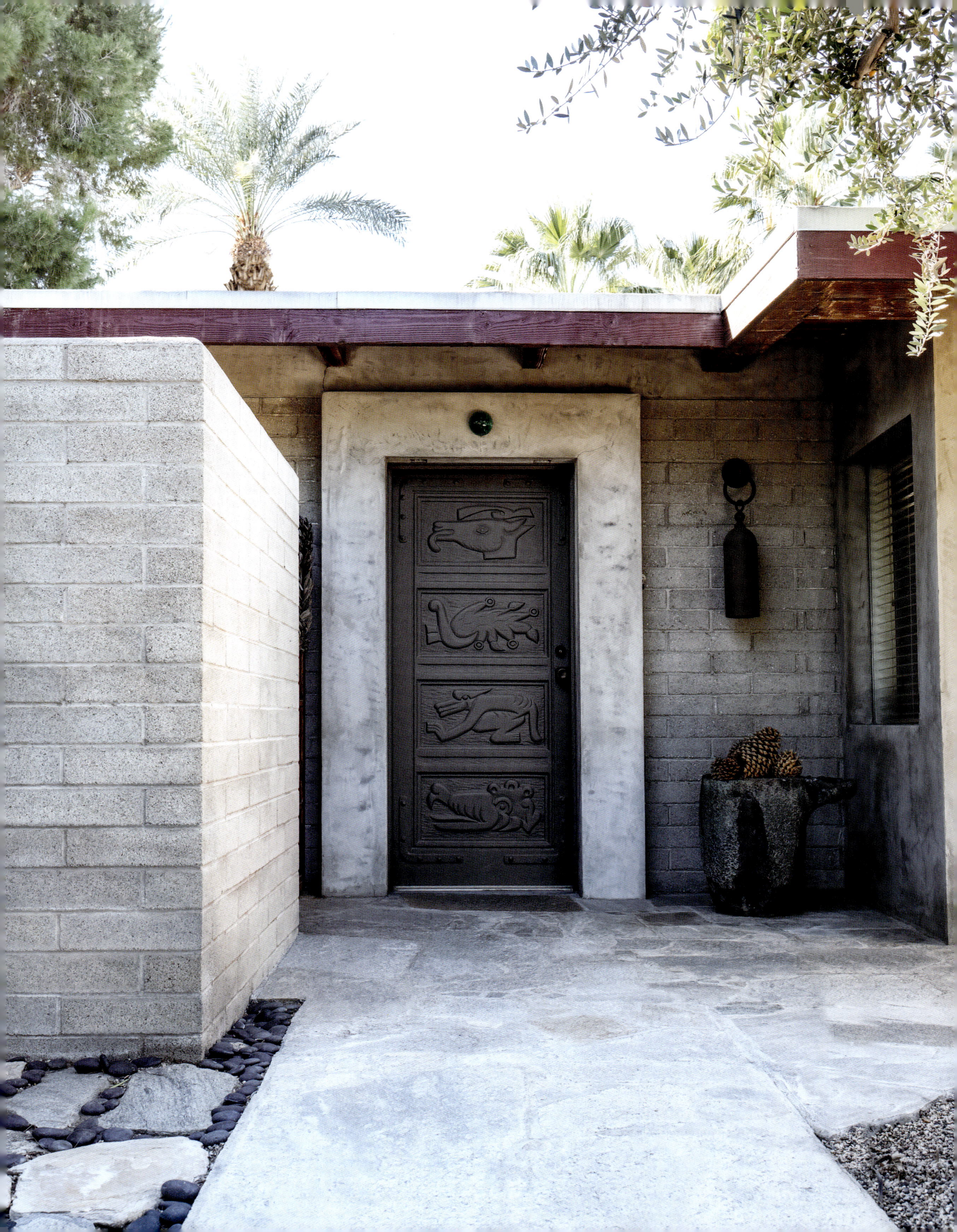

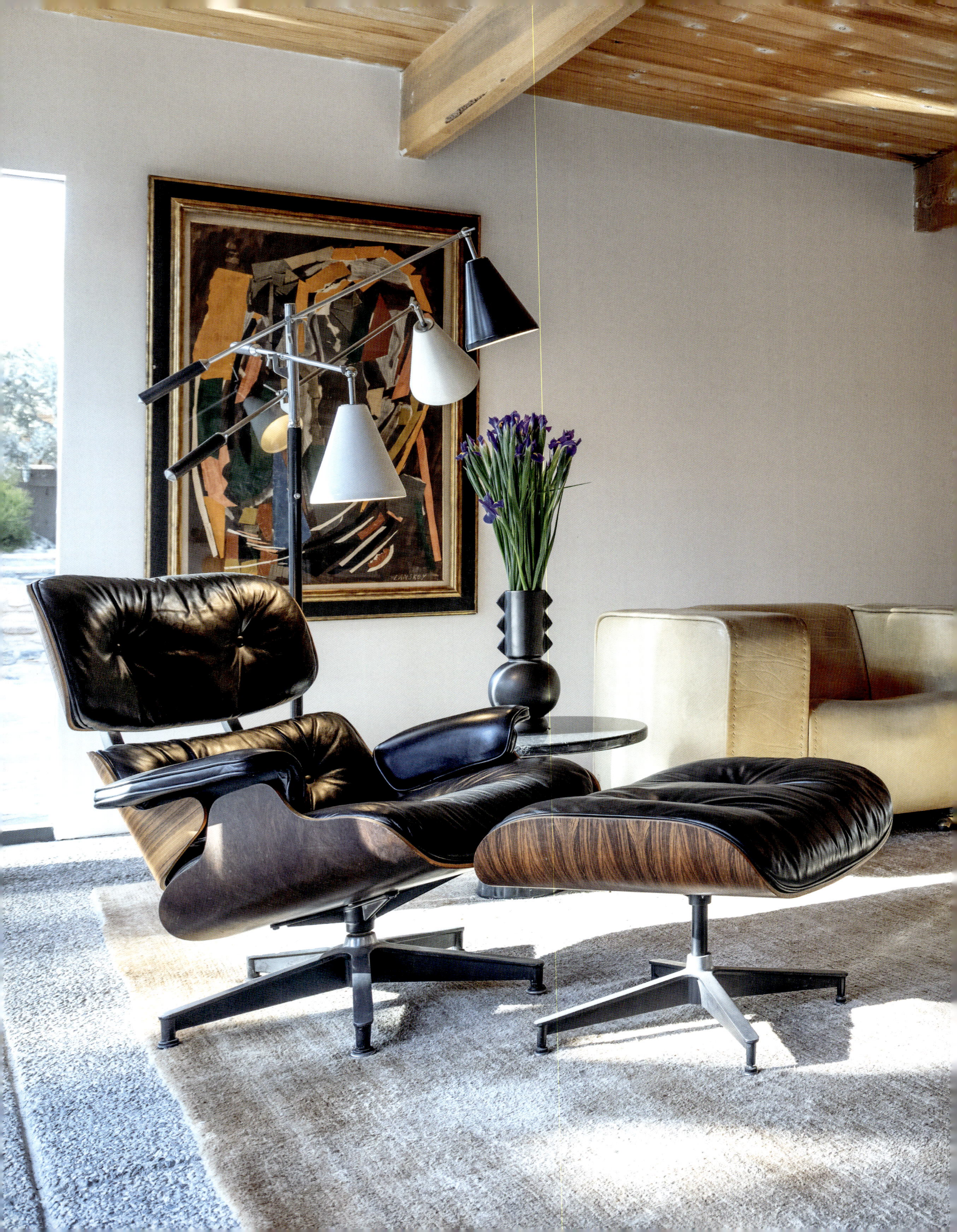

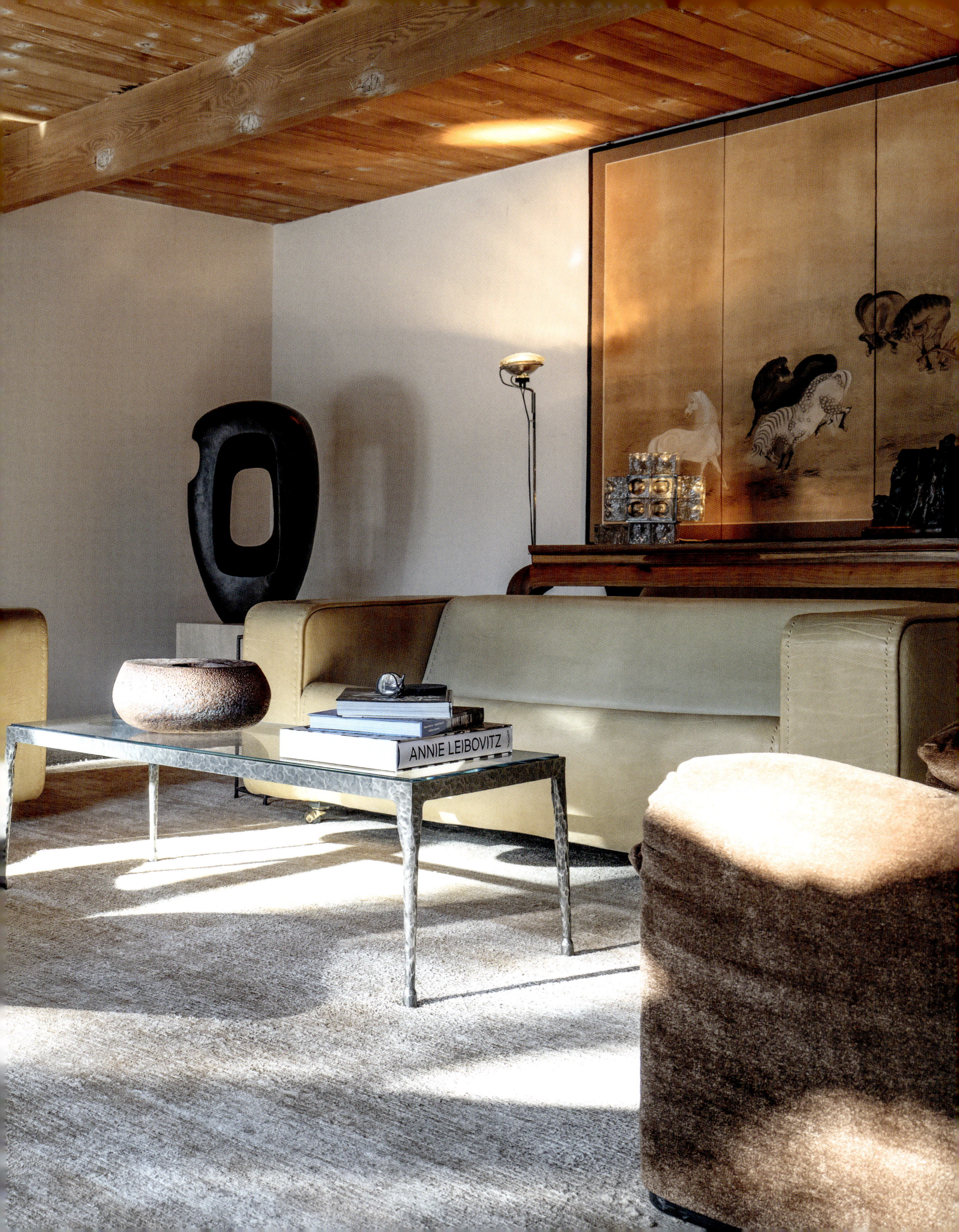
ANNIE LEIBOVITZ

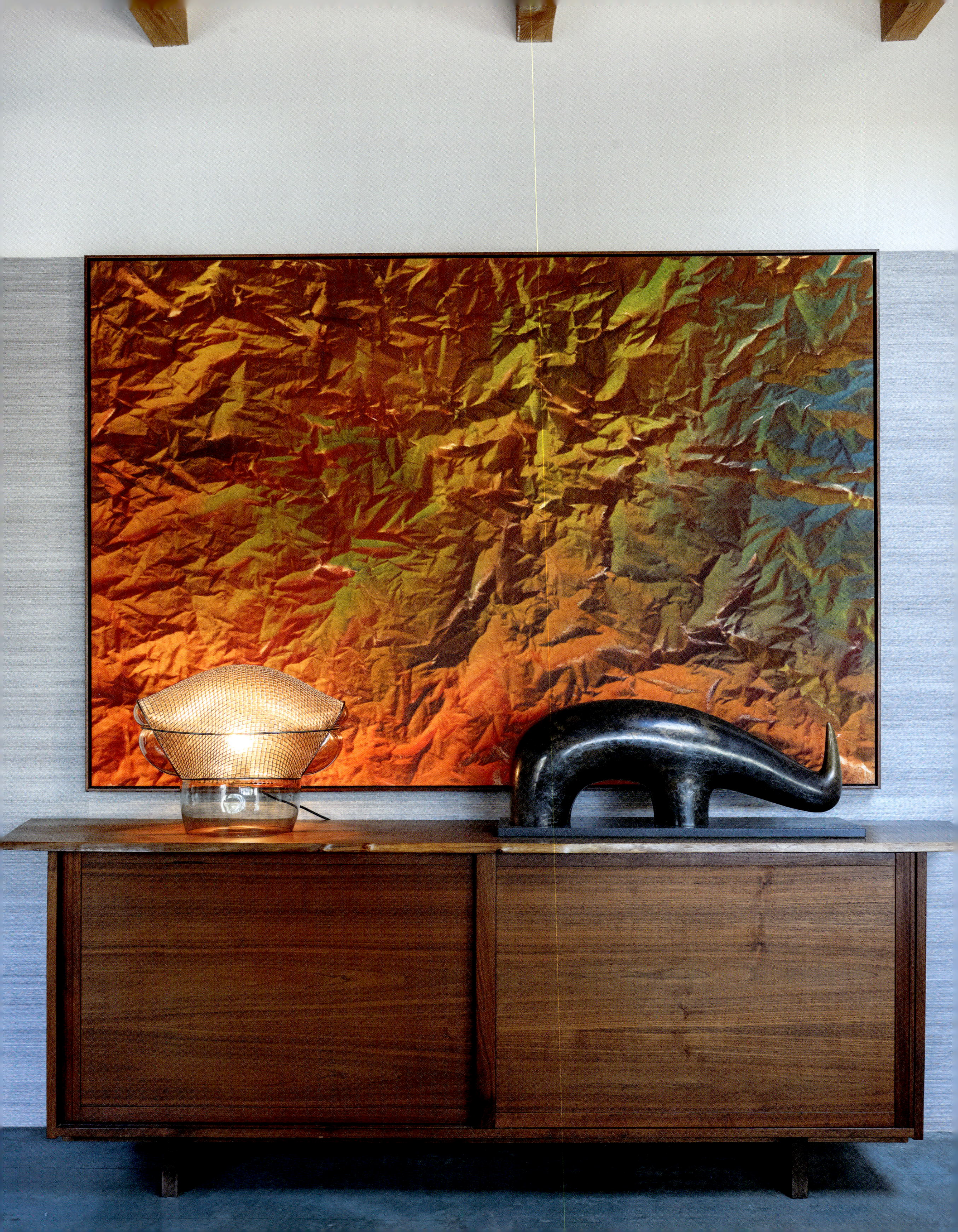

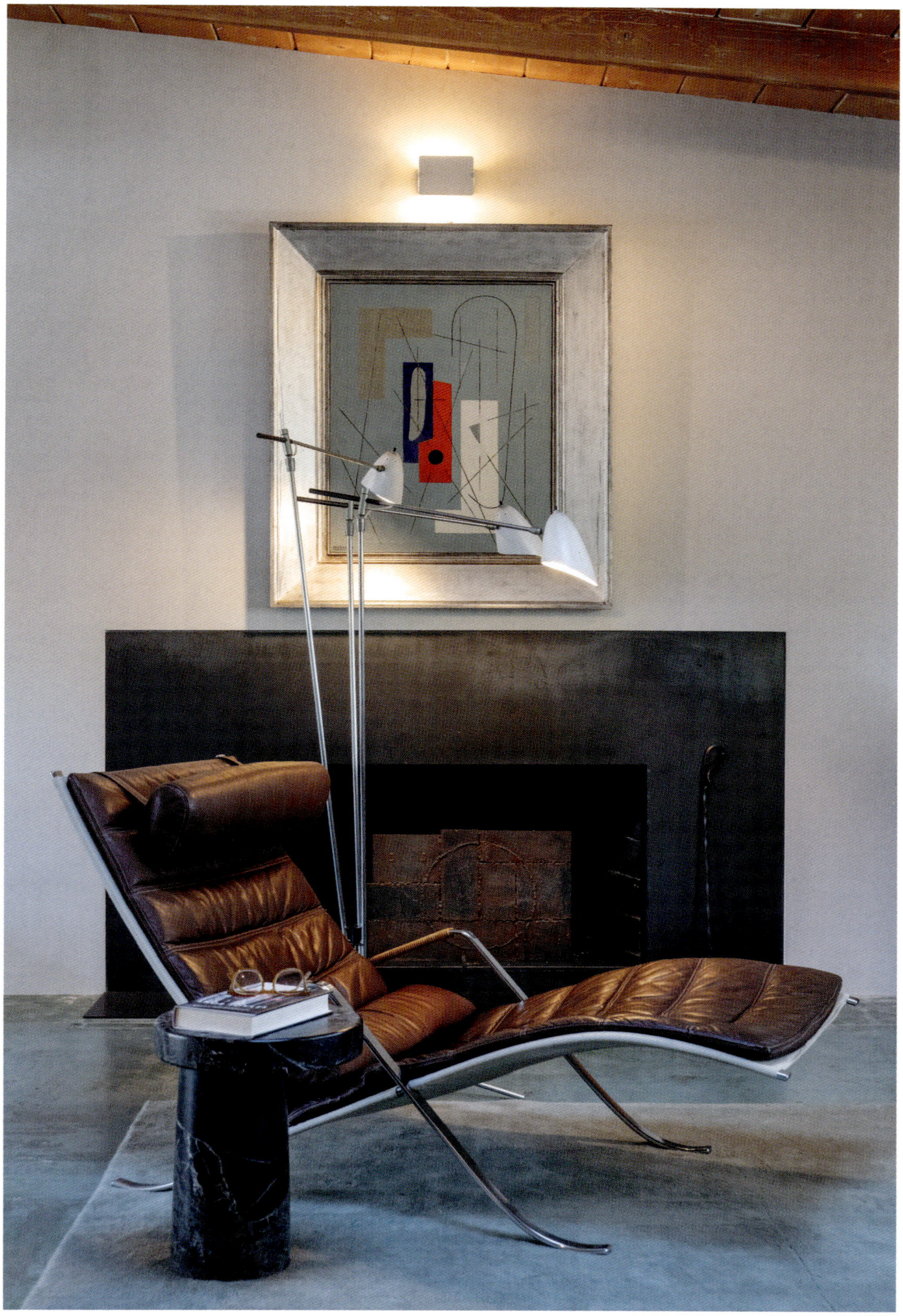

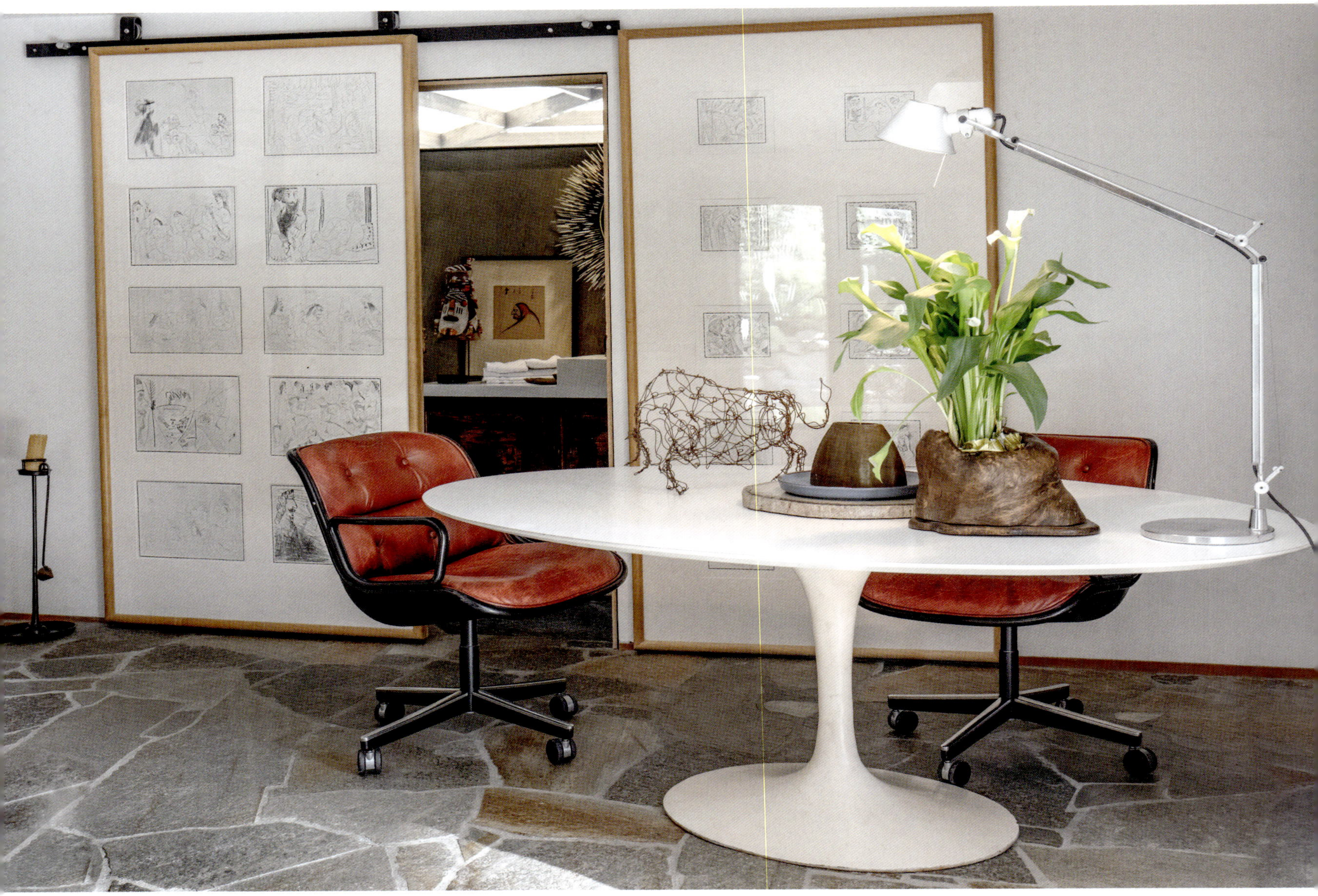

113

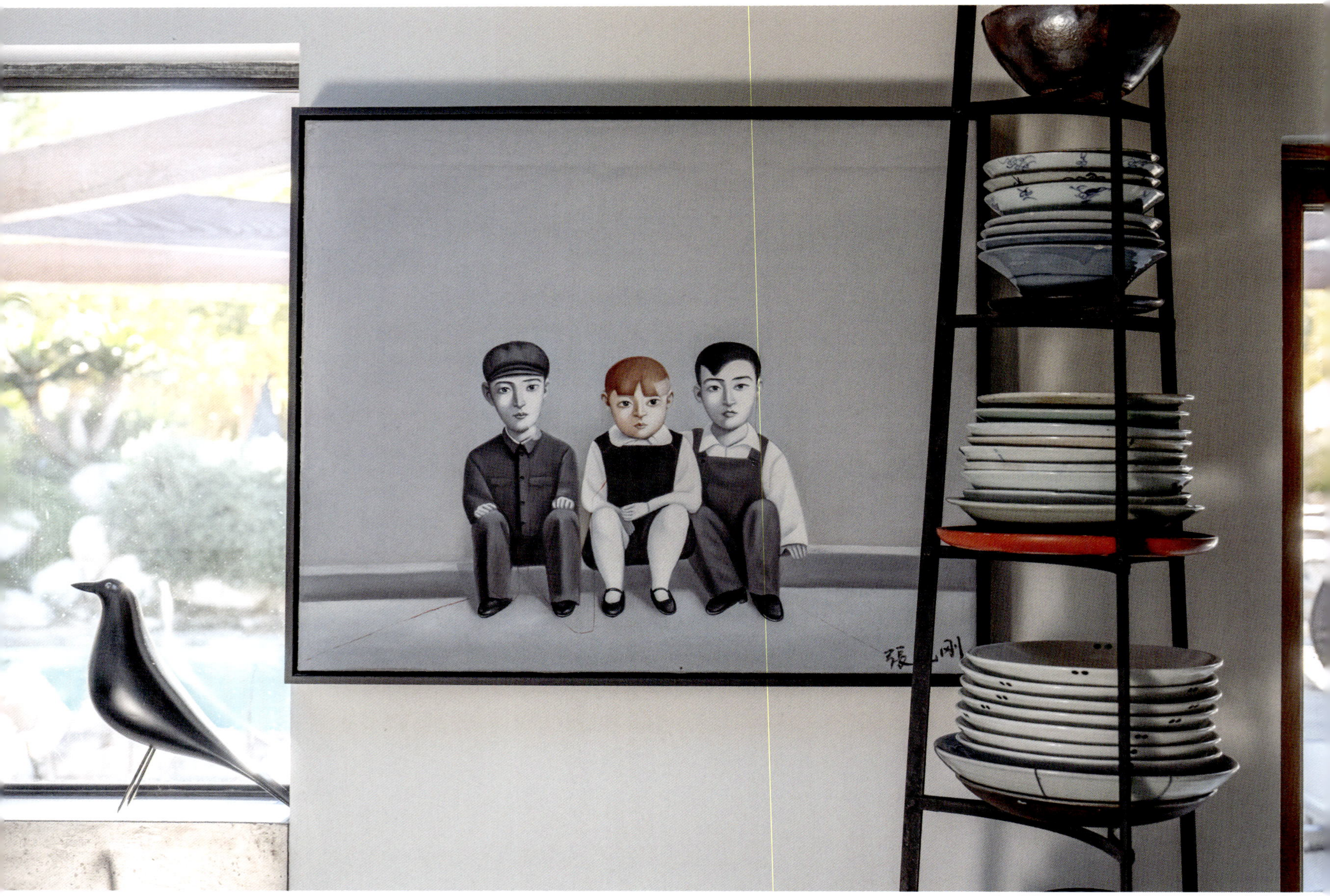

195

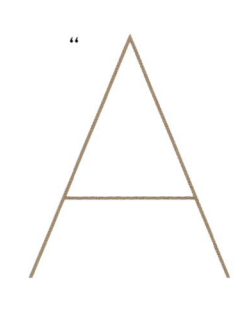

THUNDERBIRD HEIGHTS I

"ANYTHING GOES WITH EVERYTHING" is the professional tagline of Lori Goldstein, the fashion stylist behind memorable ad campaigns for Gap, American Express, and Versace. If her home in Rancho Mirage is any indication, it's also a personal credo.

Goldstein was spending a few months in Palm Springs during the pandemic when she visited a contemporary house in Thunderbird Heights with mountain and valley views she found so inspiring that she resolved to make the place her getaway from New York, instead of the Pennsylvania farmhouse she'd escaped to for years. "I packed up all my stuff and had it brought out here," she recalls, "and then it just kind of happened." When your stuff comprises a greatest-hits collection of twentieth-century design, from Art Deco to Memphis Milano, things have a way of just happening.

"I always prepare people before they turn the corner," Goldstein says of the approximately 2,500-square-foot living and dining space that now accommodates, among other things, chairs designed by Verner Panton, Gerrit Rietveld, and Pierre Paulin; tables by Paul Frankl, Joe D'Urso, and Philip and Kelvin LaVerne; lamps by Isamu Noguchi, Ferruccio Laviani, and Philippe Starck; and artwork by Roy Lichtenstein, Herman Cherry, and David Row. The Fornasetti butterfly credenza under the TV is a recent acquisition, as are a couple of sparkly Ettore Sottsass shelving units and a resin cabinet by Gaetano Pesce that sits in Goldstein's bedroom under one of Gary Lang's vibrant concentric circle paintings.

If anything goes with everything, it helps to have a fearless eye. "I'm definitely into bright and bold," says Goldstein, who now has a bright and bold clothing line, LOGO, that she markets on QVC. "But there are no rules. I'm not really worried about what anyone else thinks."

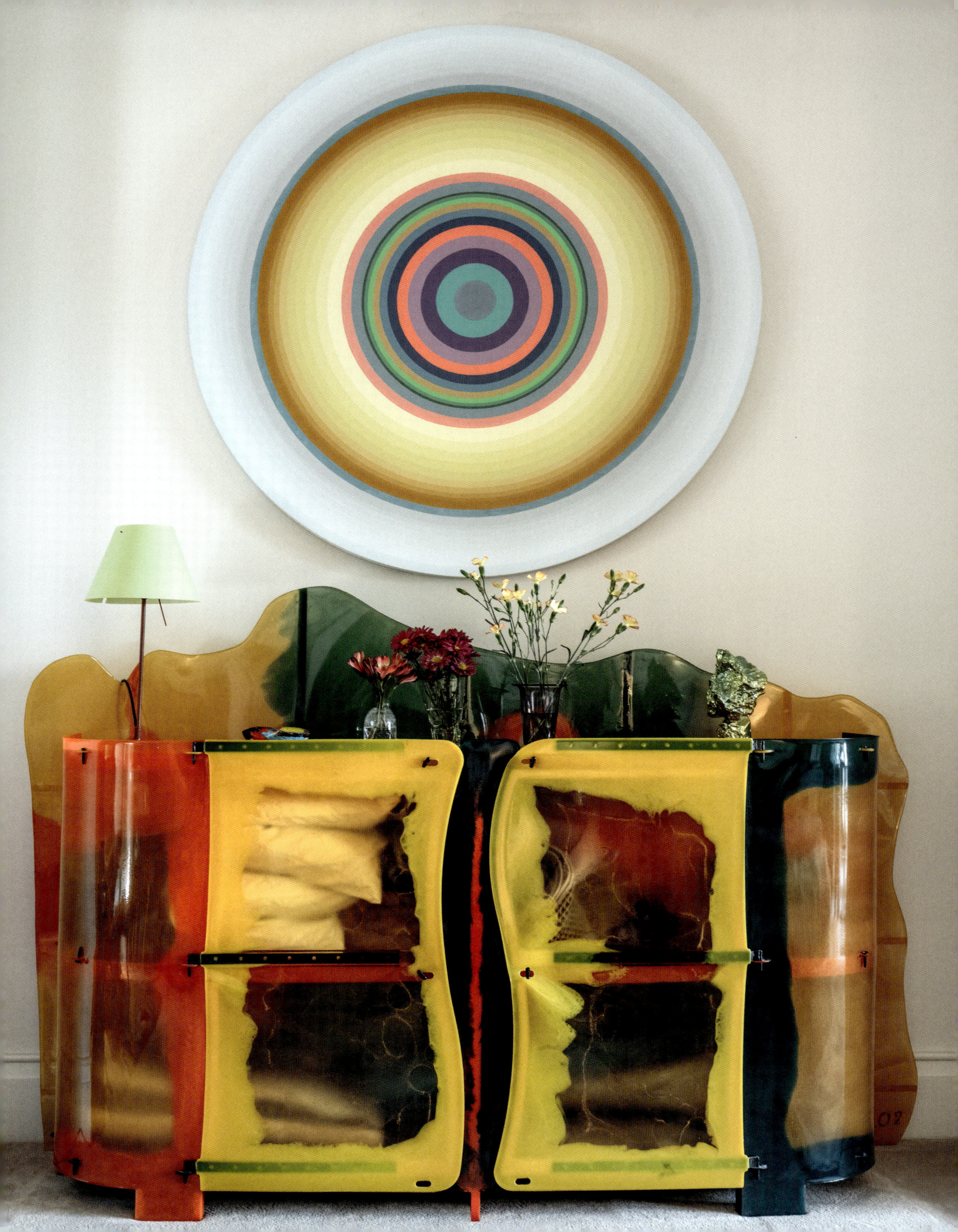

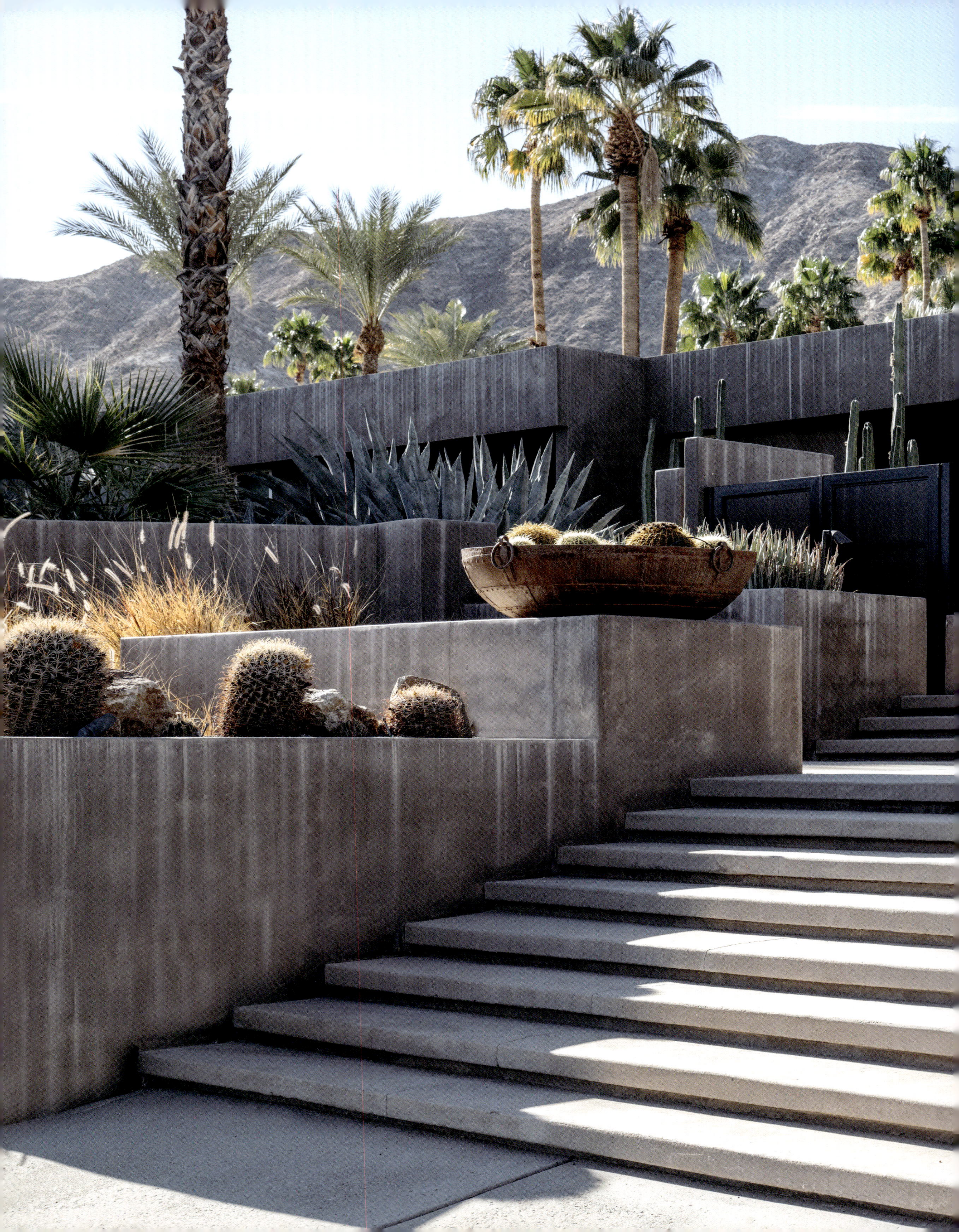

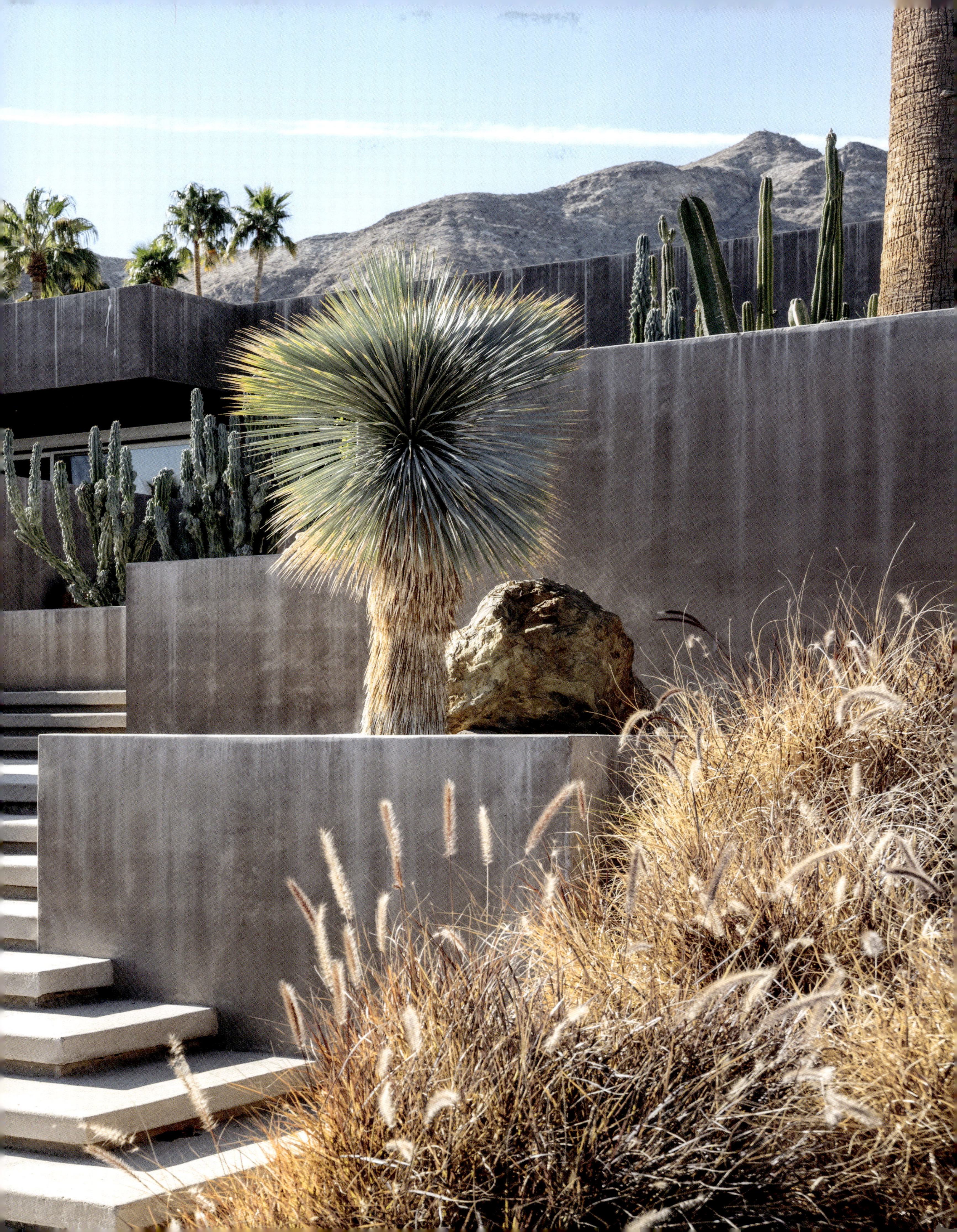

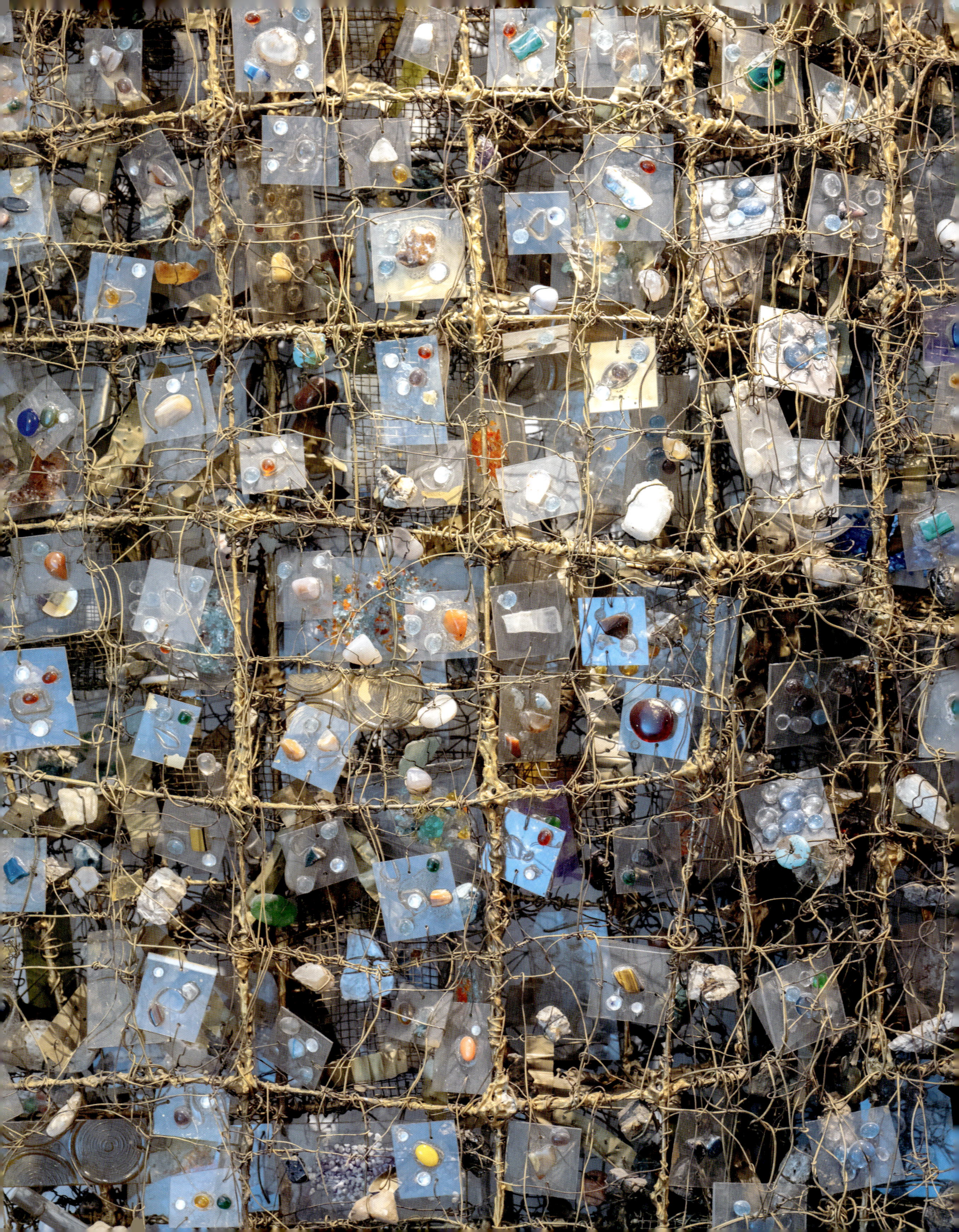

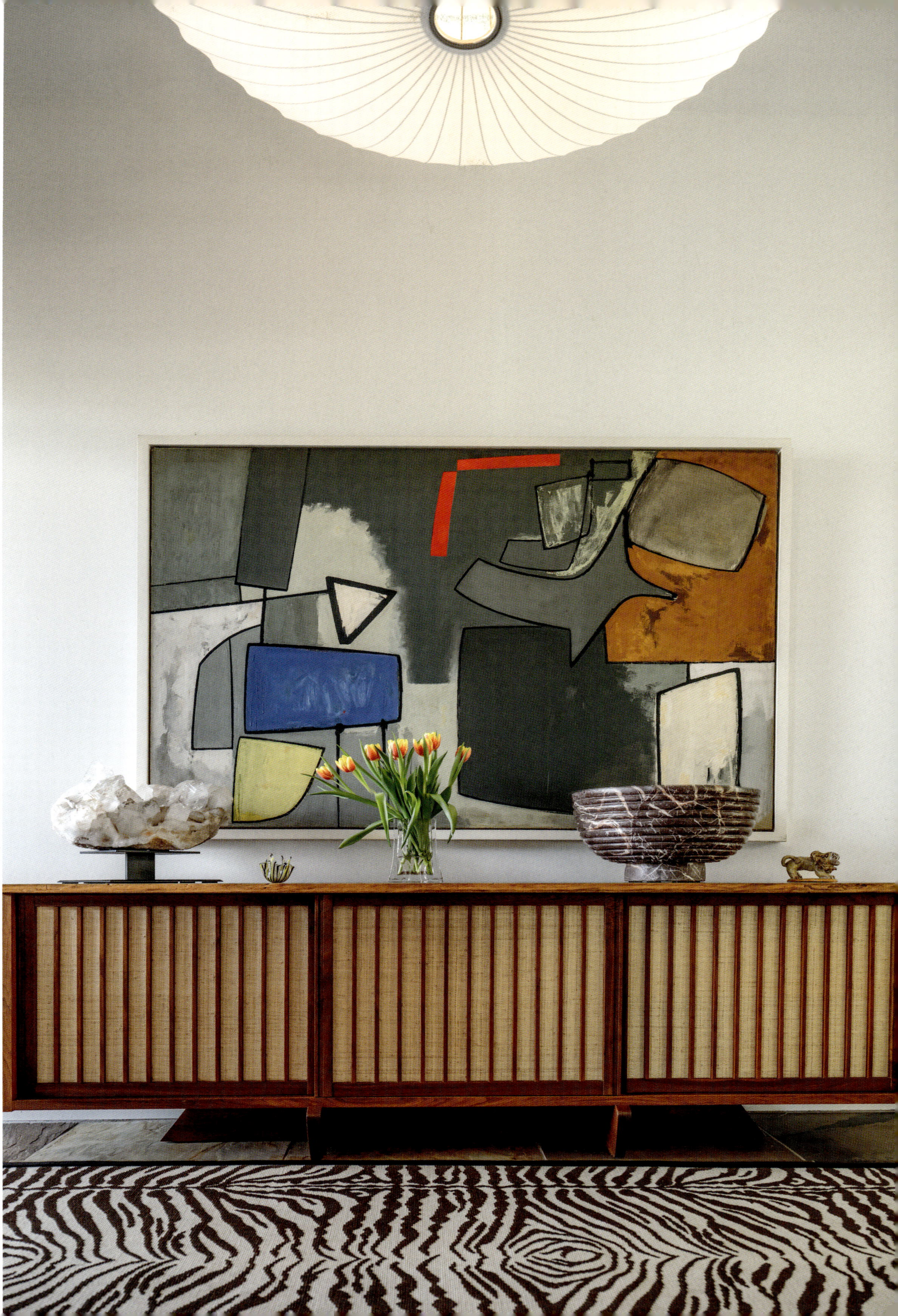

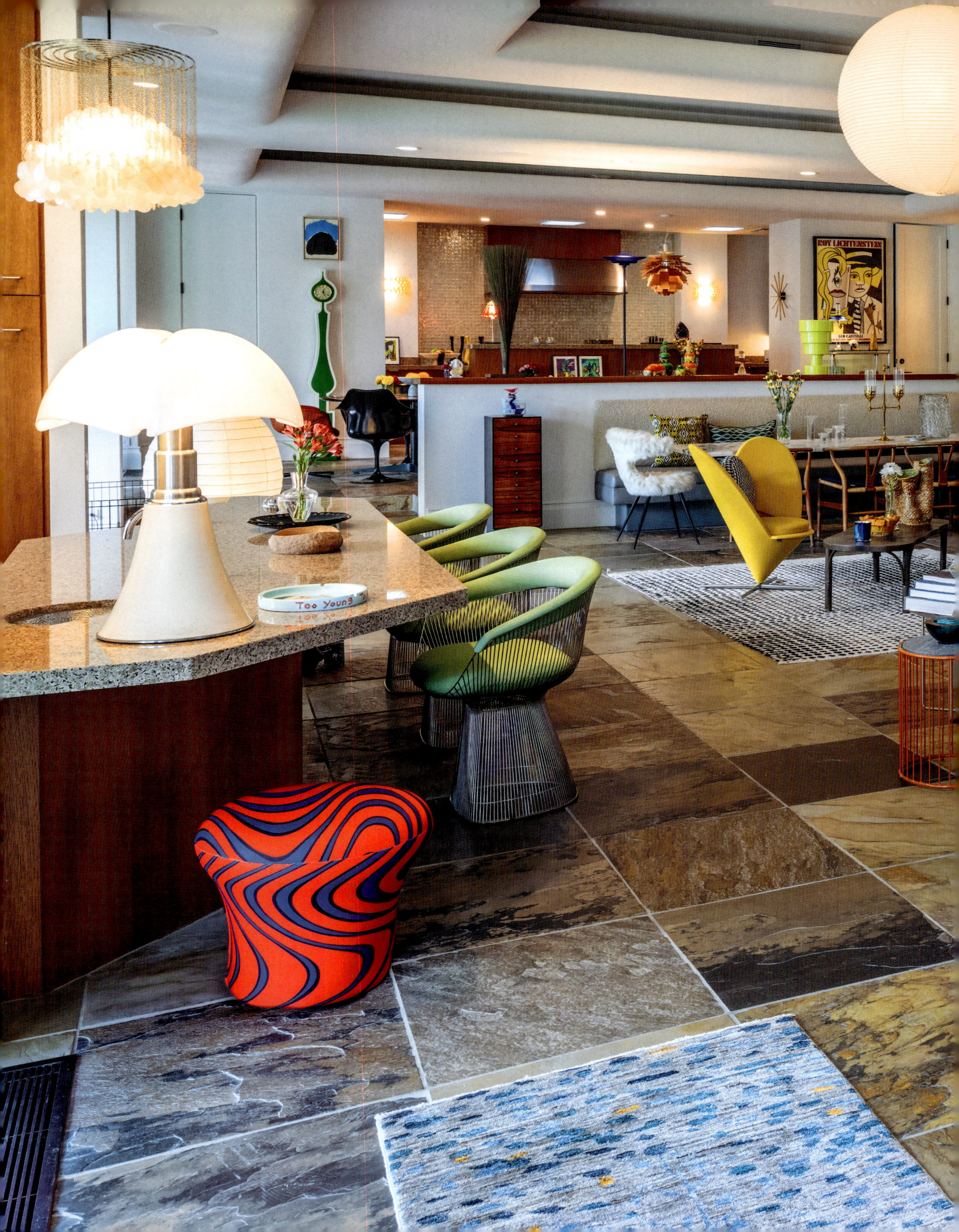
ROY LICHTENSTEIN
Too Young

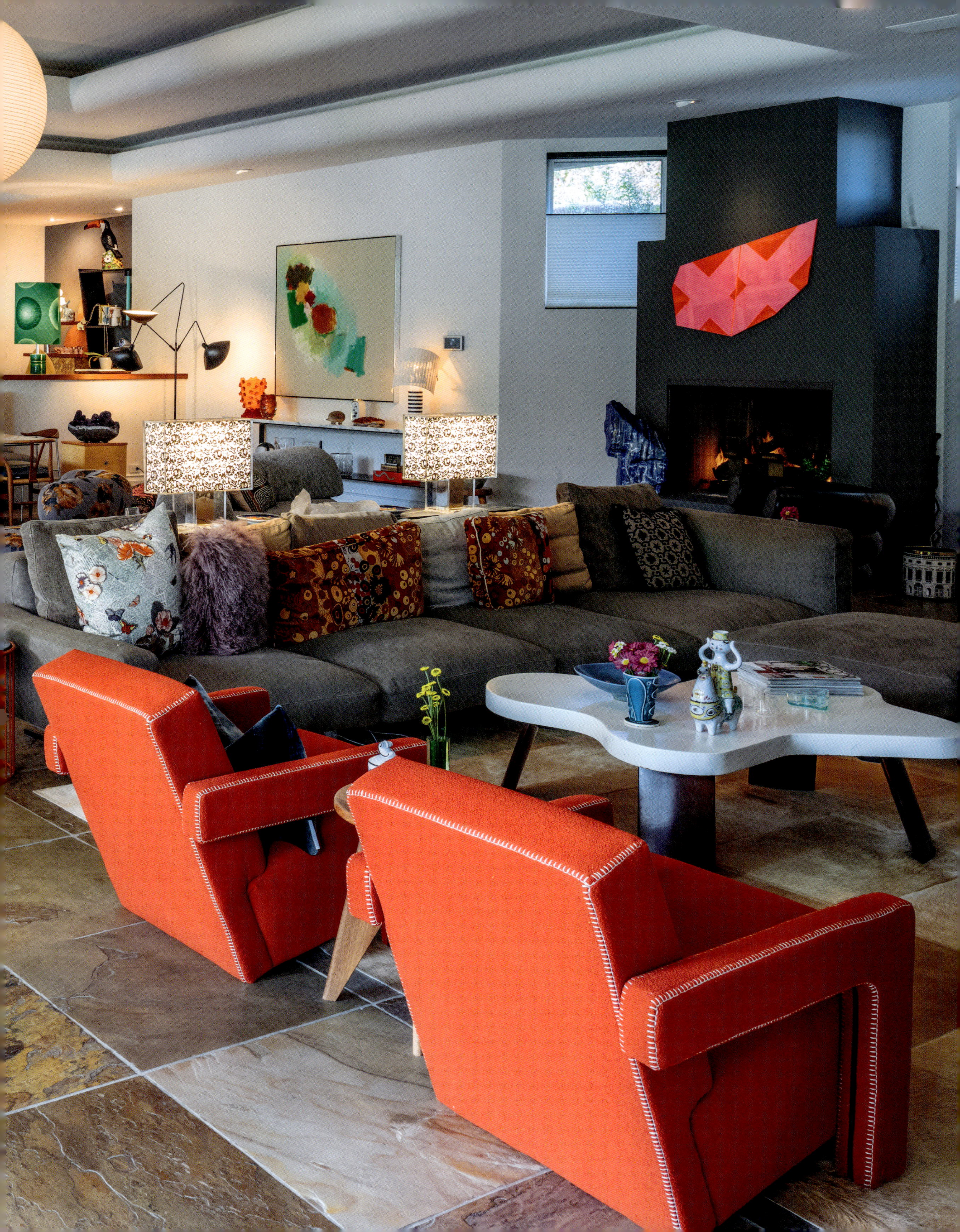

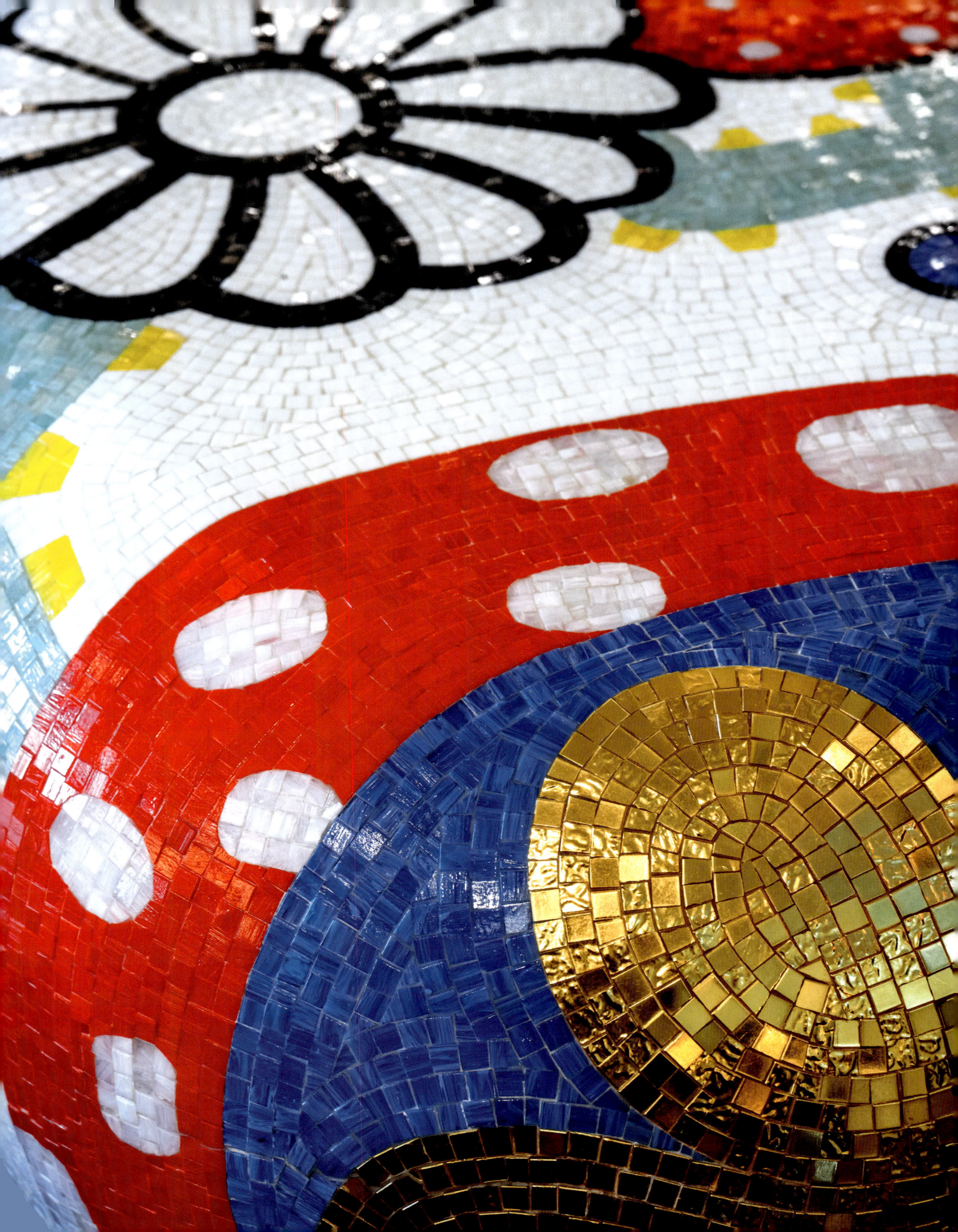

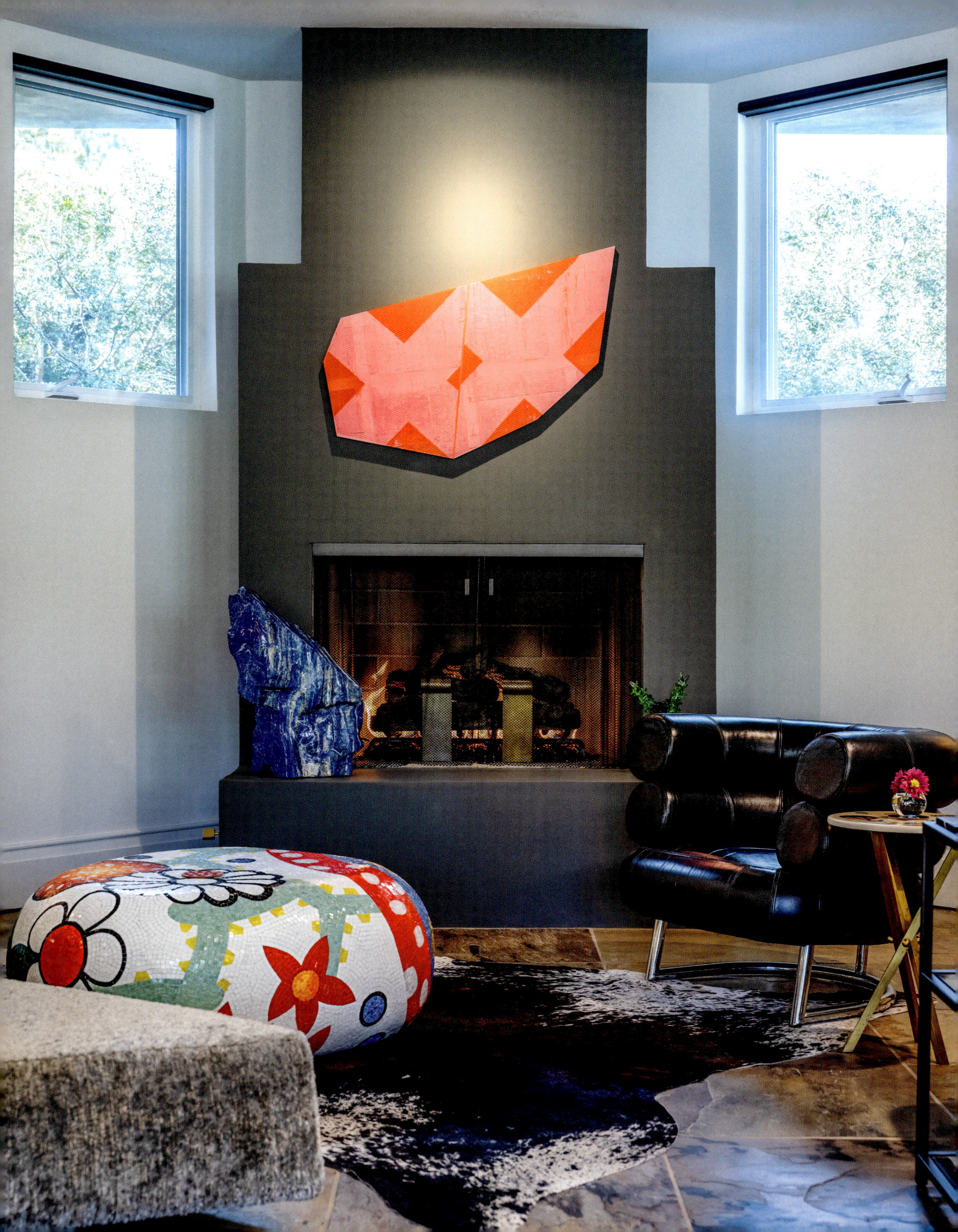

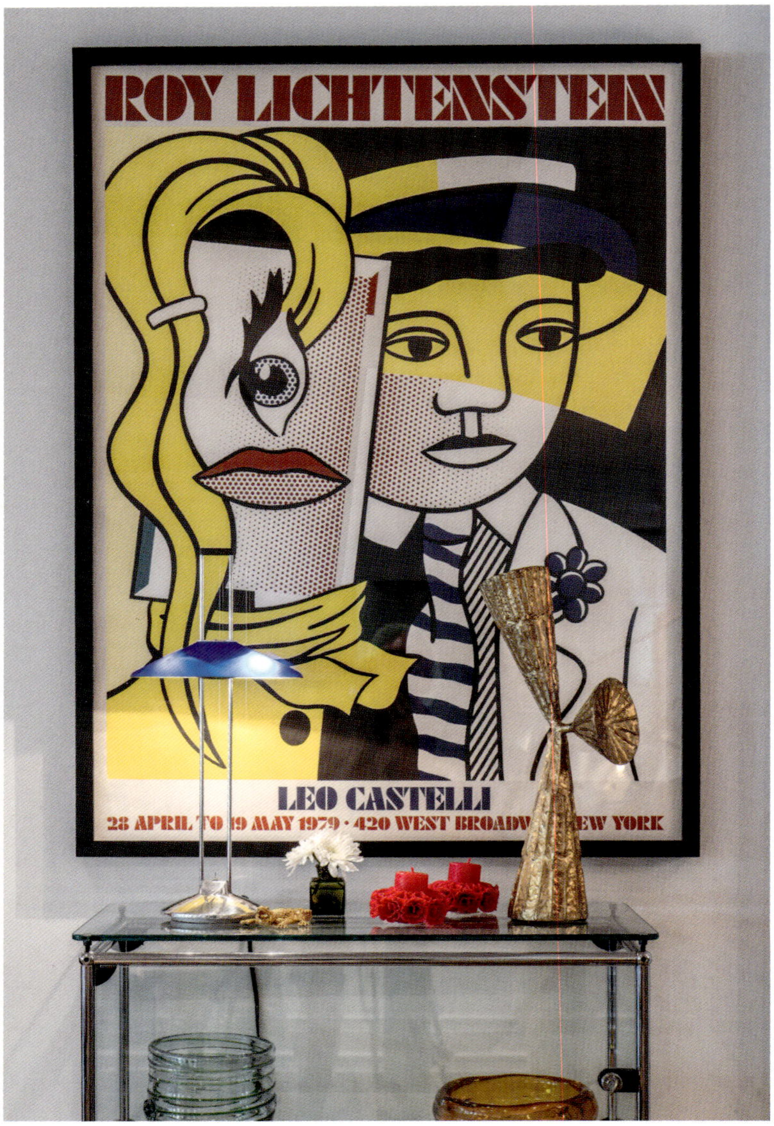
ROY LICHTENSTEIN
LEO CASTELLI

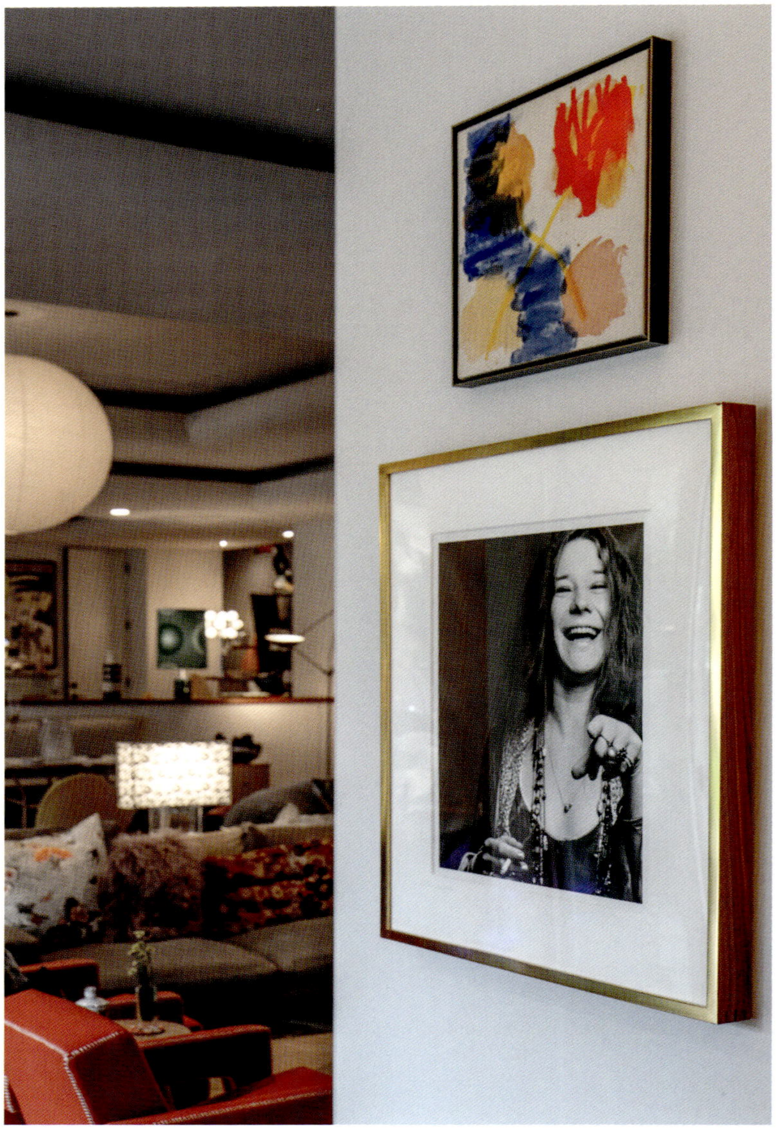

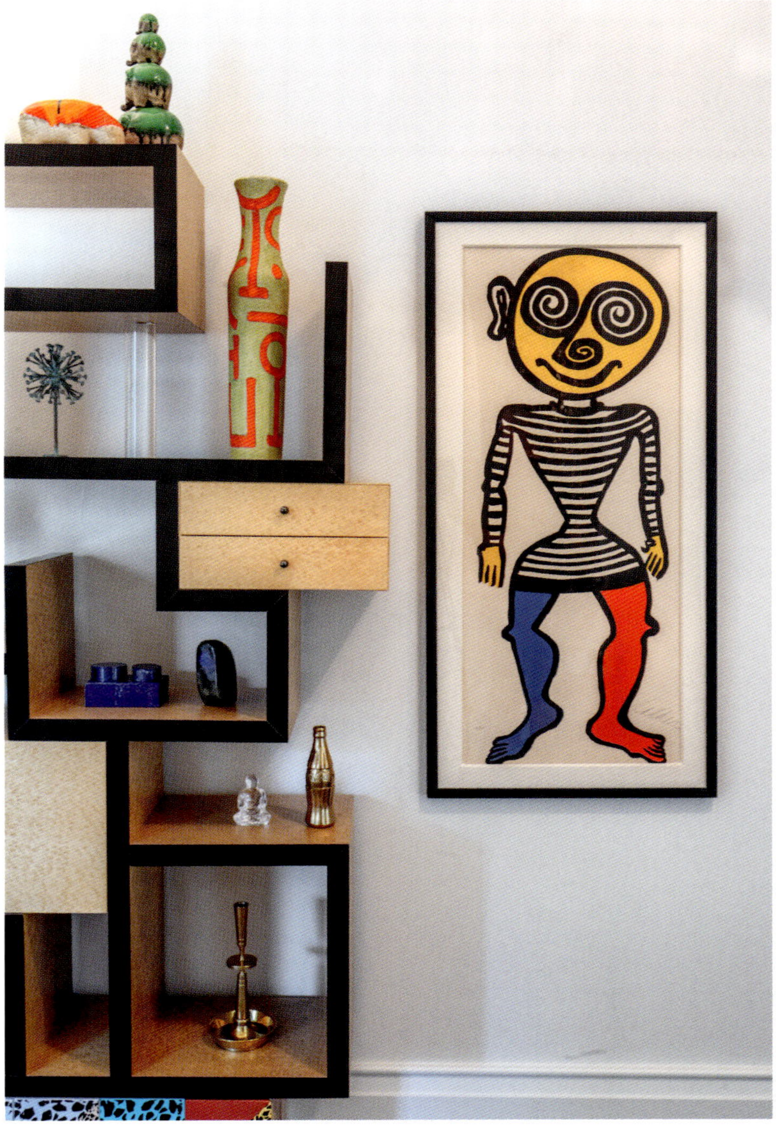

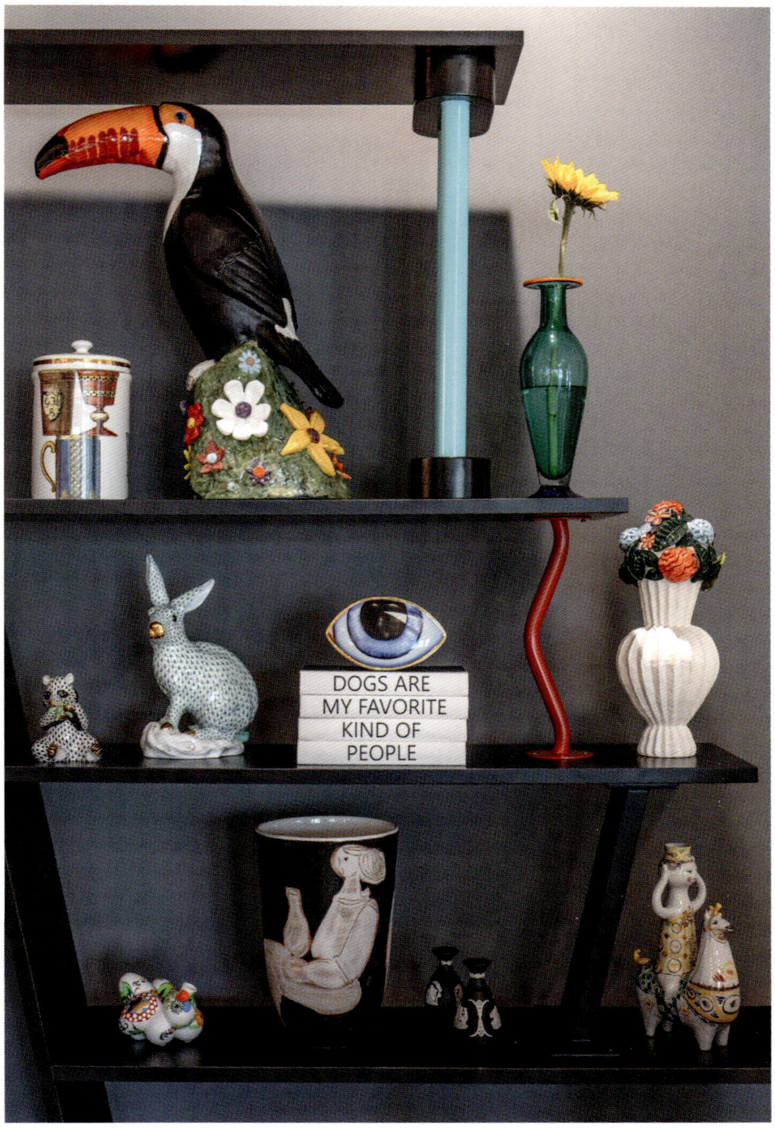
DOGS ARE
MY FAVORITE
KIND OF
PEOPLE

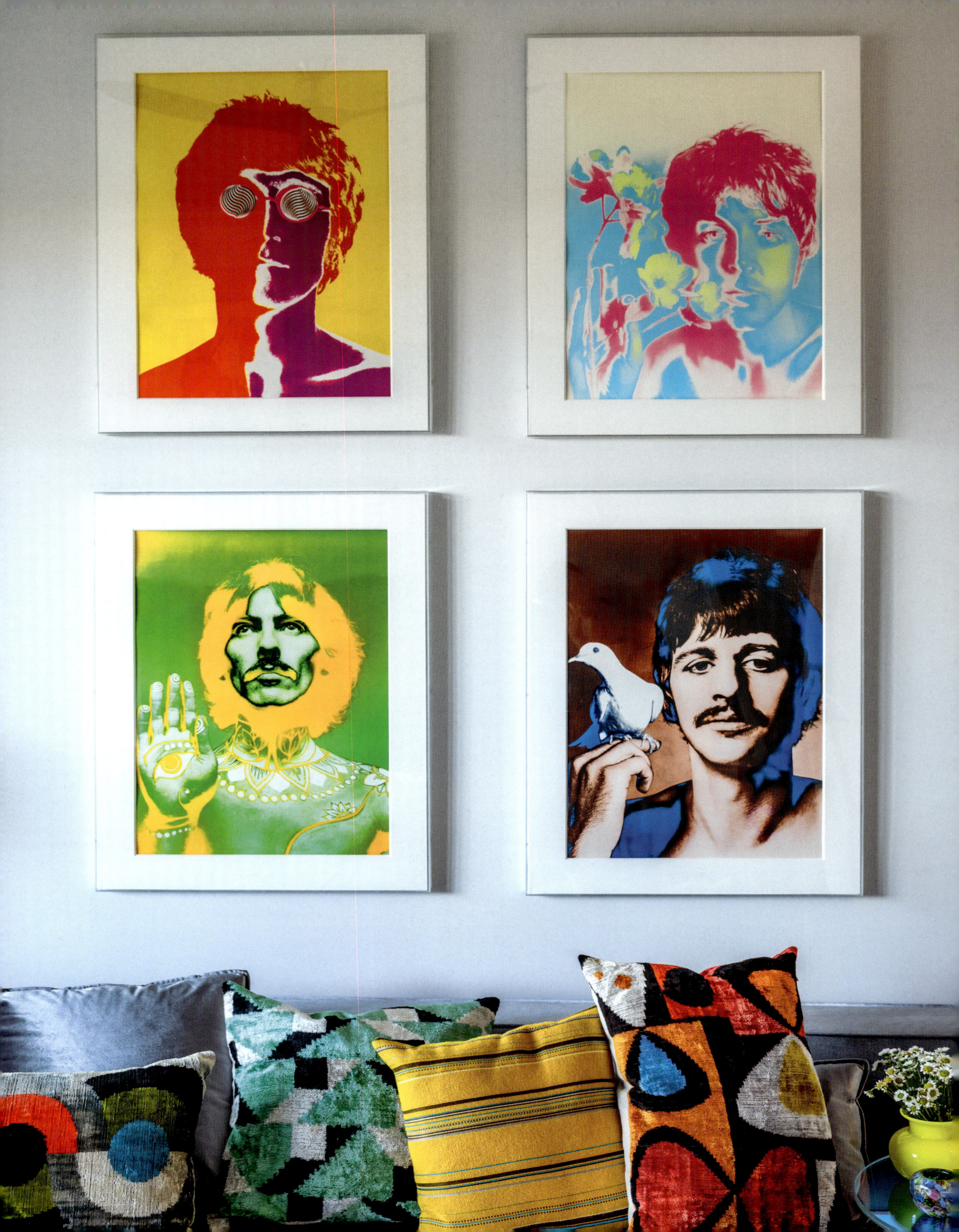

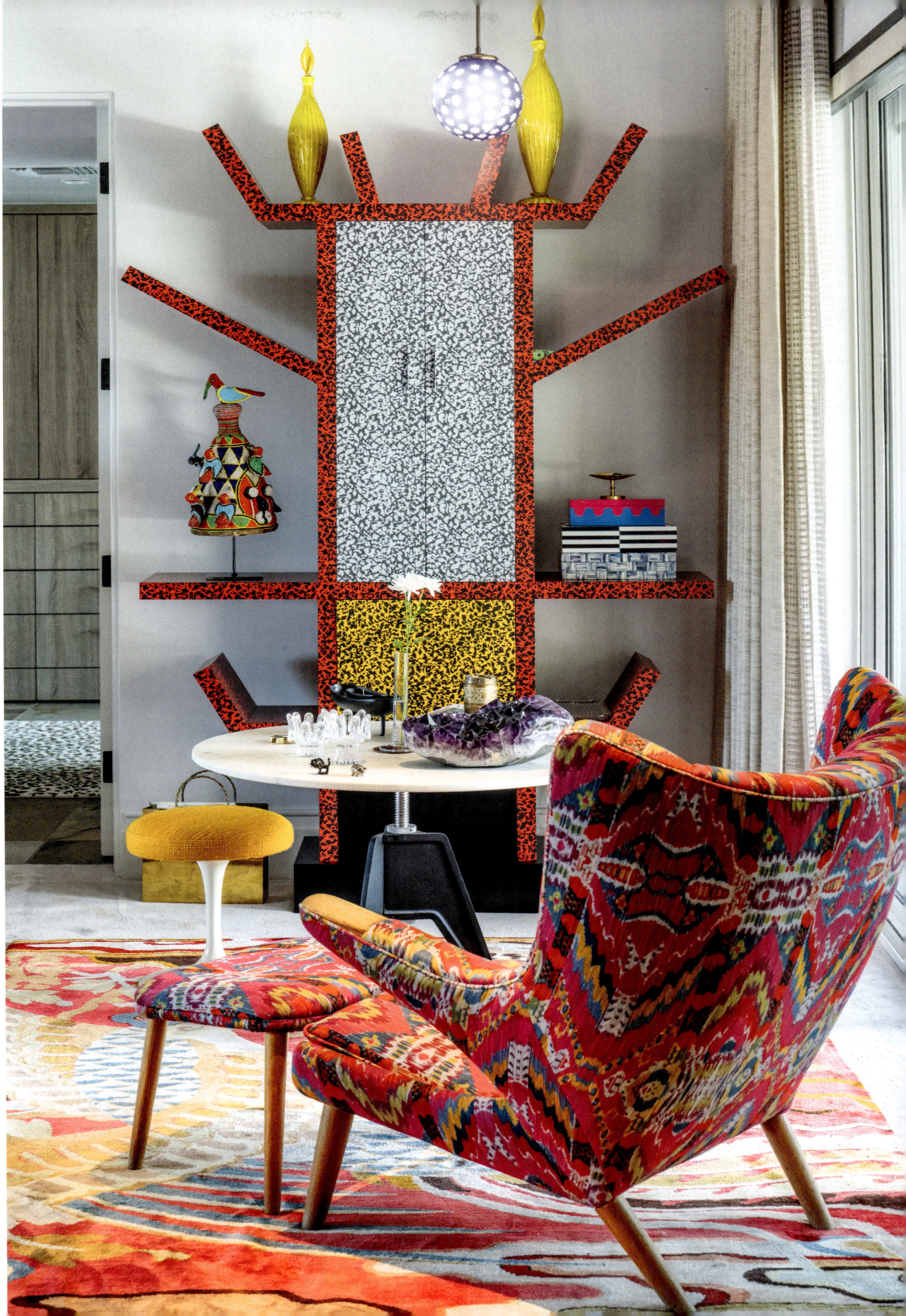

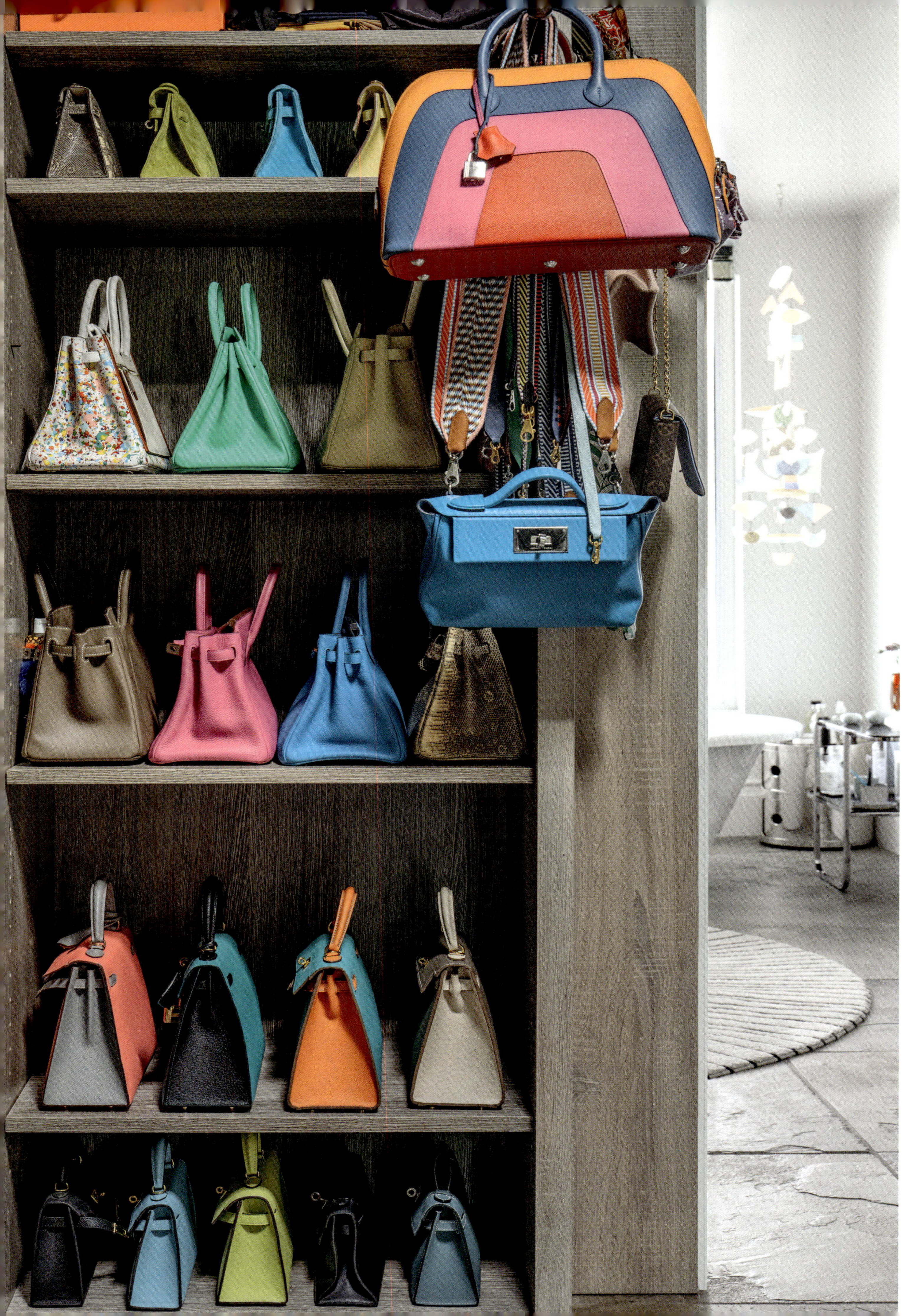

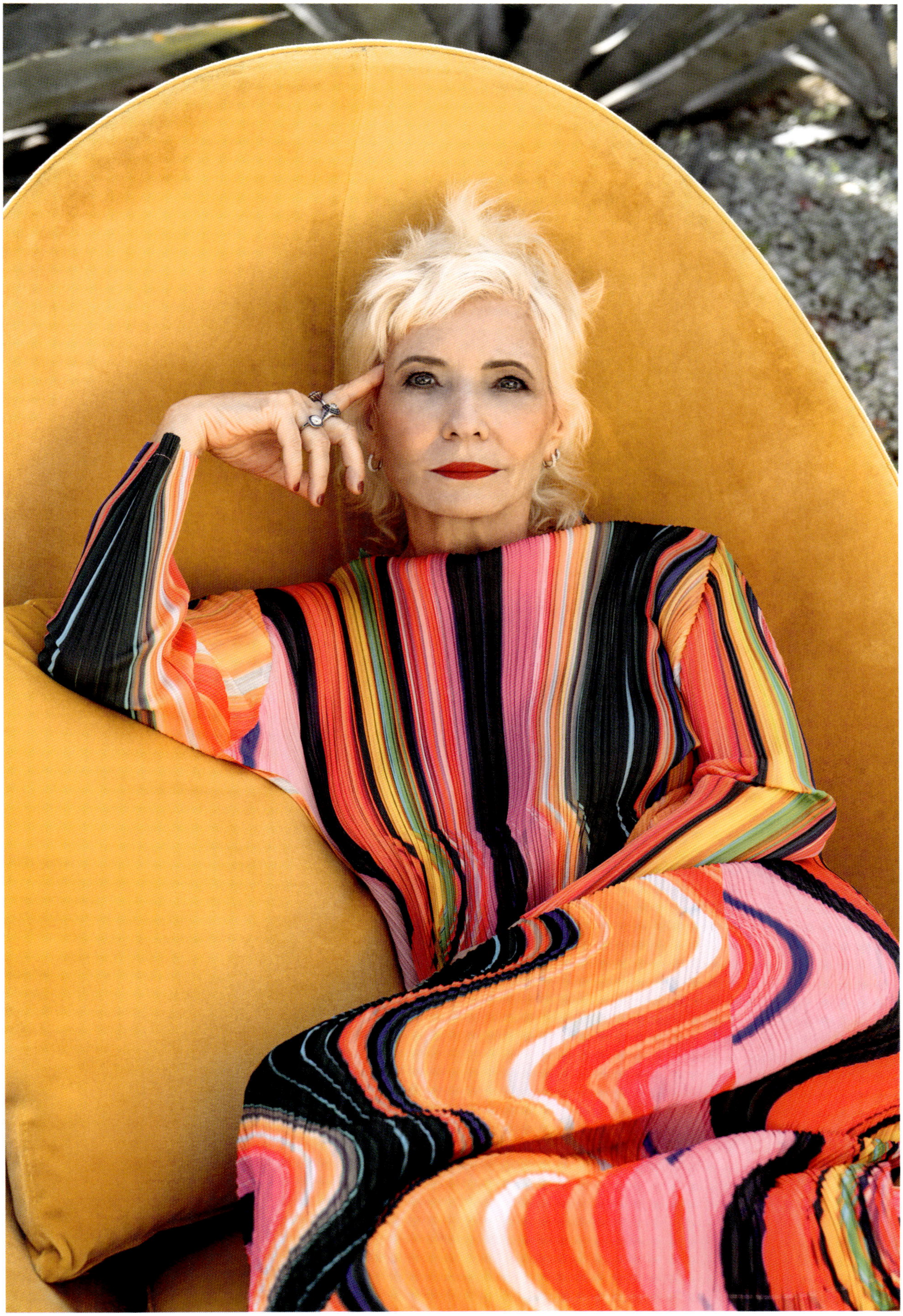

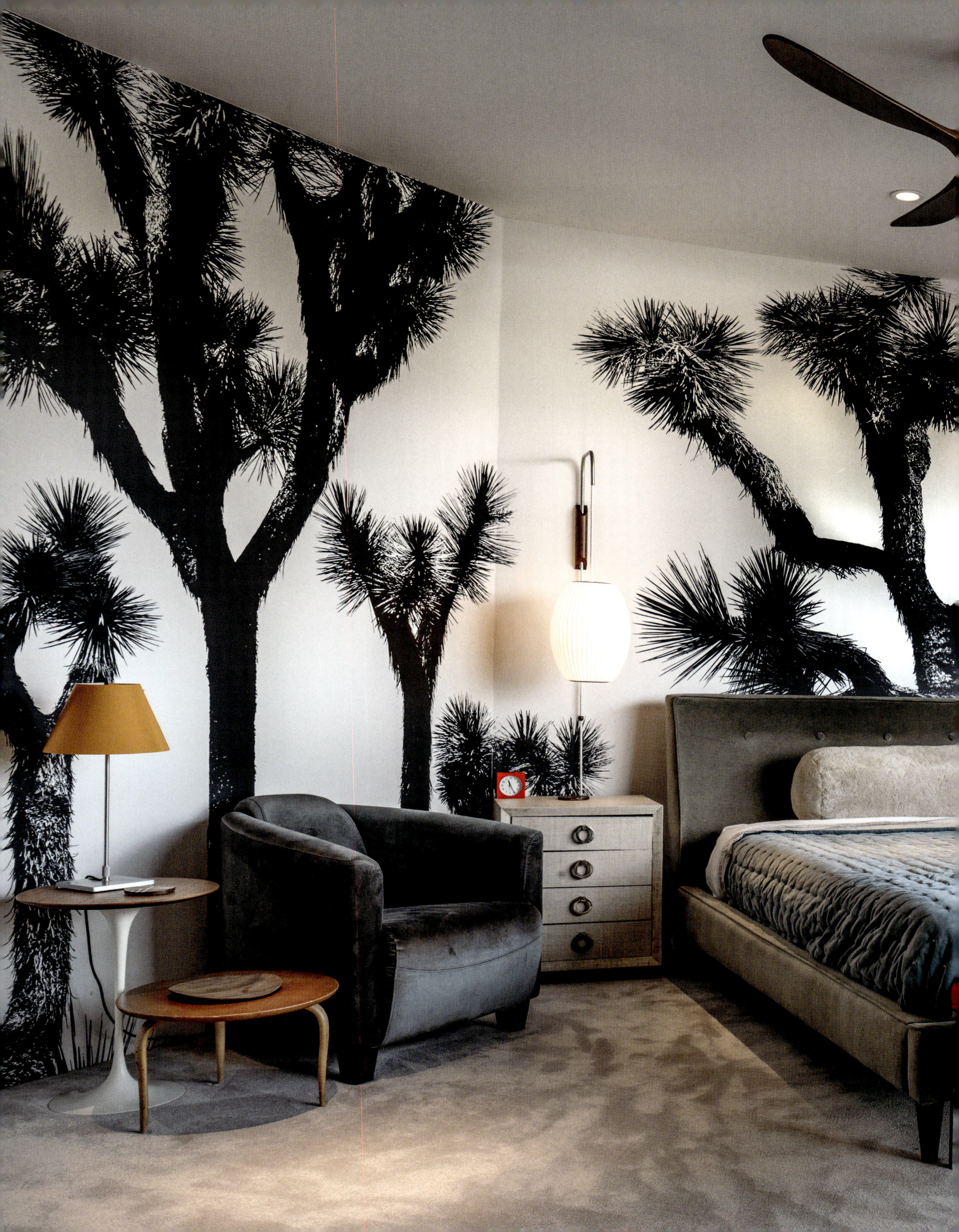

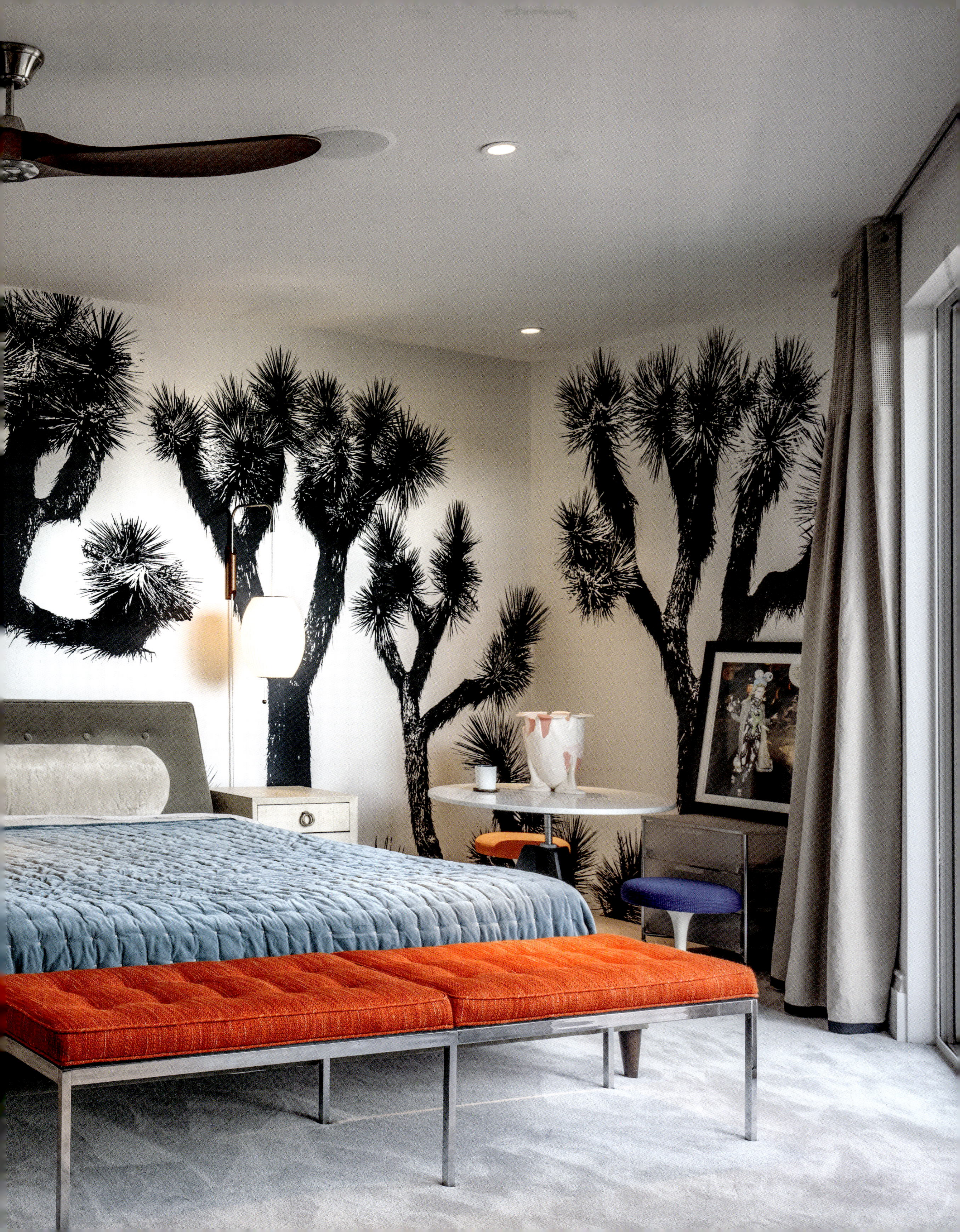

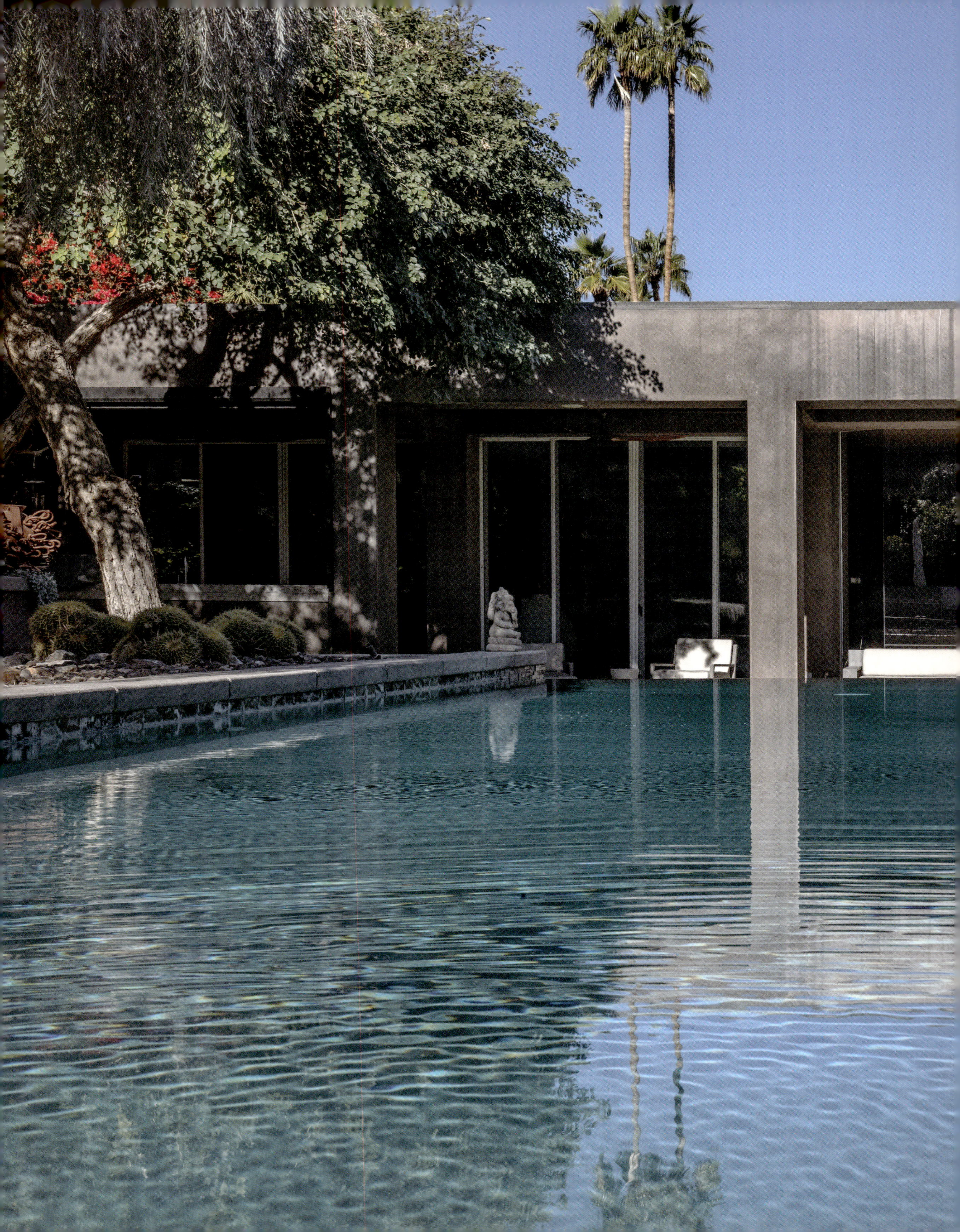

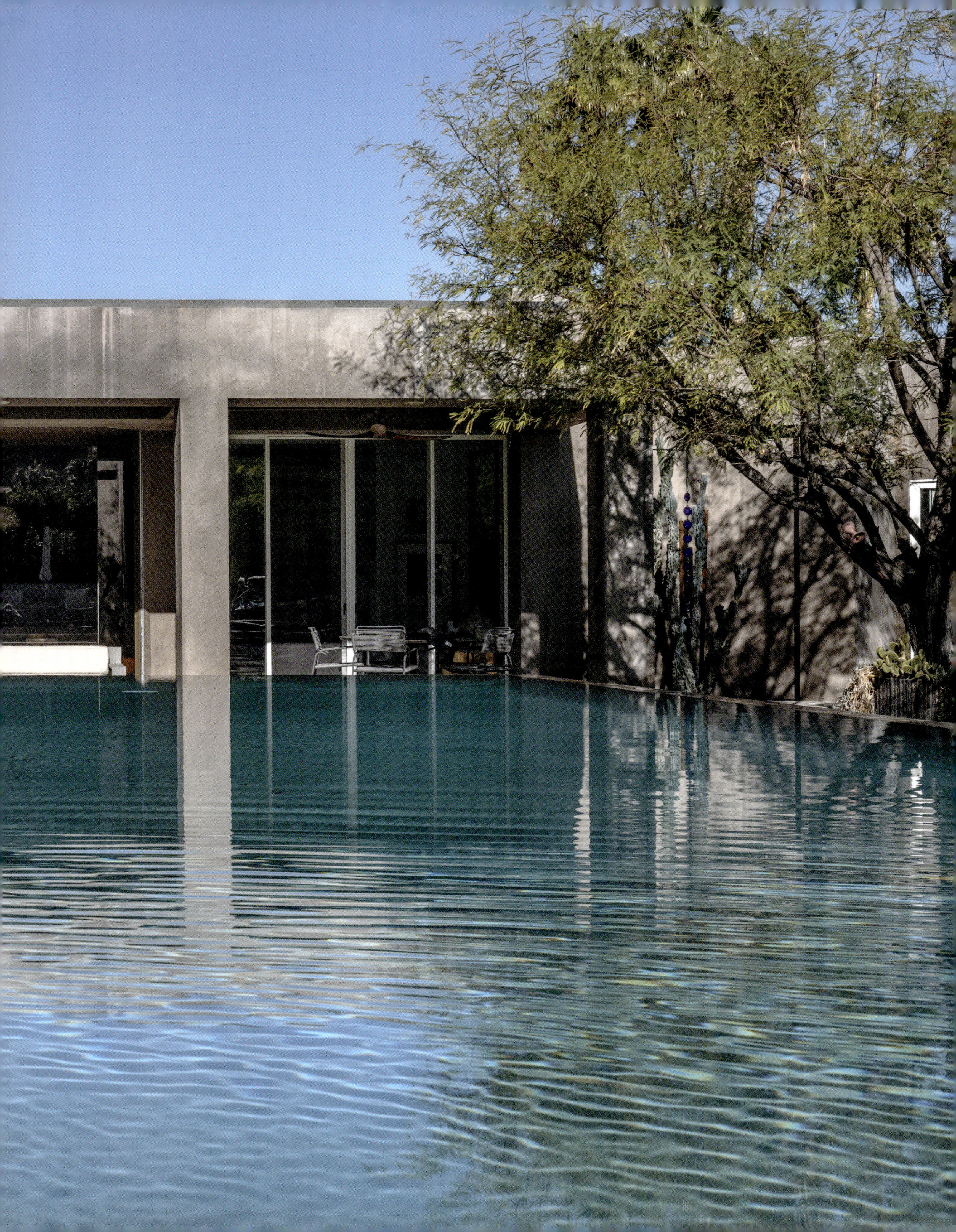

MOVIE COLONY

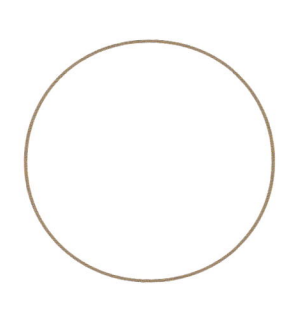

ONCE (IN 2007), A MAN (DANIEL GILES) drove to Palm Springs to look at a house that the architect Donald Wexler had built for himself and his family in 1955. More recently, the house had been used as a vacation rental, and it was not in good shape—think glass bricks, linoleum tile, stained carpeting. But Giles, the founder of a fragrance brand, Perfumehead, was entranced. "I sat in the living room and just followed the line of the house," he remembers, "and you could see that it was very pure, with a very special energy."

He bought the house, then enlisted Wexler, in his eighties at the time, to help him restore it. They incorporated features that the architect had originally planned for the house but couldn't afford, like terrazzo floors and a larger window in the living room to frame the old olive tree outside. Giles loved the house—"It was my sanctuary," he says—but in 2016, facing some difficult professional and personal challenges, he decided to sell it. The buyer was a friend of his, someone he knew would be a good steward, but, he admits, "I immediately thought, 'What have I done?'"

Seven years later the friend bought another property in the desert and agreed to sell the house back to Giles. There were tears in Giles's eyes as he was handed the keys for the second time. His appreciation for the house had only grown over the years, and he hired the interior designer Darren Brown to develop a paint color just for it—"Wexler white"—and to help him "pare all the furniture back to shapes and forms that complemented its architecture." He even came up with a fragrance inspired by the scents outside the house: pine, verbena, orange blossom. It's called 1272. True story.

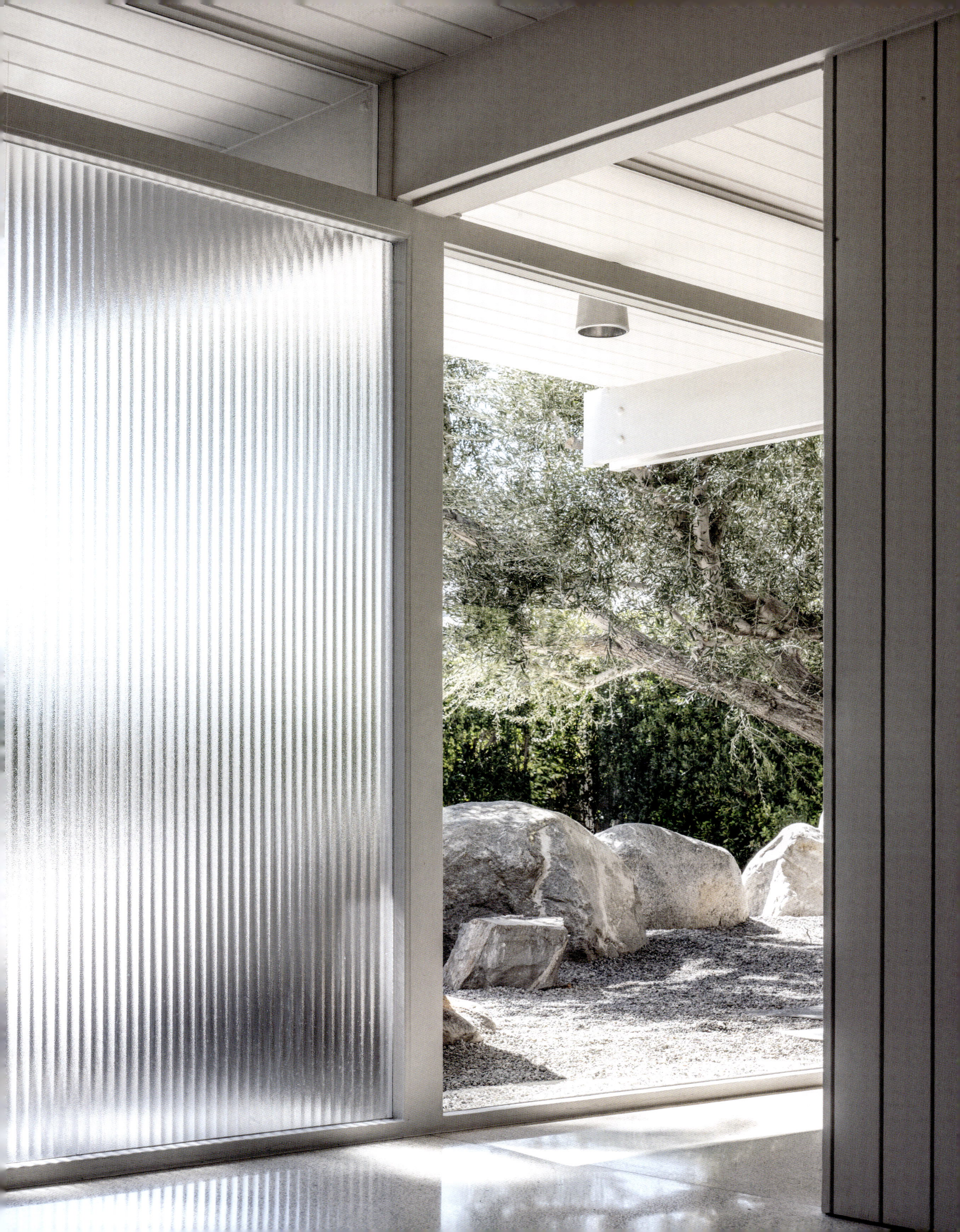

218

219

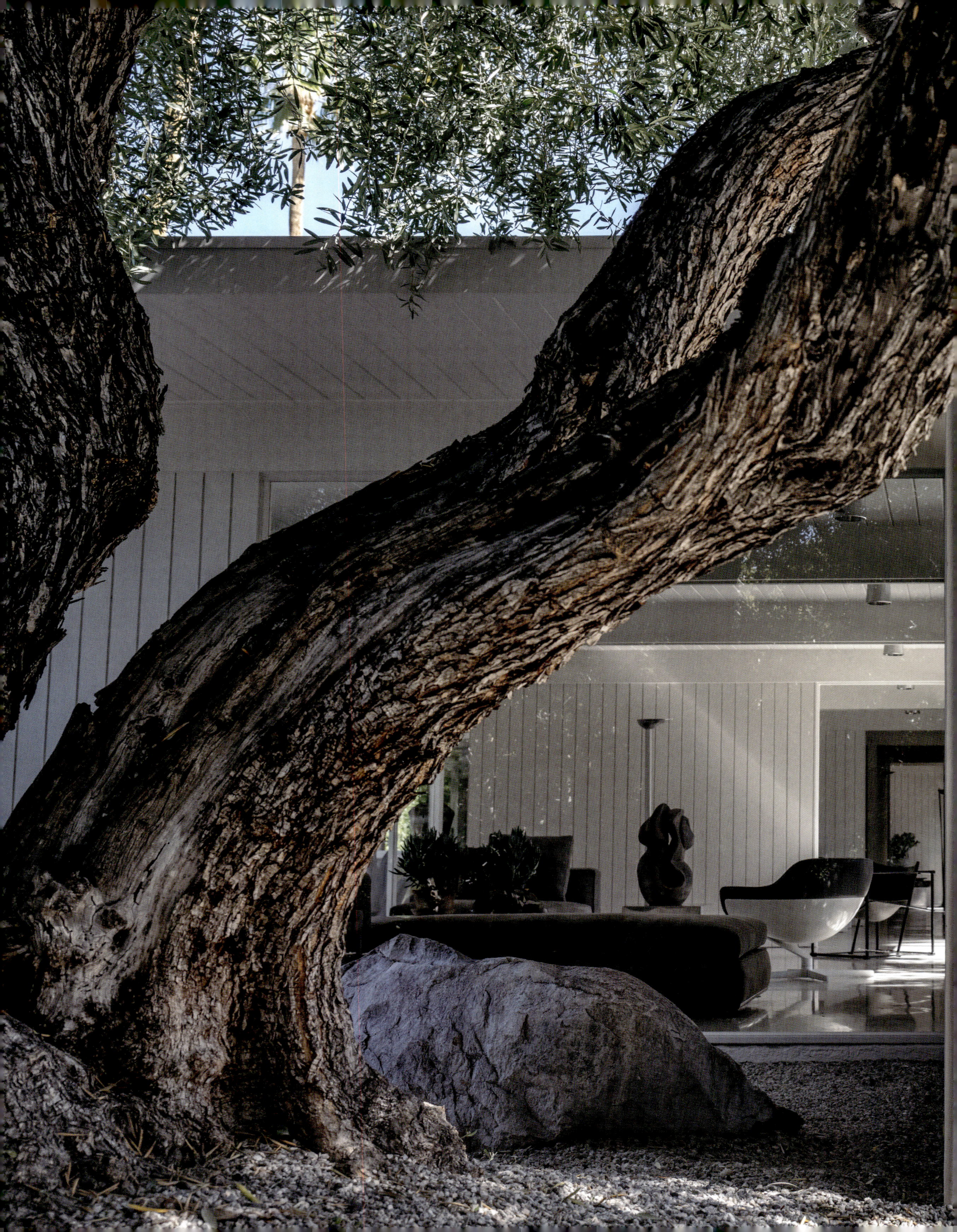

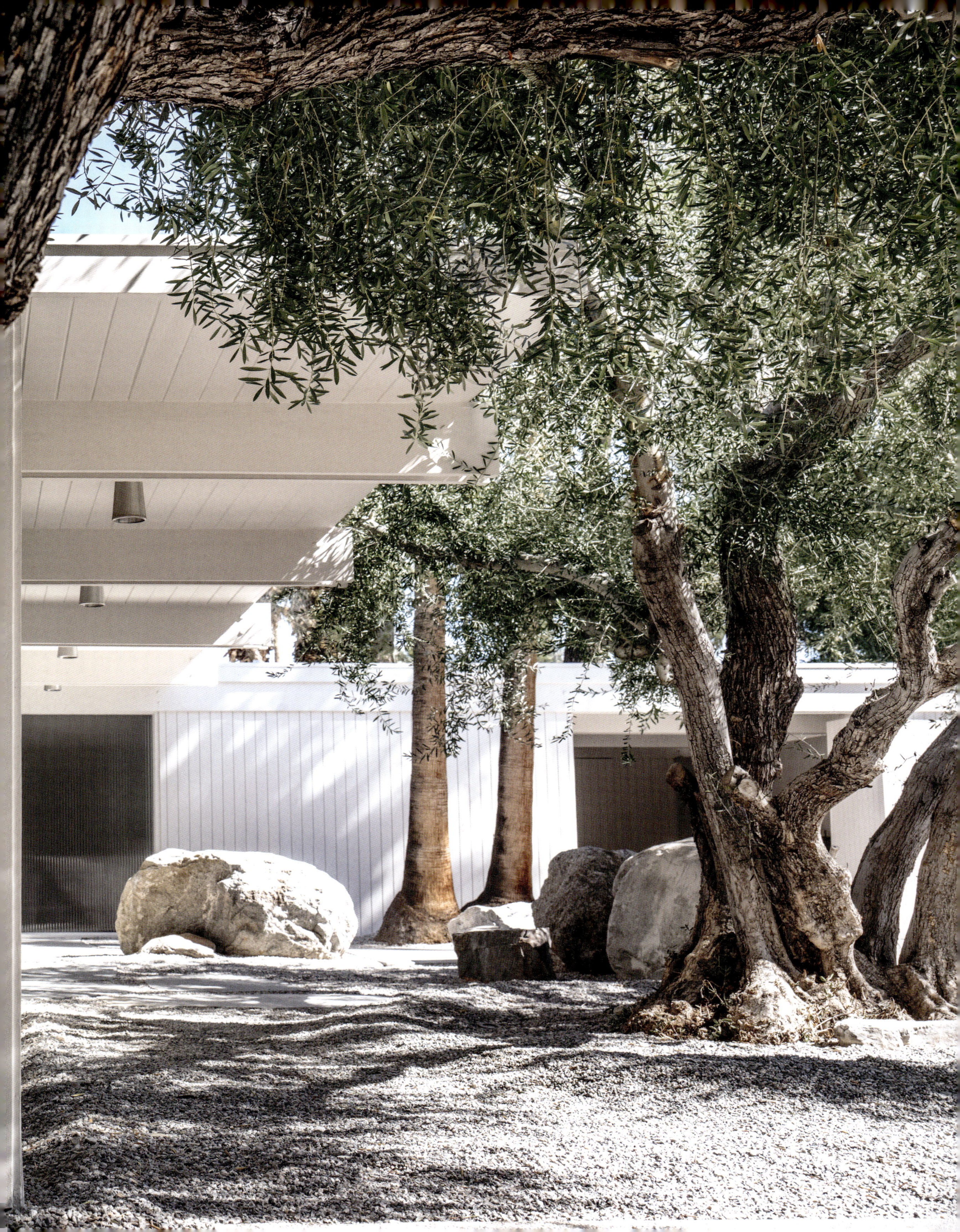

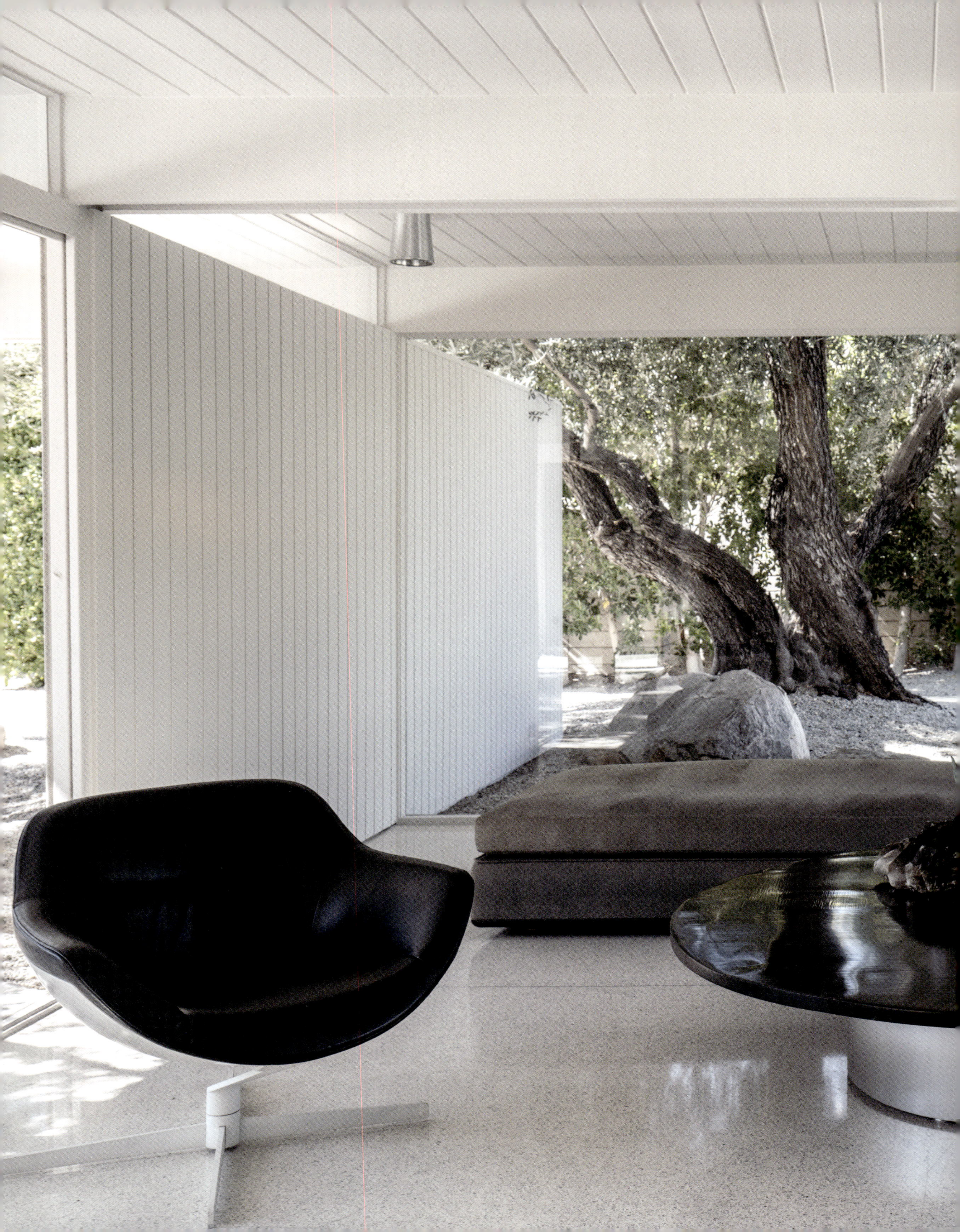

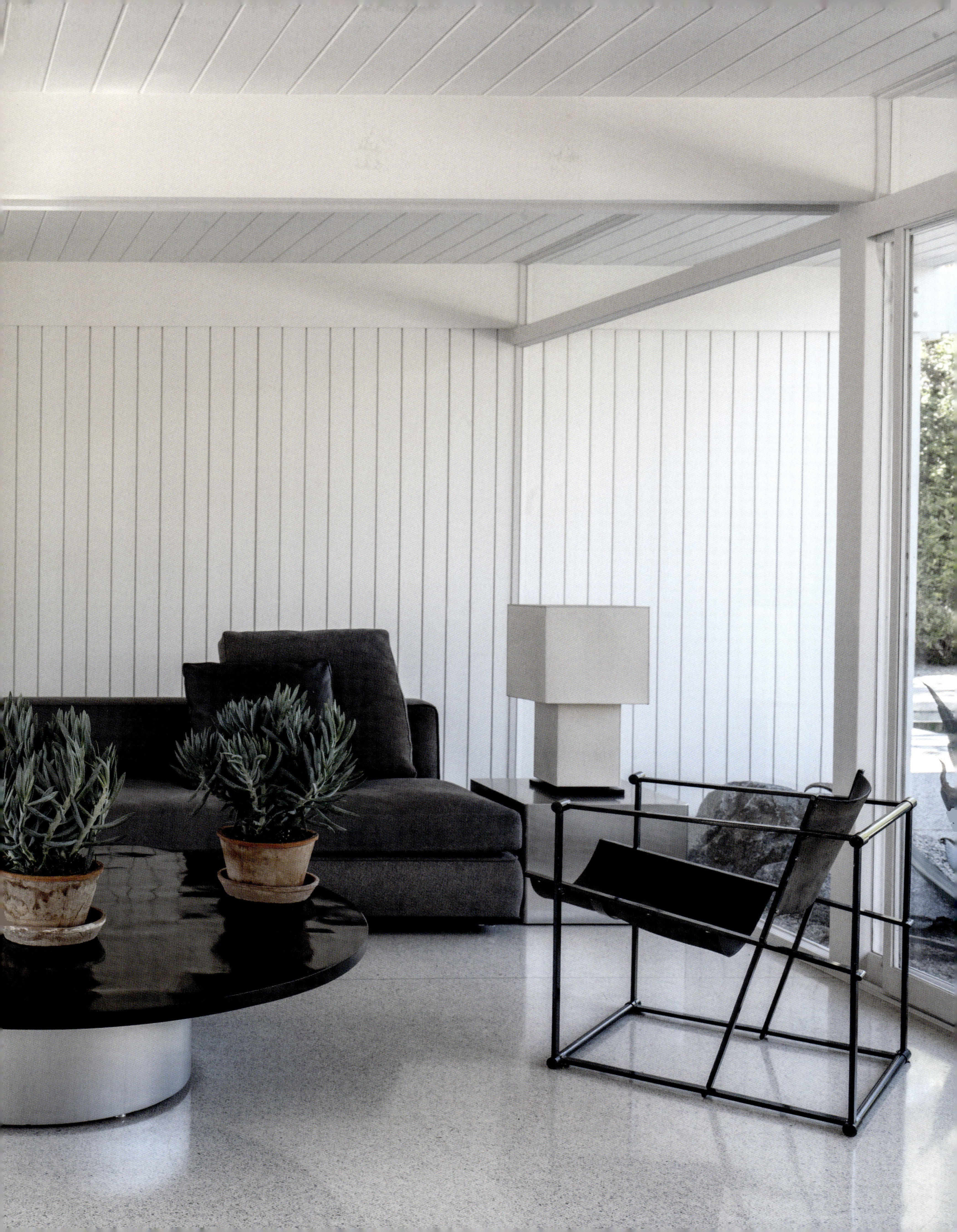

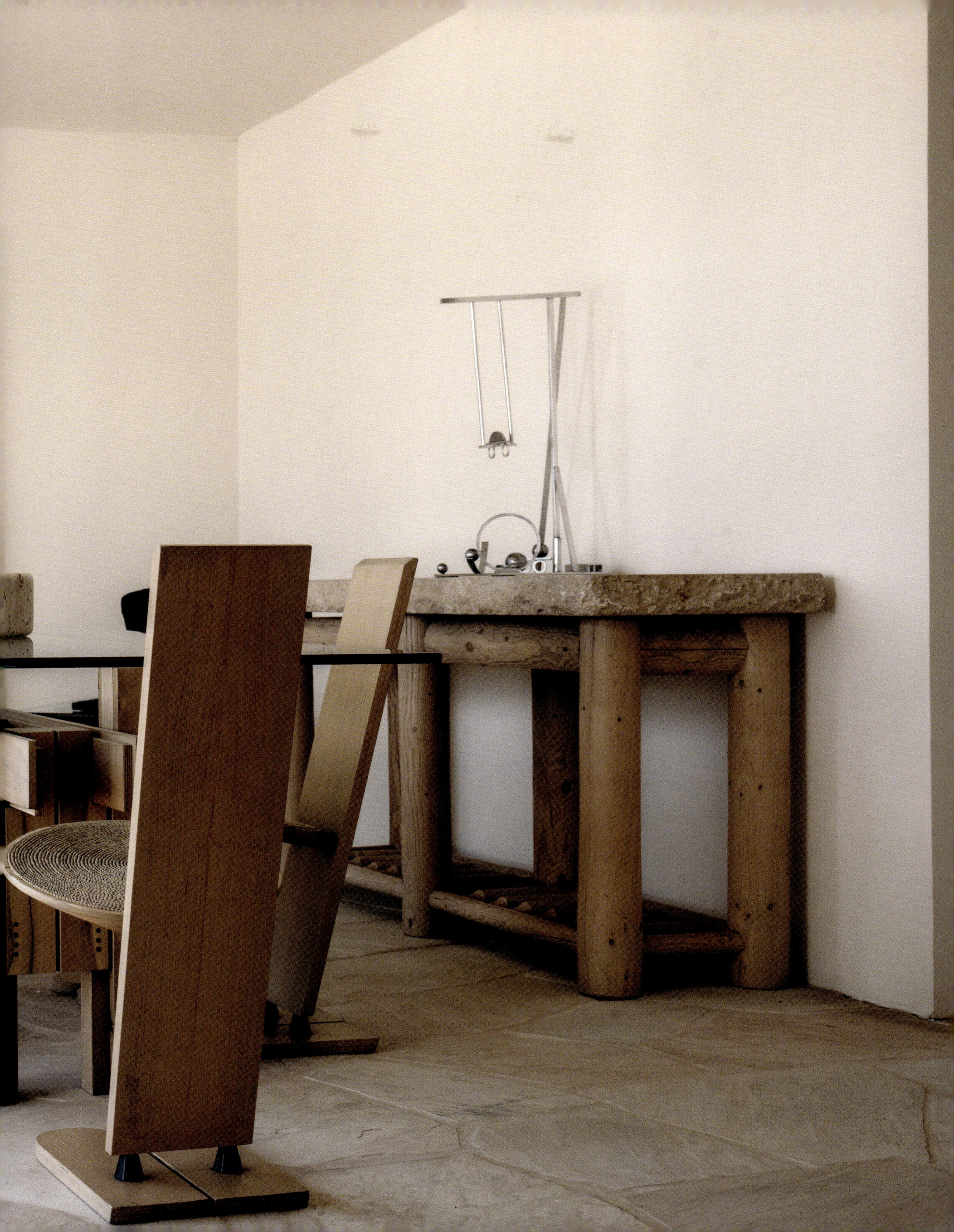

238

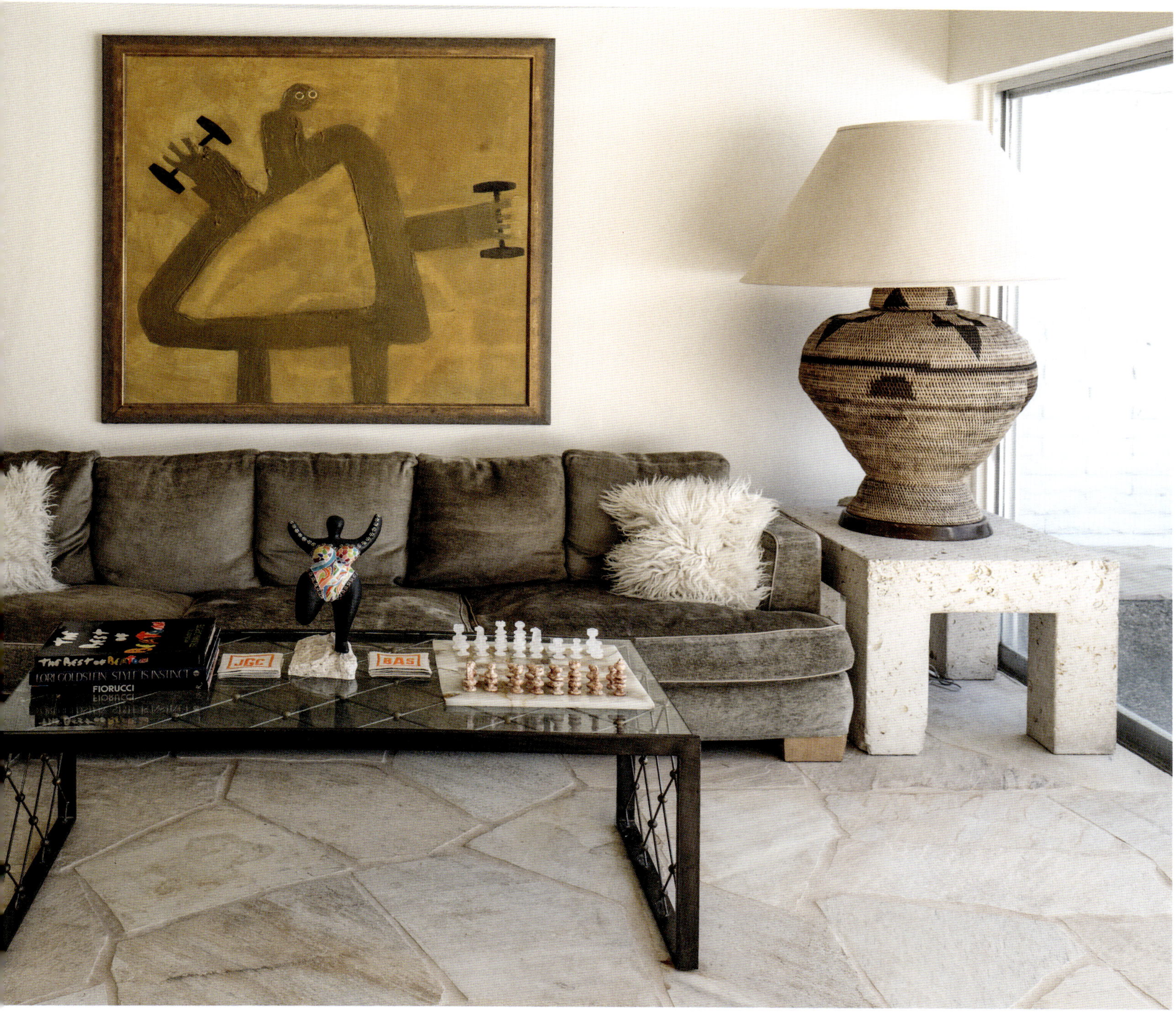
LORI GOLDSTEIN STYLE IS INSTINCT
FIORUCCI
JGC
BAS

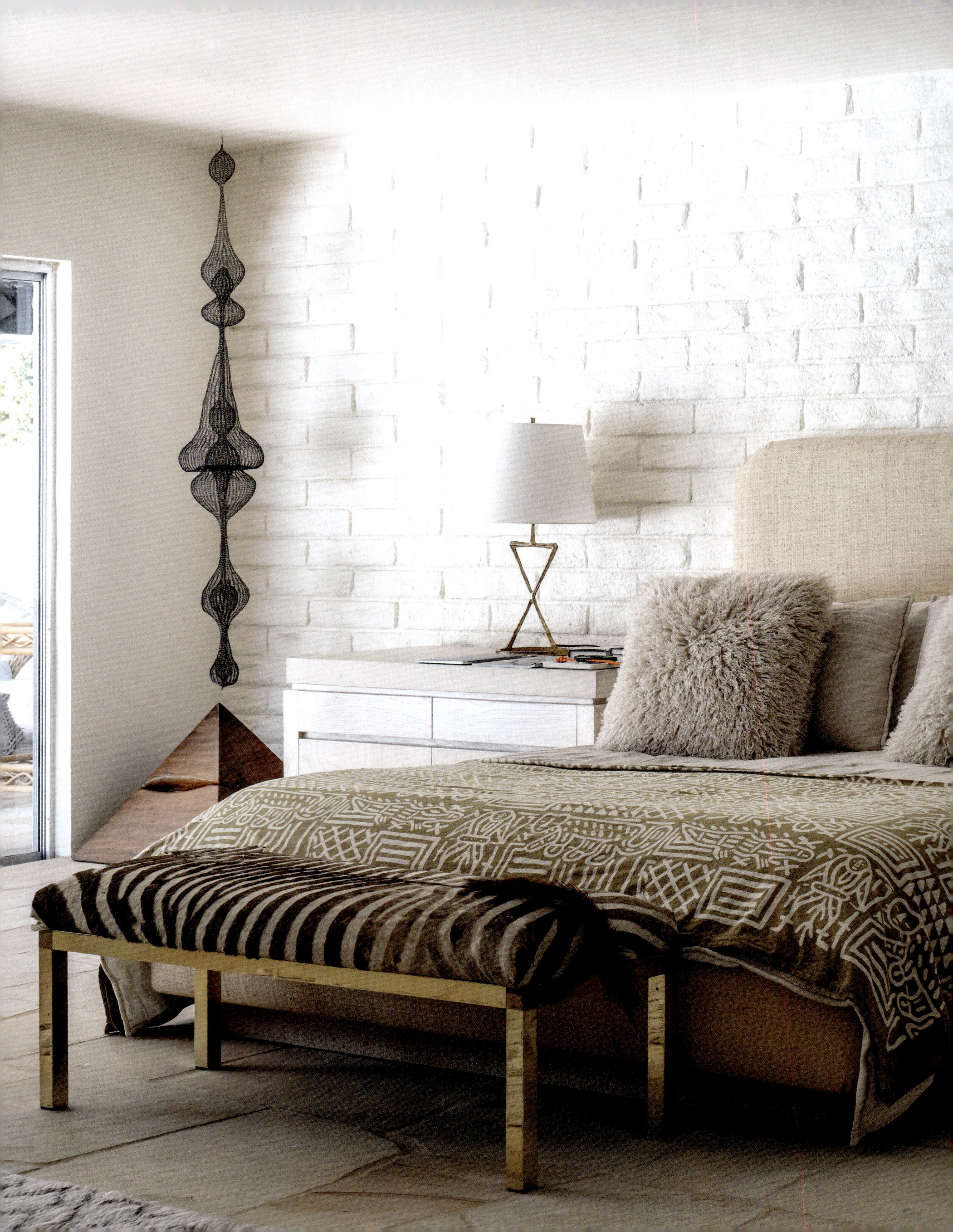

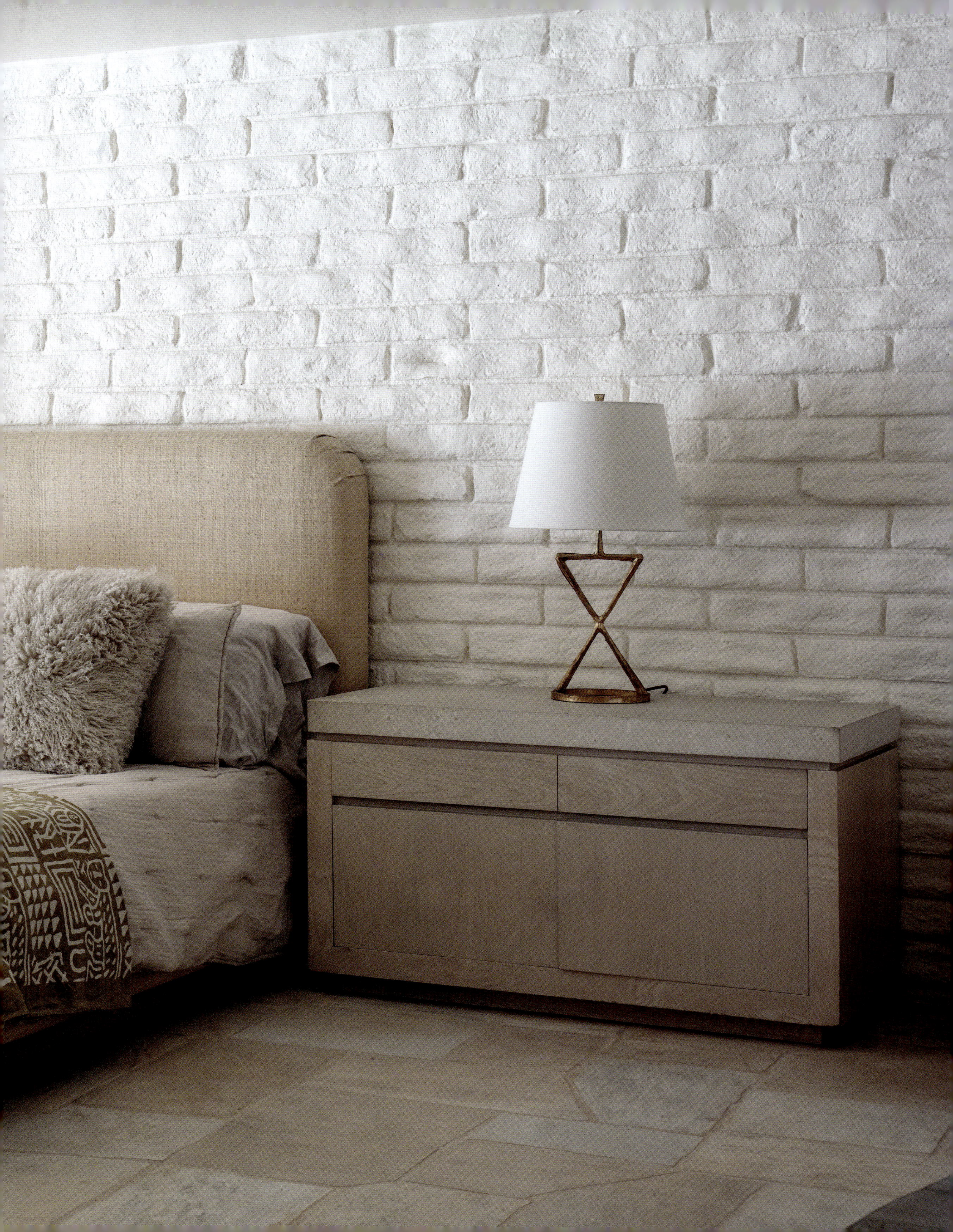

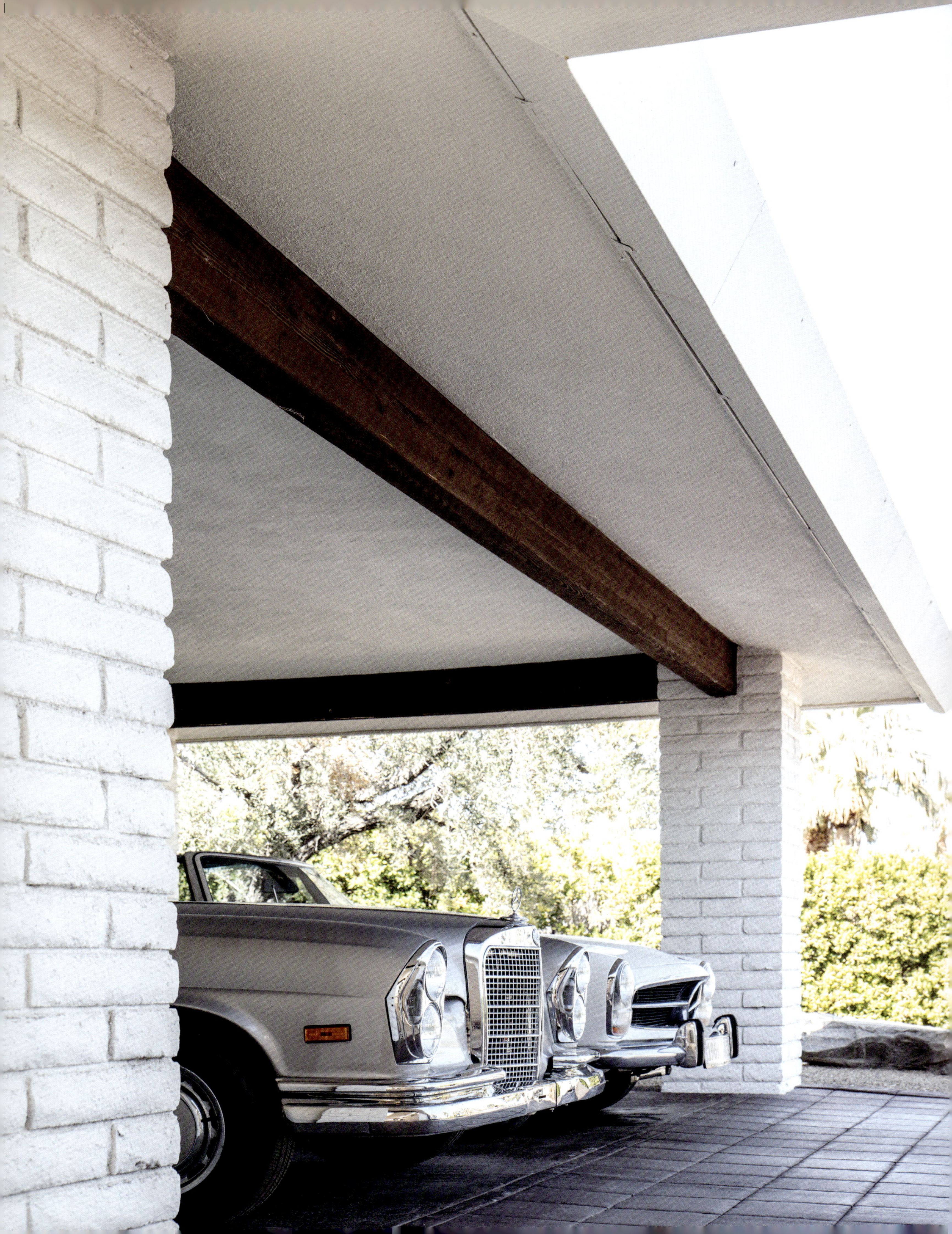

243

MARRAKESH

WHAT ACCOUNTS FOR THE NEWFOUND popularity of the pink-walled Brigadoon known as the Marrakesh Country Club? The Palm Desert resort's executive golf course? Its Moroccan-themed clubhouse, recently made over by the designer Tom Scheerer? The 364 improbably formal villas overlooking the fairways like so many Petit Trianon duplexes? Yes, yes, and yes!

The villas, also pink, were designed in 1968 by the architect John Elgin Woolf, the father of what's known as the Hollywood Regency style, and they're being snapped up by a new generation of design-savvy buyers eager to put their high-voltage spin on the idiom (giant sectionals, geometric wallpaper).

There are a few outliers, including Stephen Drucker, a former magazine editor—and the editor of this book—who bought his own three-bedroom Marrakesh villa in 2019. "Don't call any of this 'Hollywood Regency,' please," he implores. "The term has become so devalued and murky." Woolf, Drucker insists, was about so much more than over-the-top glamour. "His underpinning was neoclassicism. The houses at Marrakesh have the harmony and elegance of Palladian villas." Drucker's own decorating inspiration, which Scheerer helped him flesh out, was the Athens apartment of the neoclassical-inclined designer T. H. Robsjohn-Gibbings.

Pass through the courtyard, with its bougainvillea-draped walls, fragrant lemon tree, and trickling fountain. A tole lemon tree sculpture greets you just inside Woolf's signature ten-foot-tall "Pullman" doors. Robsjohn-Gibbings materializes in the living room, where a pair of the designer's armchairs flank a ten-foot-long contemporary Italian sofa beneath a charcoal abstraction by Christine Hiebert. Everything seems to float against white walls and bare white terrazzo floors. A plaster model of the Parthenon and a set of nineteenth-century sepia photographs of classical ruins nod to the great civilizations. "The hardest thing to create in architecture is a sense of tranquility," Drucker says. "John Woolf gave us that at Marrakesh. I just kept going."

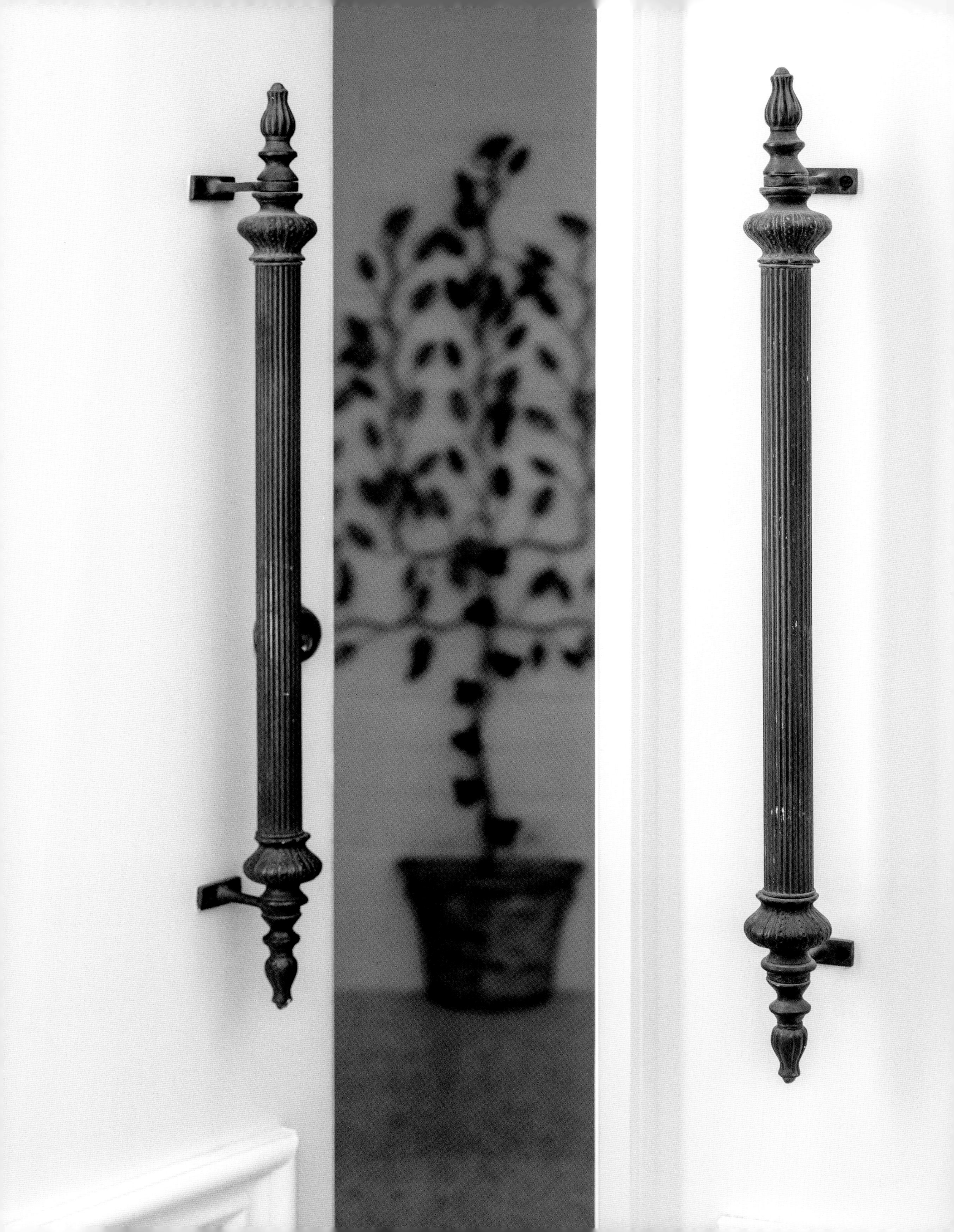

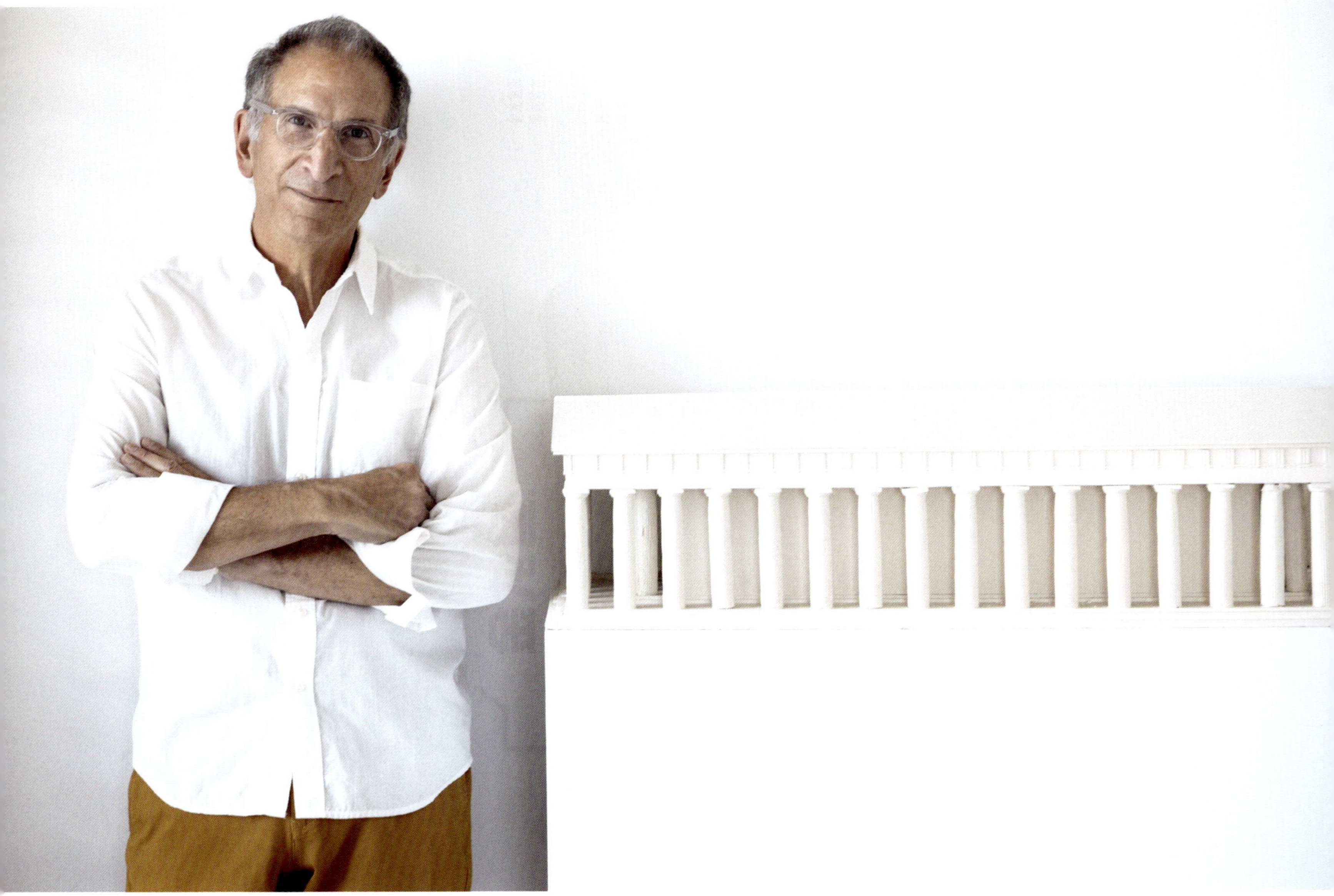

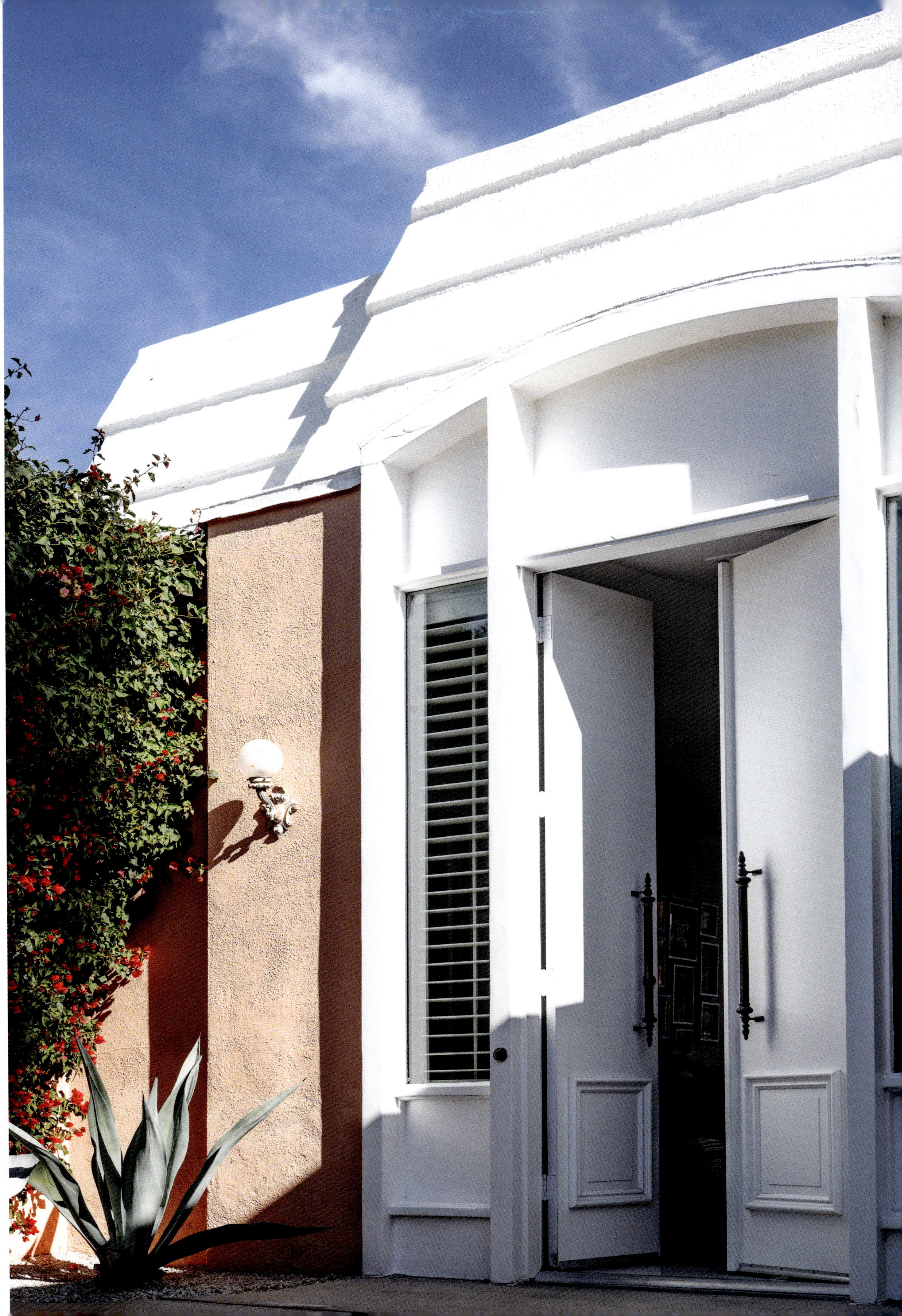

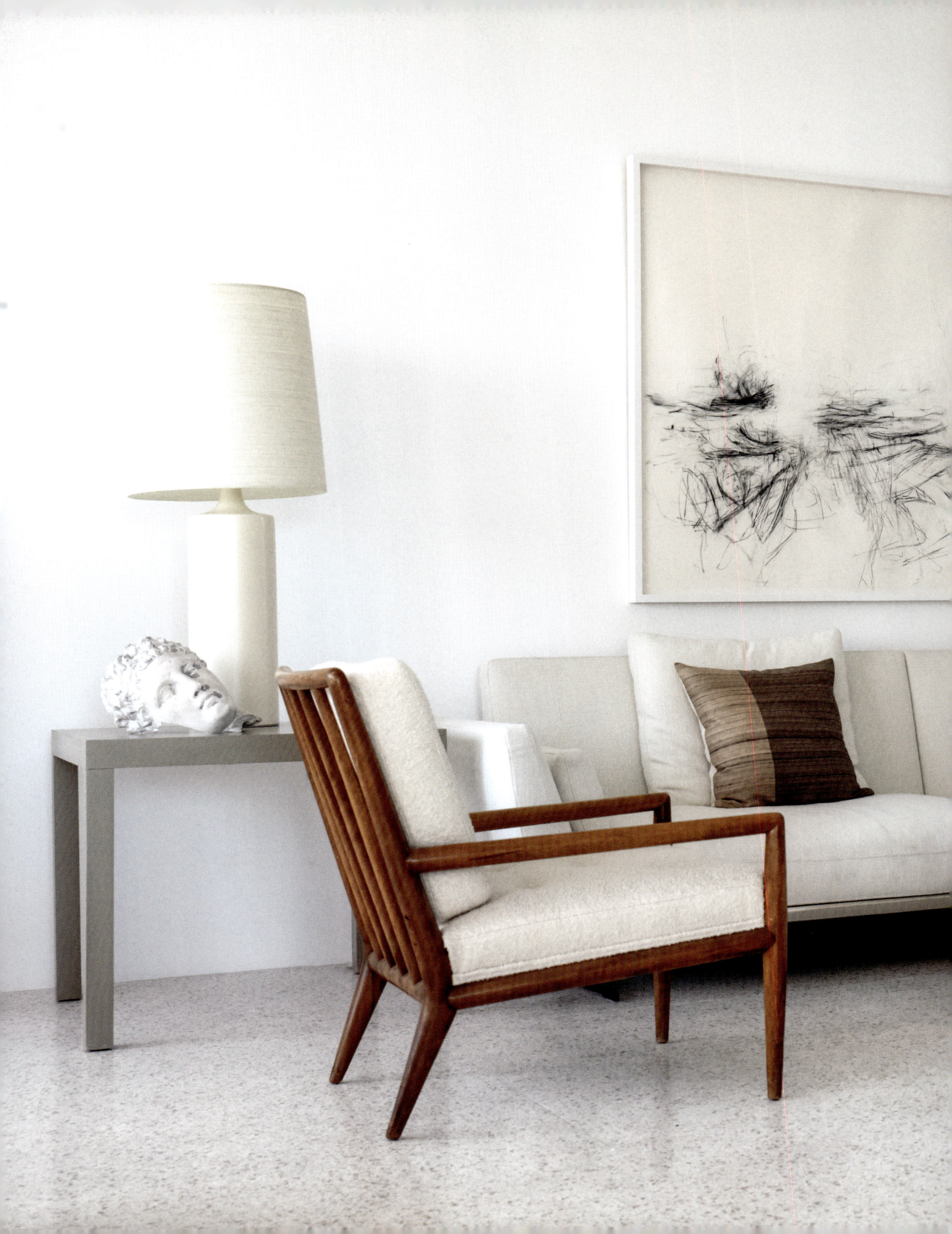

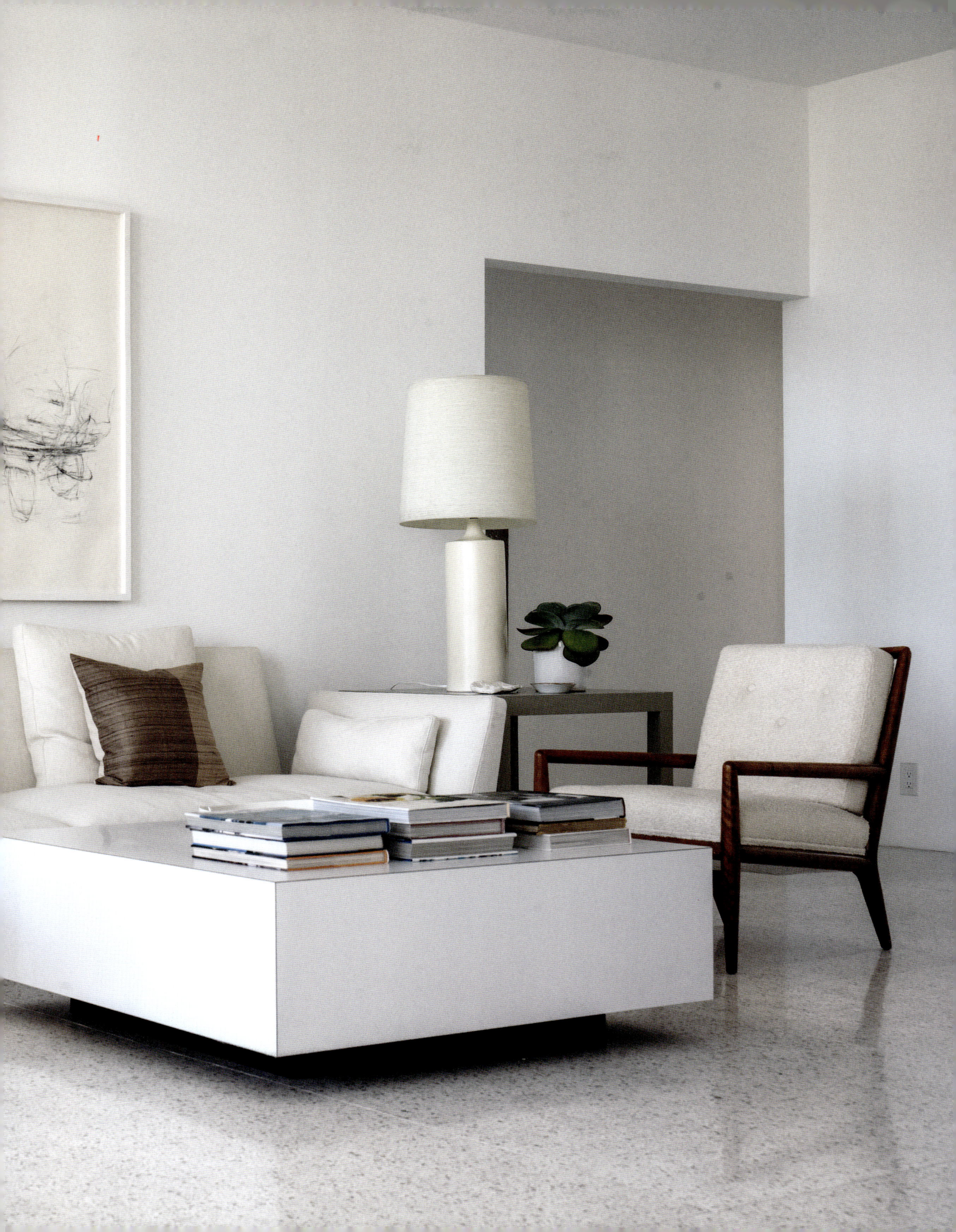

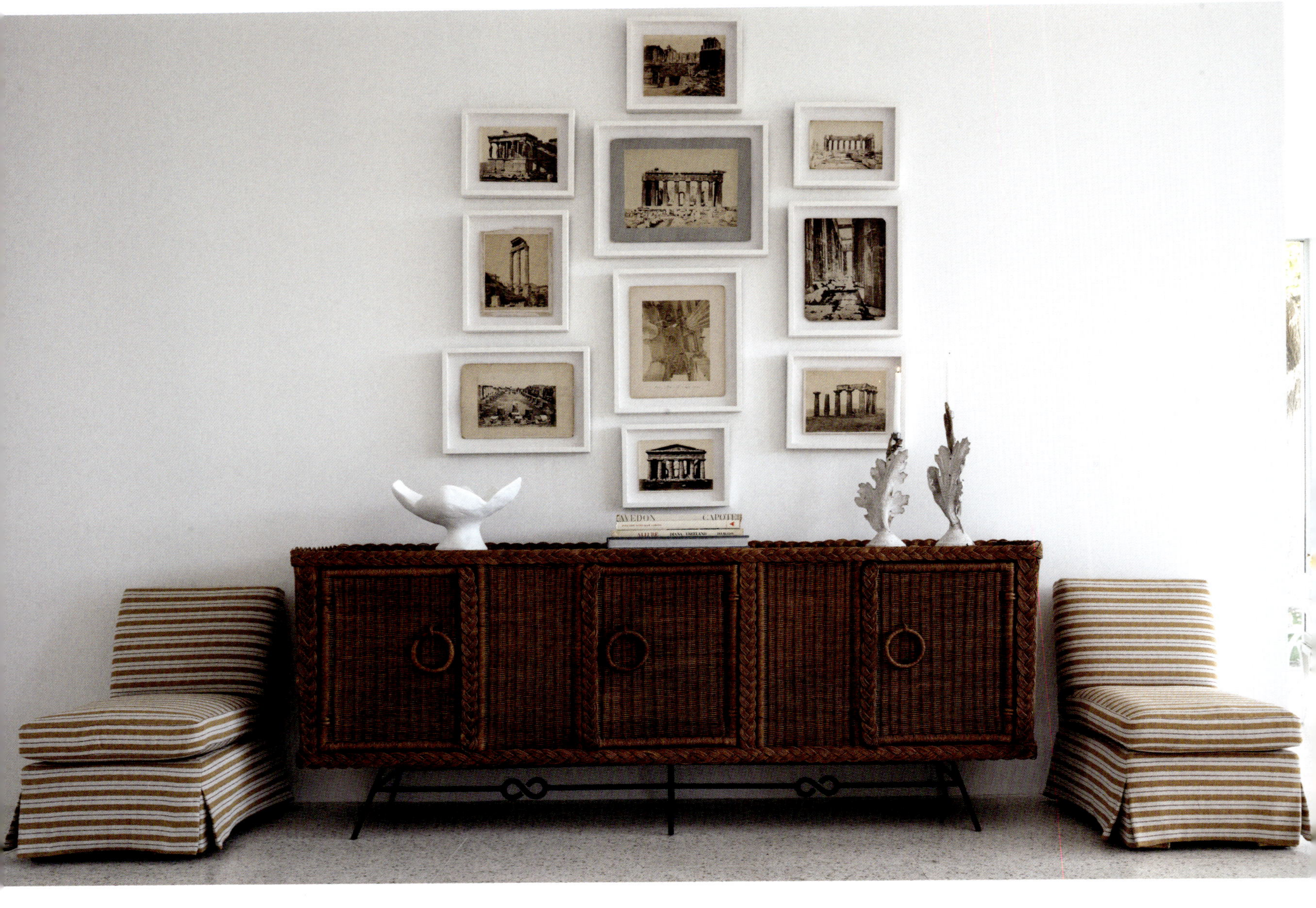
AVEDON
CAPOTE

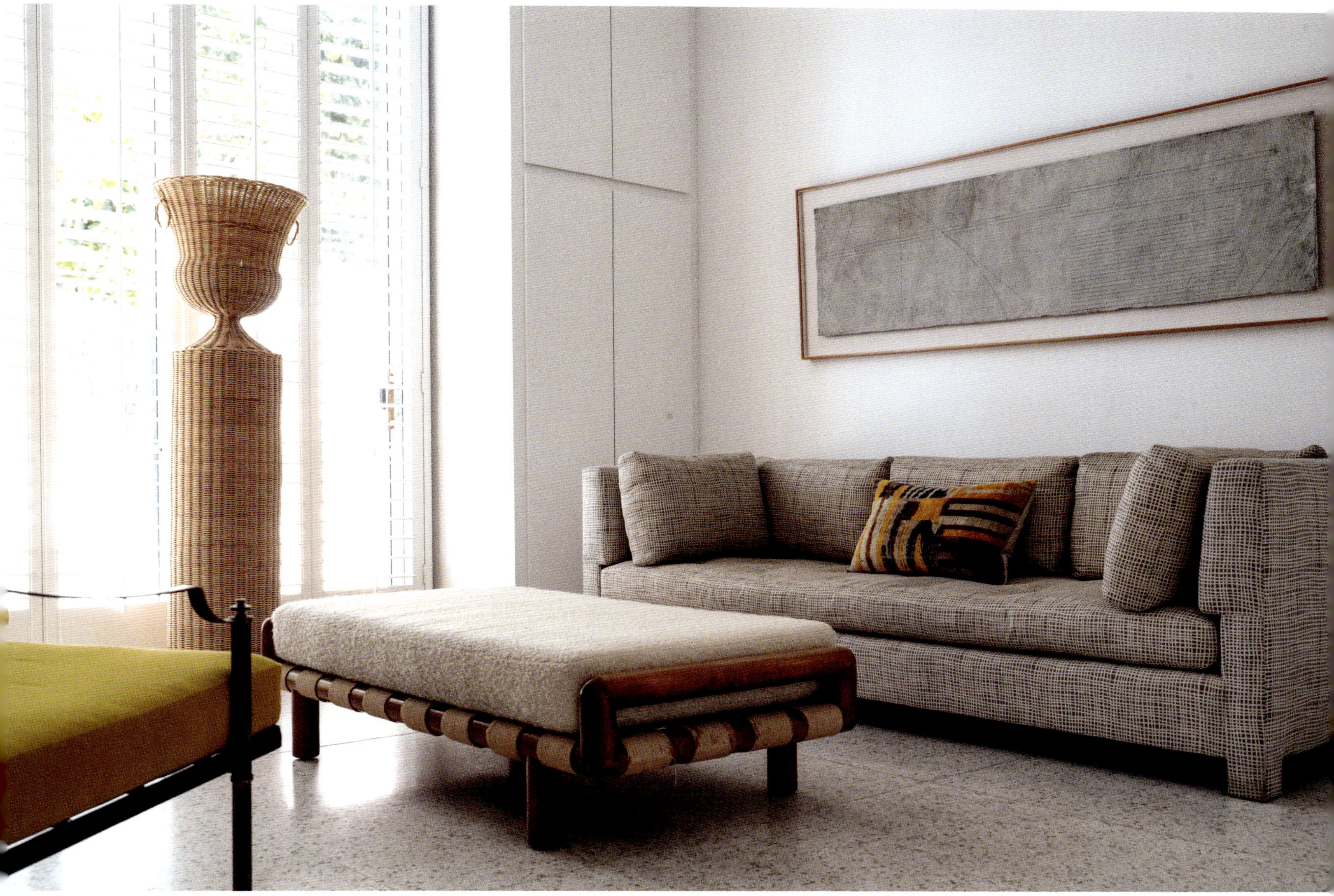

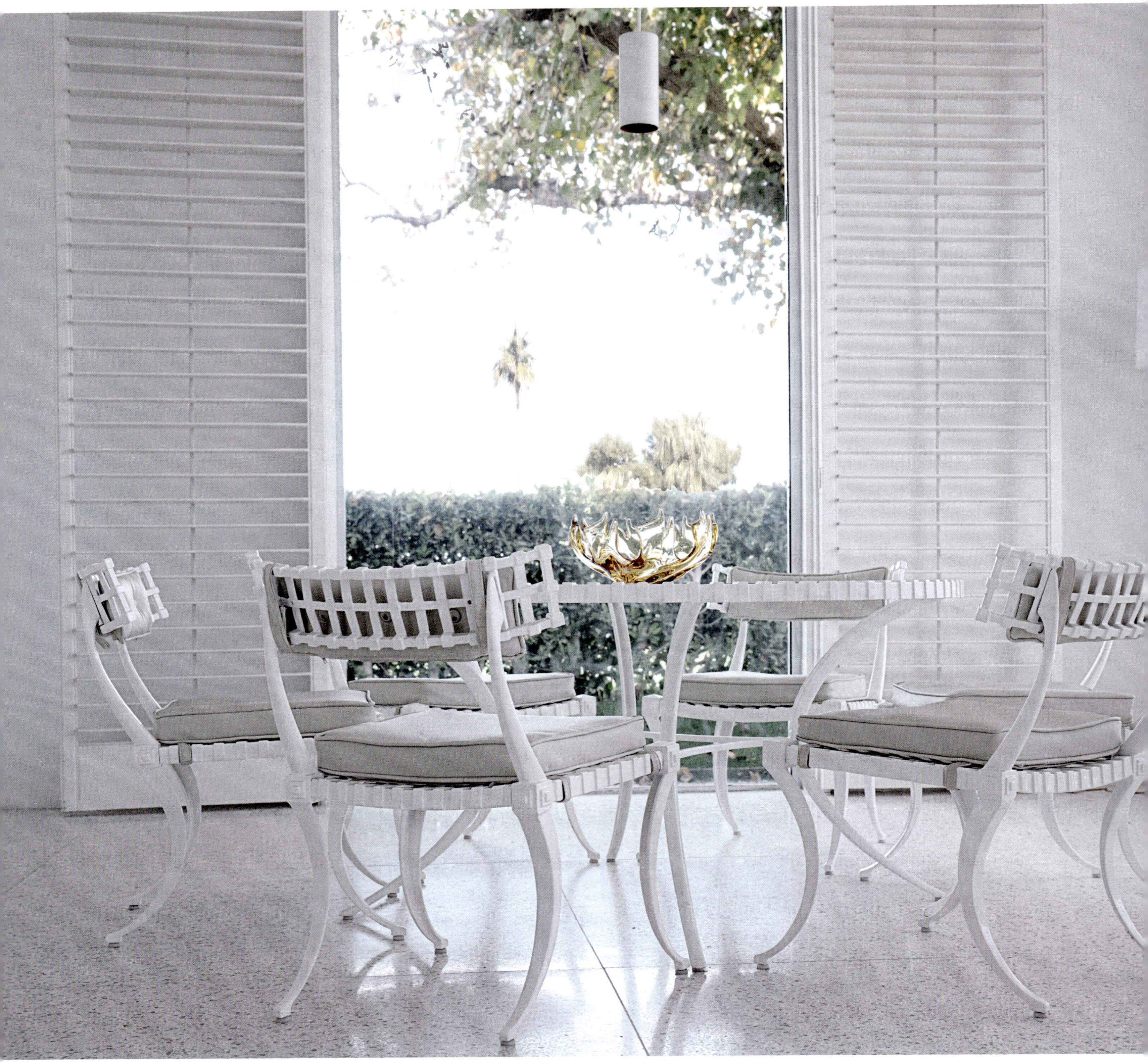

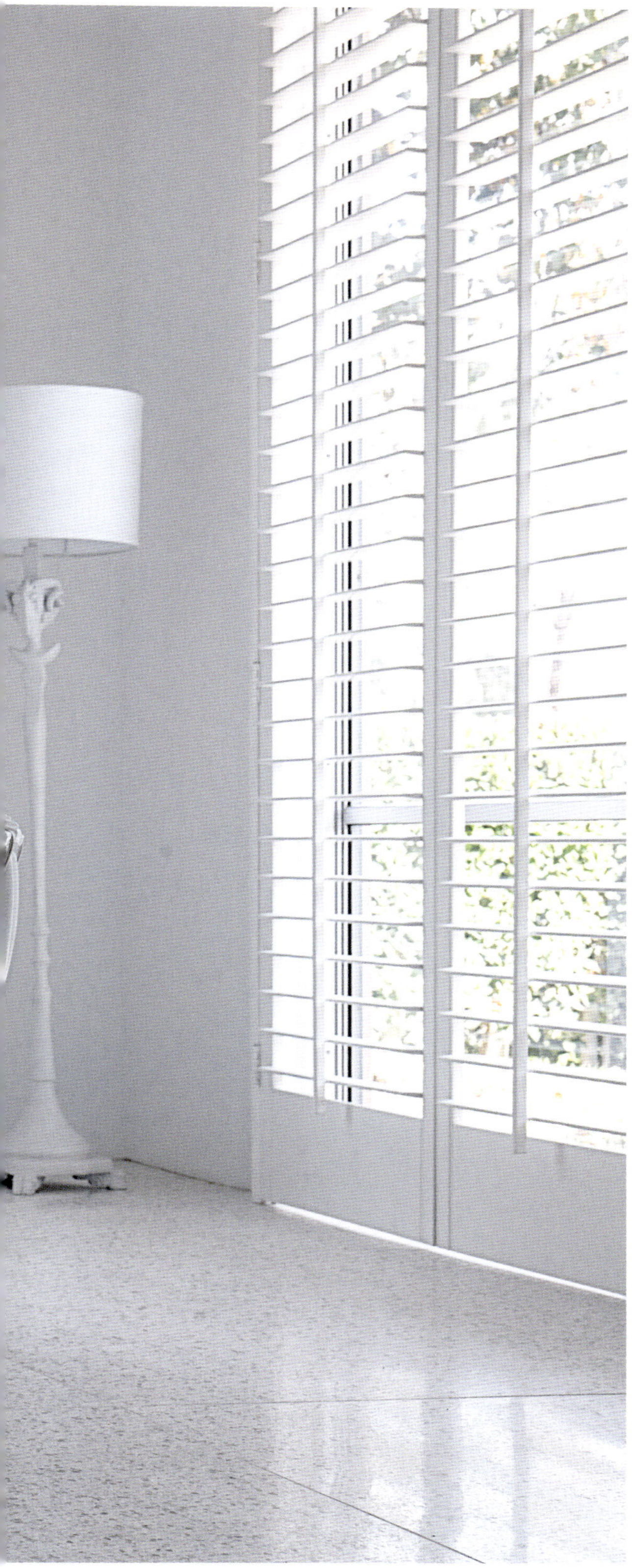

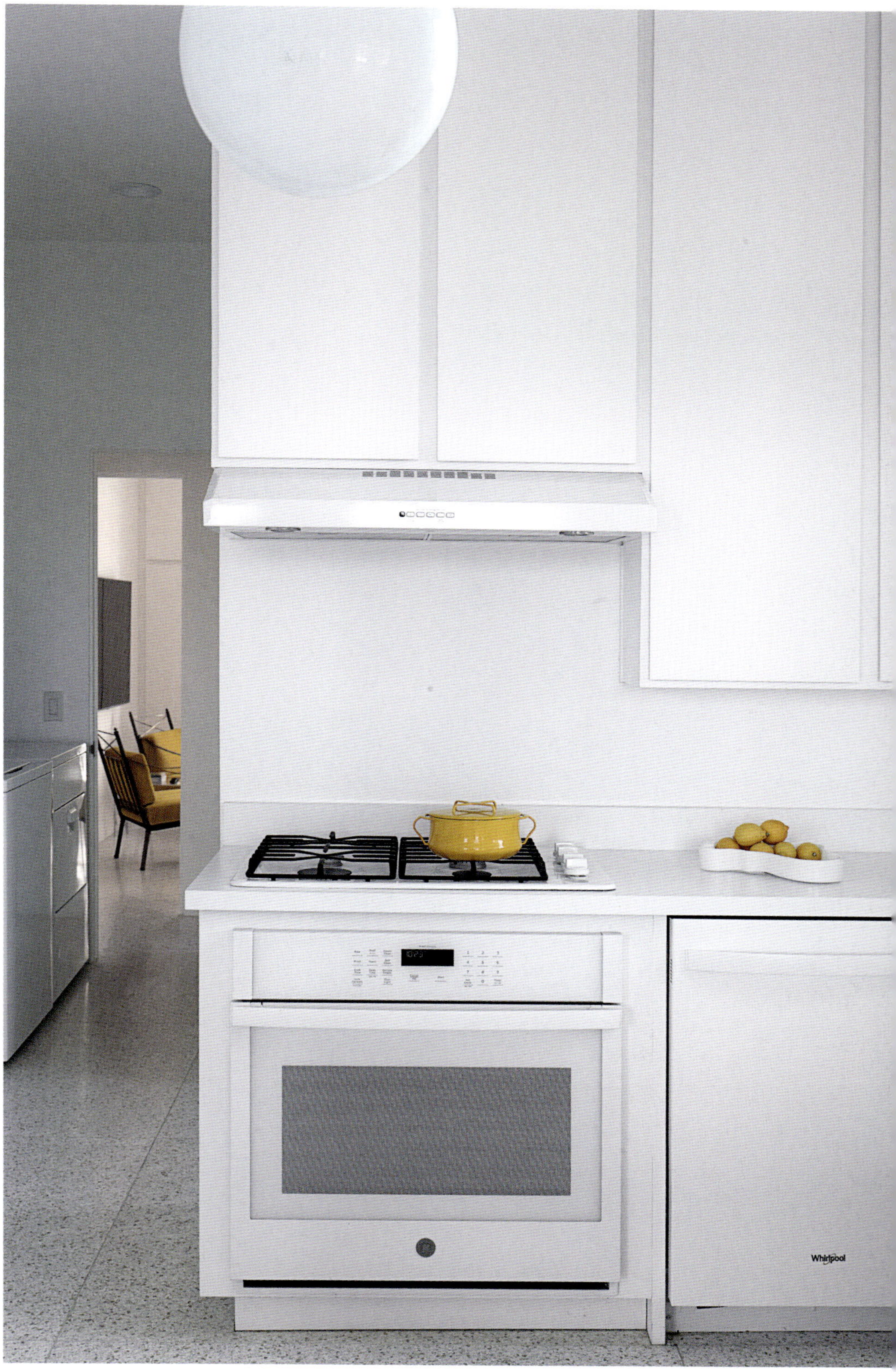
Whirlpool

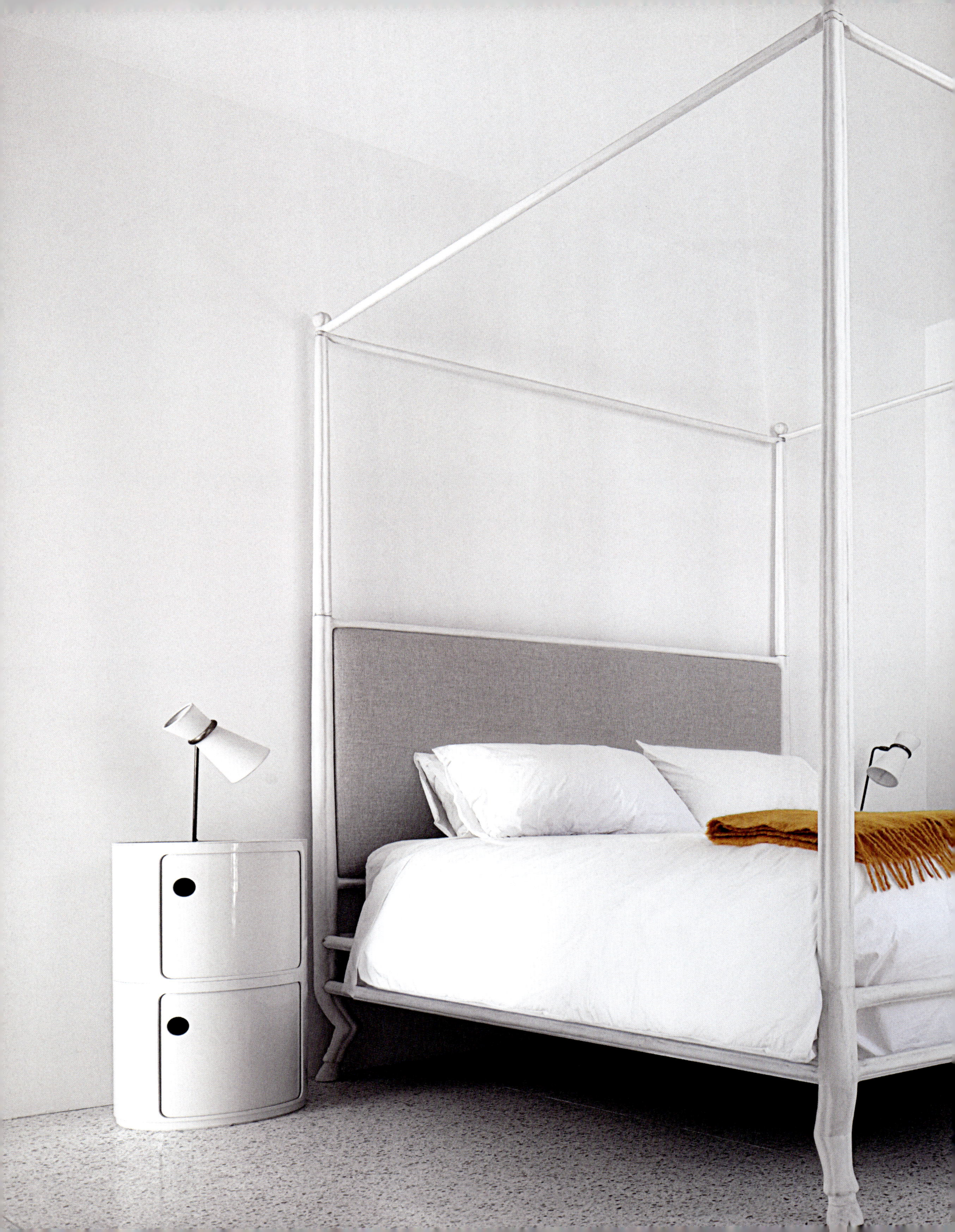

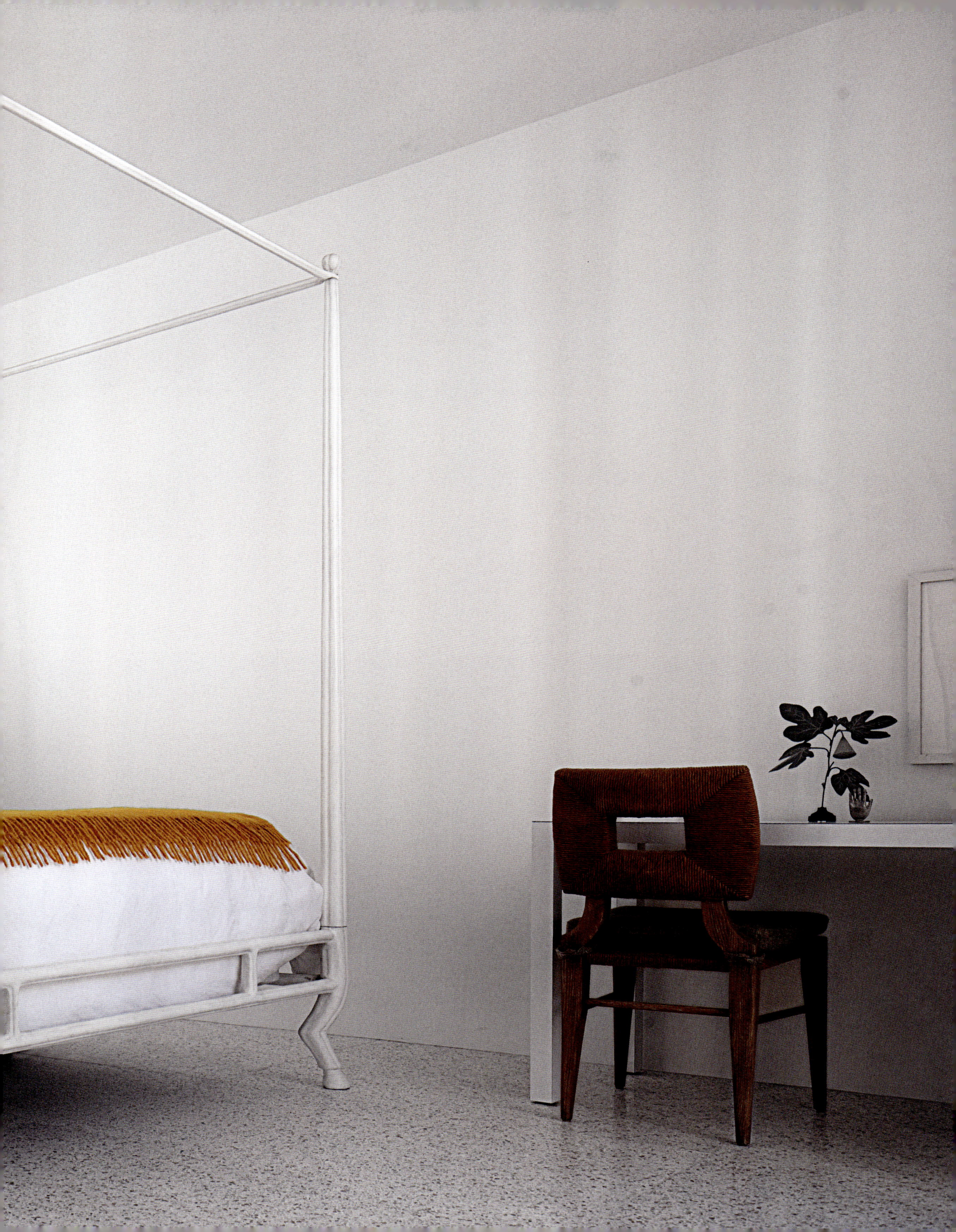

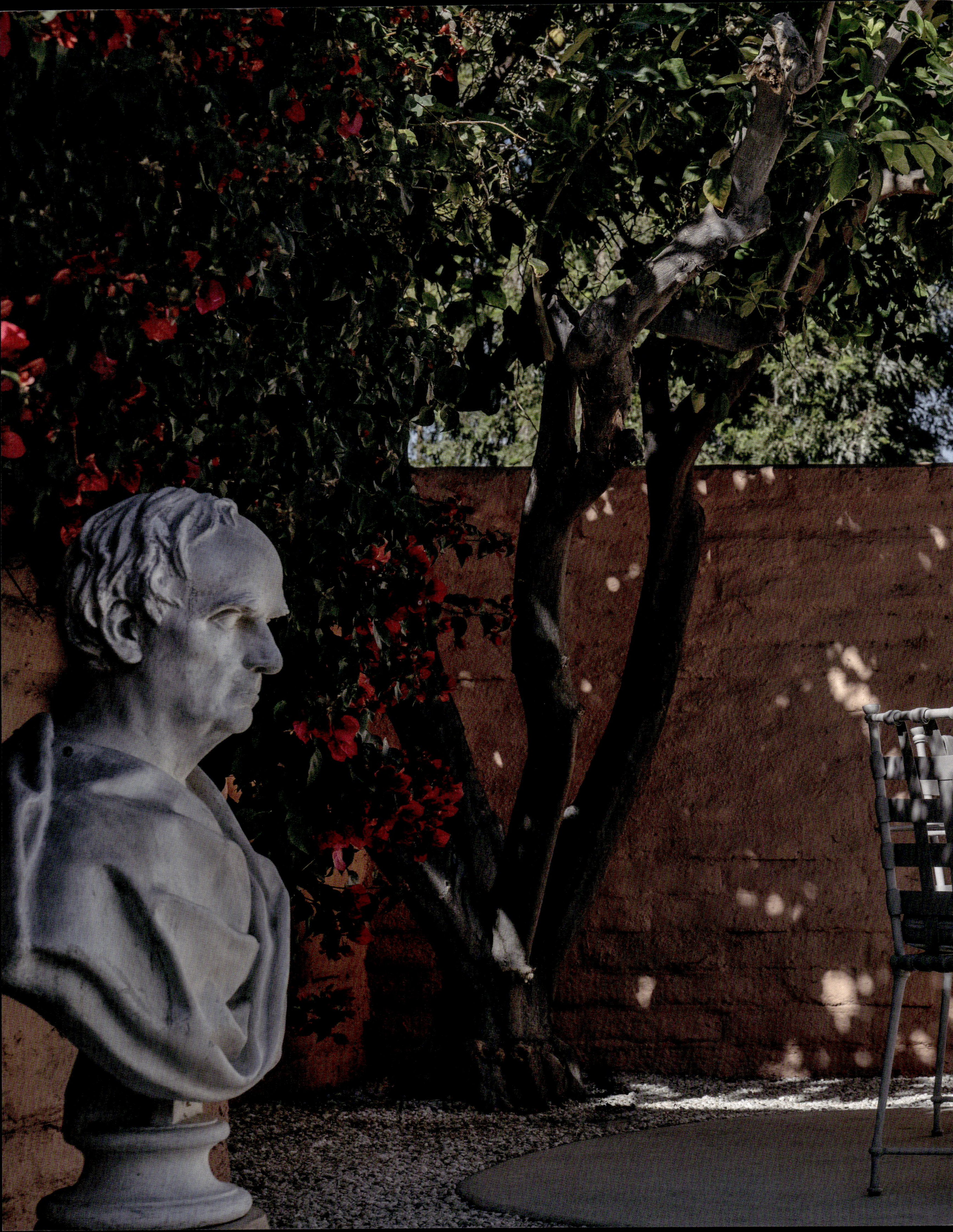

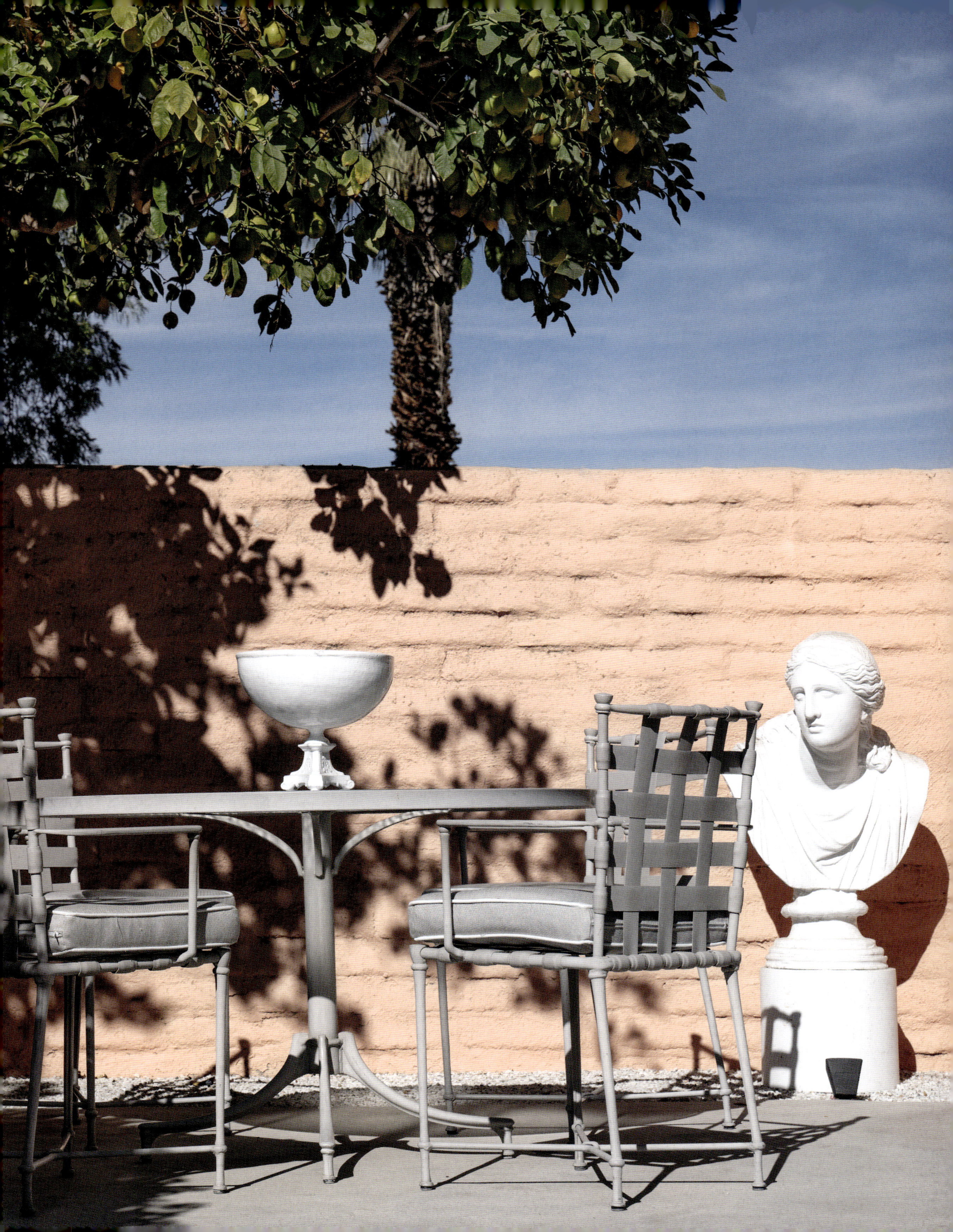

INDIAN CANYONS II

PEOPLE HAVE ALWAYS COME TO THE desert to heal. In the early 1900s patients with respiratory ailments found relief in the hot, dry climate of Palm Springs; more recently, New Agers have sought spiritual renewal in the mountains of Joshua Tree and the hot springs of Twentynine Palms. In 2021, following the sudden, tragic death of her nine-year-old son, Pierce, Lesley Hu and her boyfriend, Jim Baaden, left San Francisco in search of a quiet desert refuge. They found a place that spoke to them in Indian Canyons, at the base of the San Jacinto Mountains: a clean-lined post-and-beam built around a central atrium and two other outdoor areas. A friend, designer Jean-Claude Huon, helped them add a couple of bathrooms and a bedroom to the house—one room is dedicated to Pierce's memory—and together they fashioned a calm, restorative environment.

"Our orientation was toward natural materials in a neutral palette," says Baaden, "whether it was stone or leather or wood." Favoring organic textures and muted earth tones—including touches of green, Pierce's favorite color—they brought together artwork and furniture that had personal meaning to them, particularly things from their travels. A tapestry by the Thai weaving artist Kachama Perez hangs in the living room. Bouclé-covered chairs and a resin coffee table in the same room were purchased on a trip to Paris. The bearskin rug in Baaden's office was brought back from Japan. Baaden enjoyed "nerding out on all the details" with Huon, especially acquiring pieces for the outdoor spaces by Willy Guhl, David Cressey, and other midcentury and contemporary ceramists and sculptors. But he never lost sight of the larger objective: "This was always about giving Lesley and Pierce a place we could all be comfortable in."

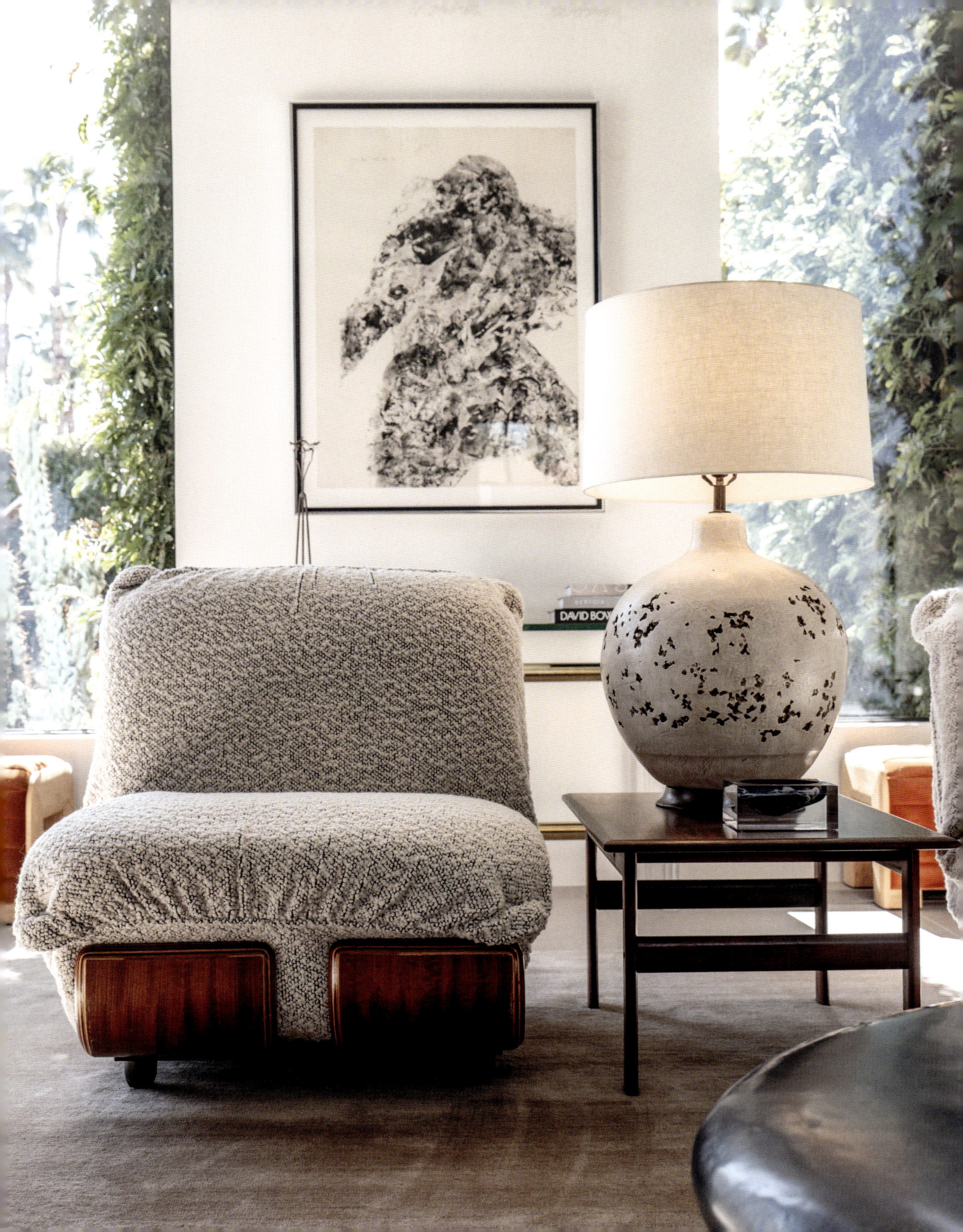
DAVID BOW

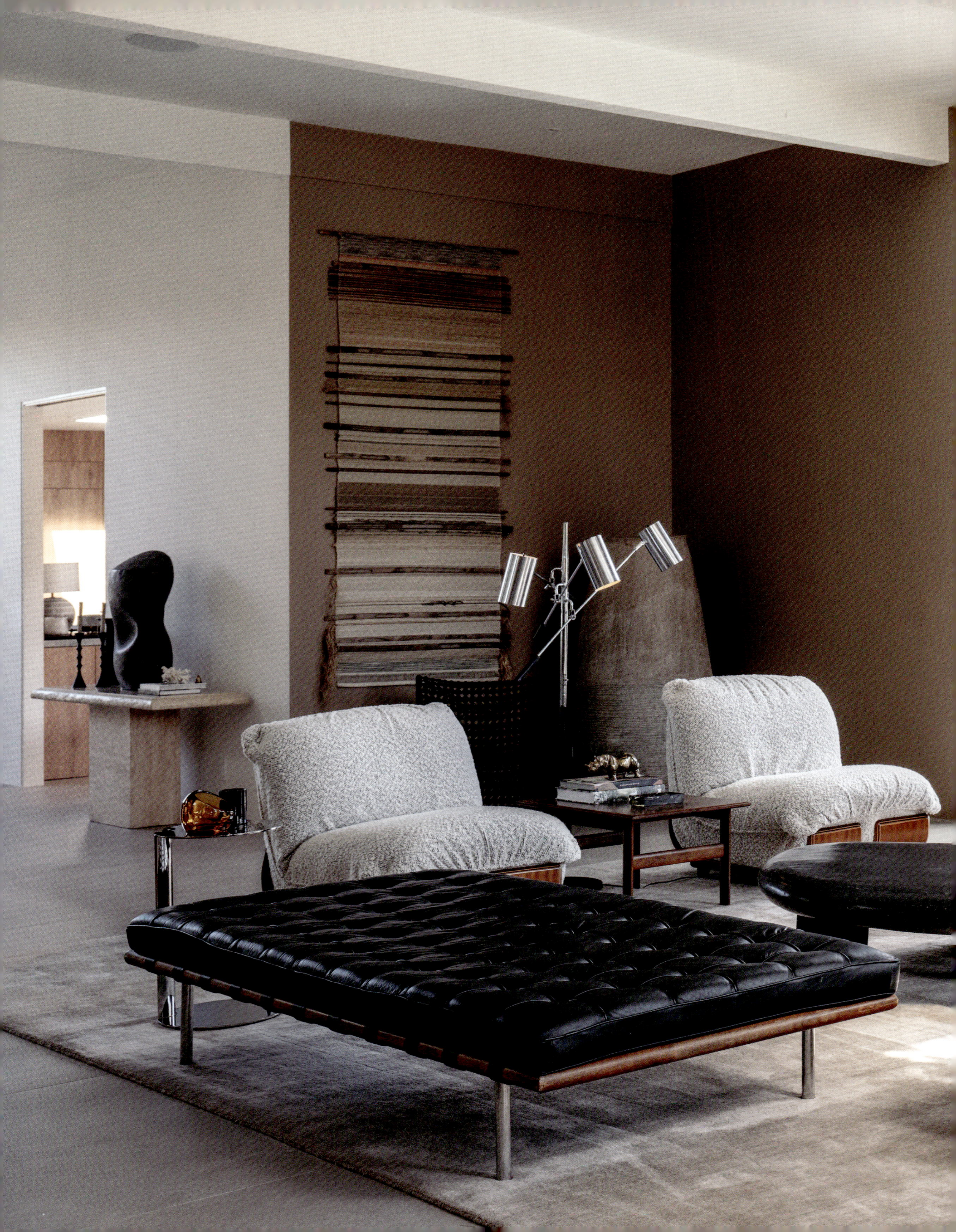

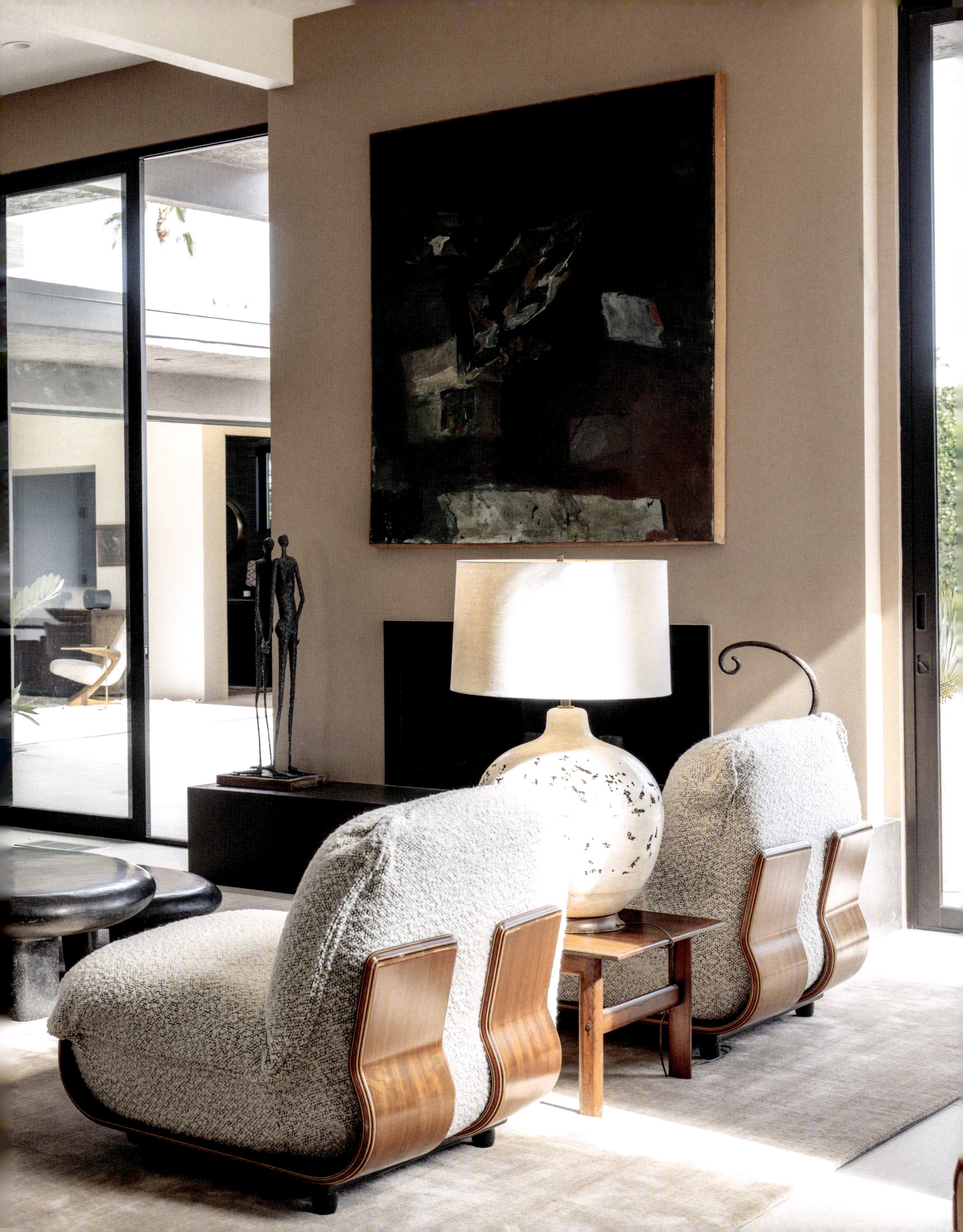

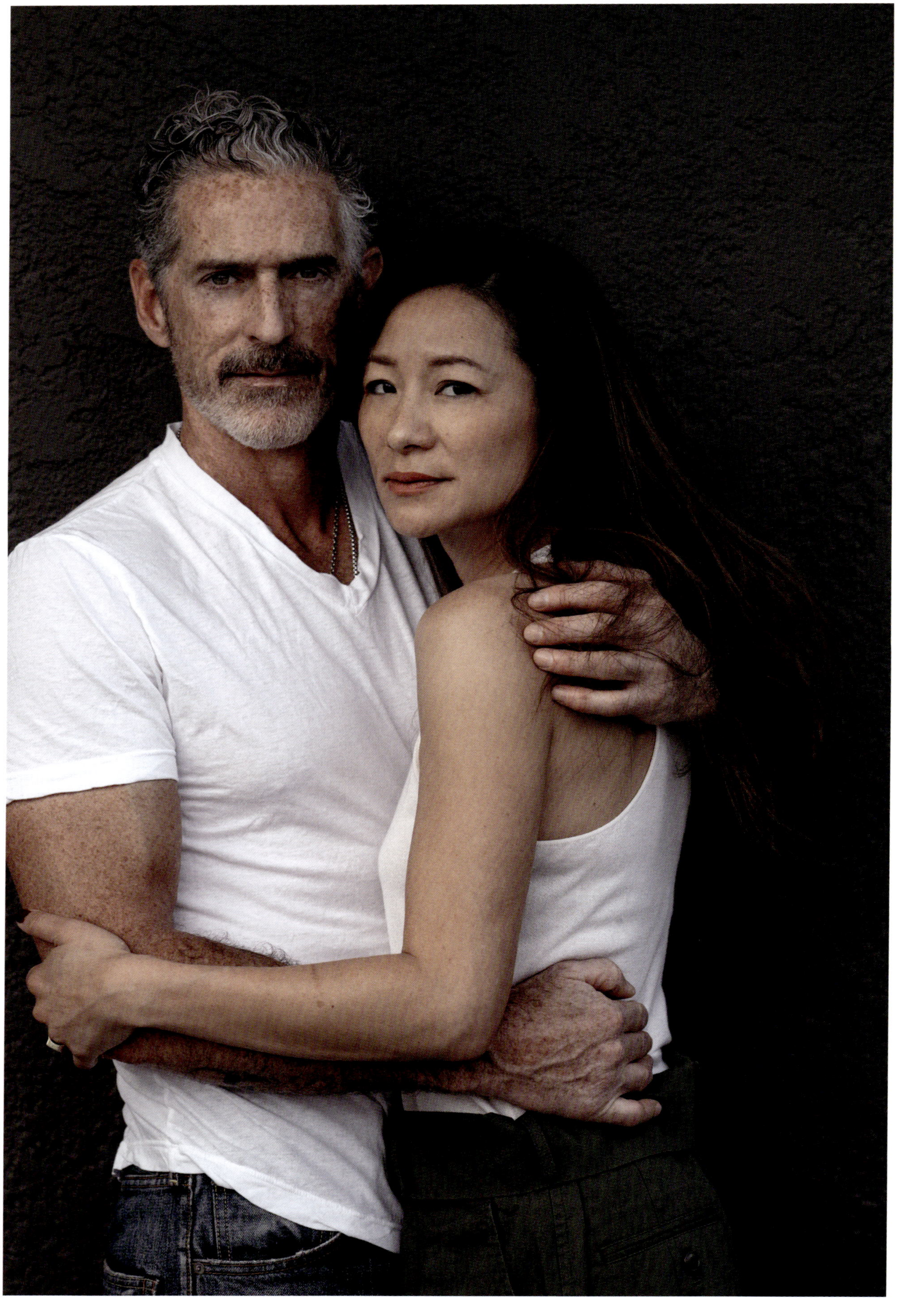

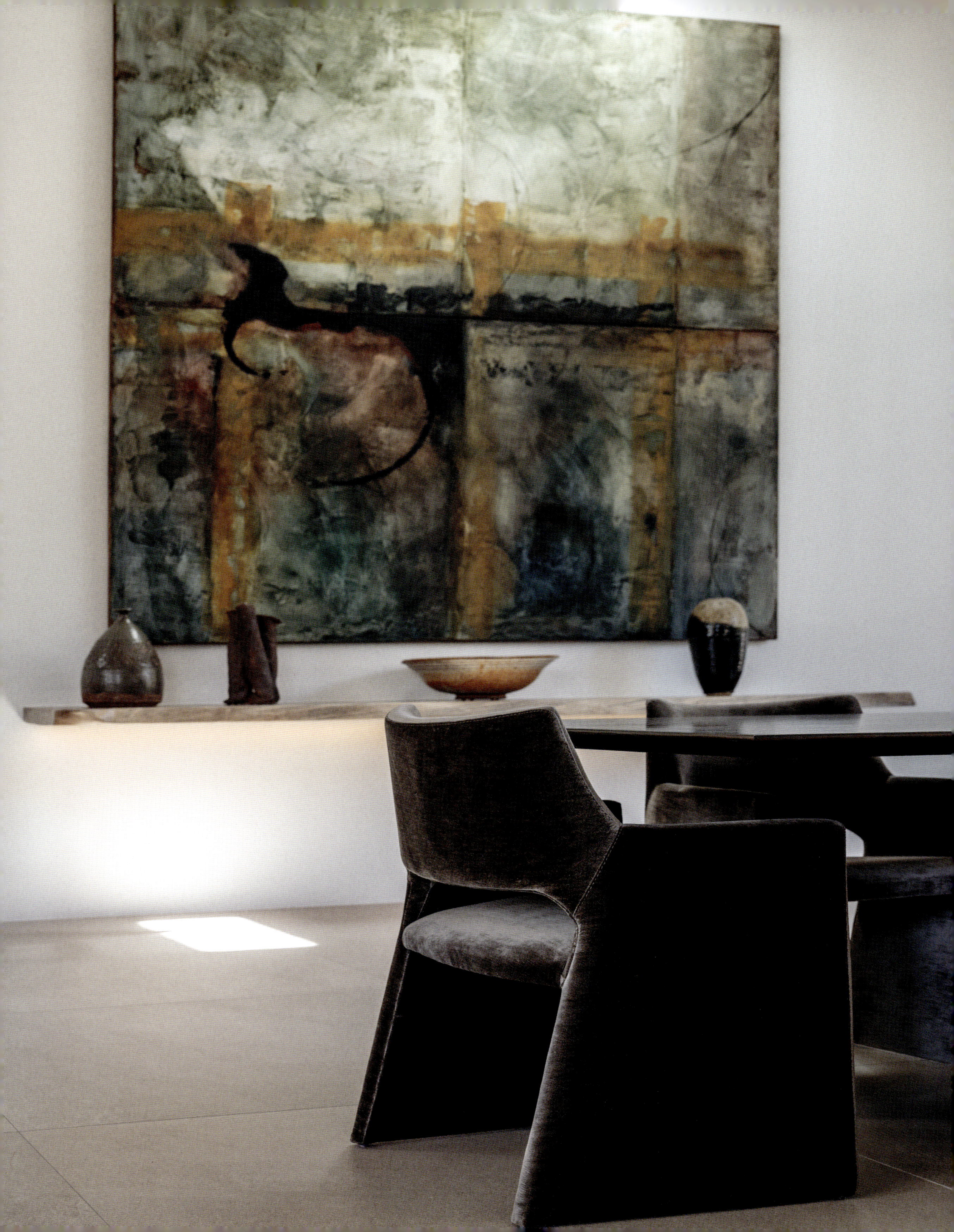

264

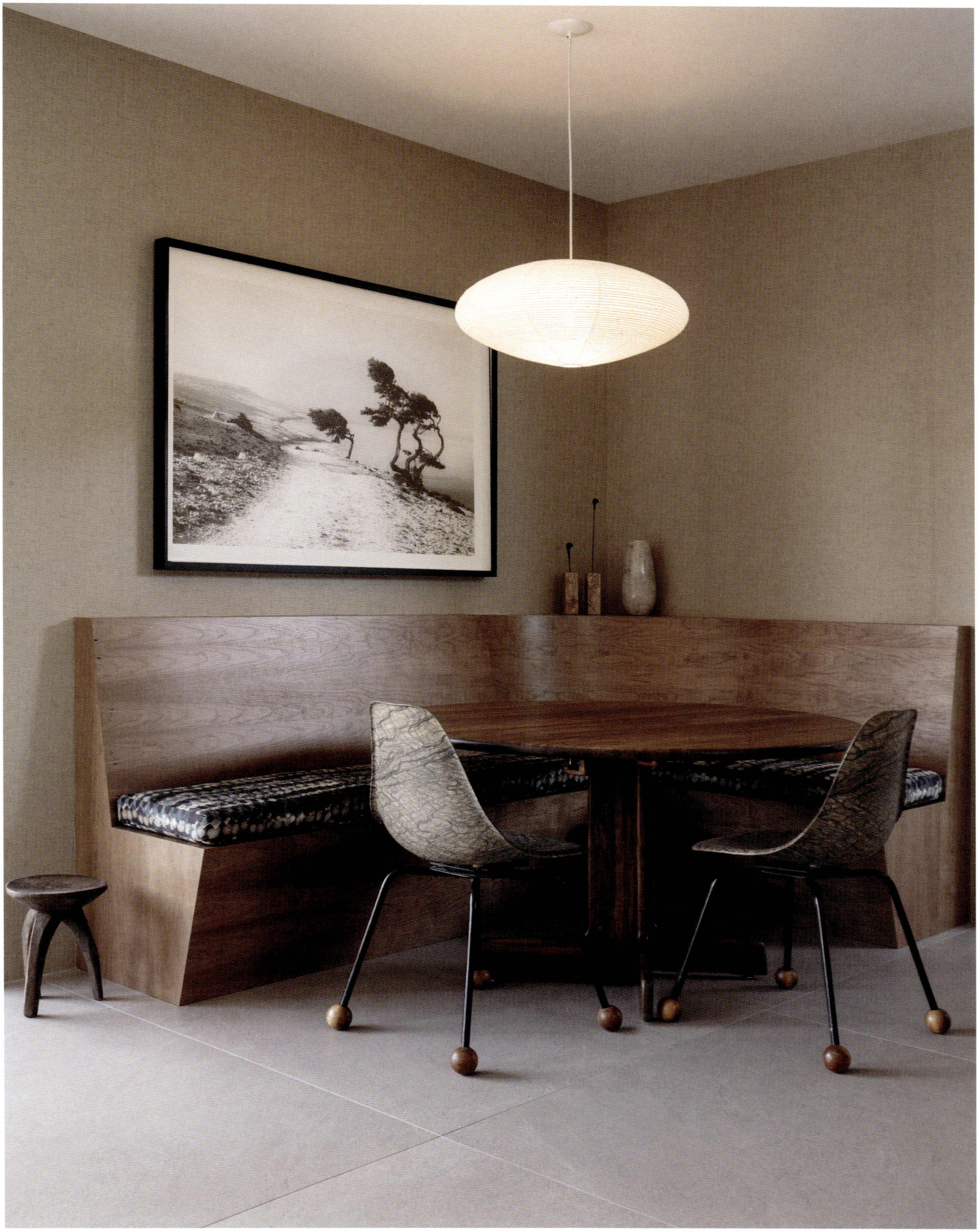

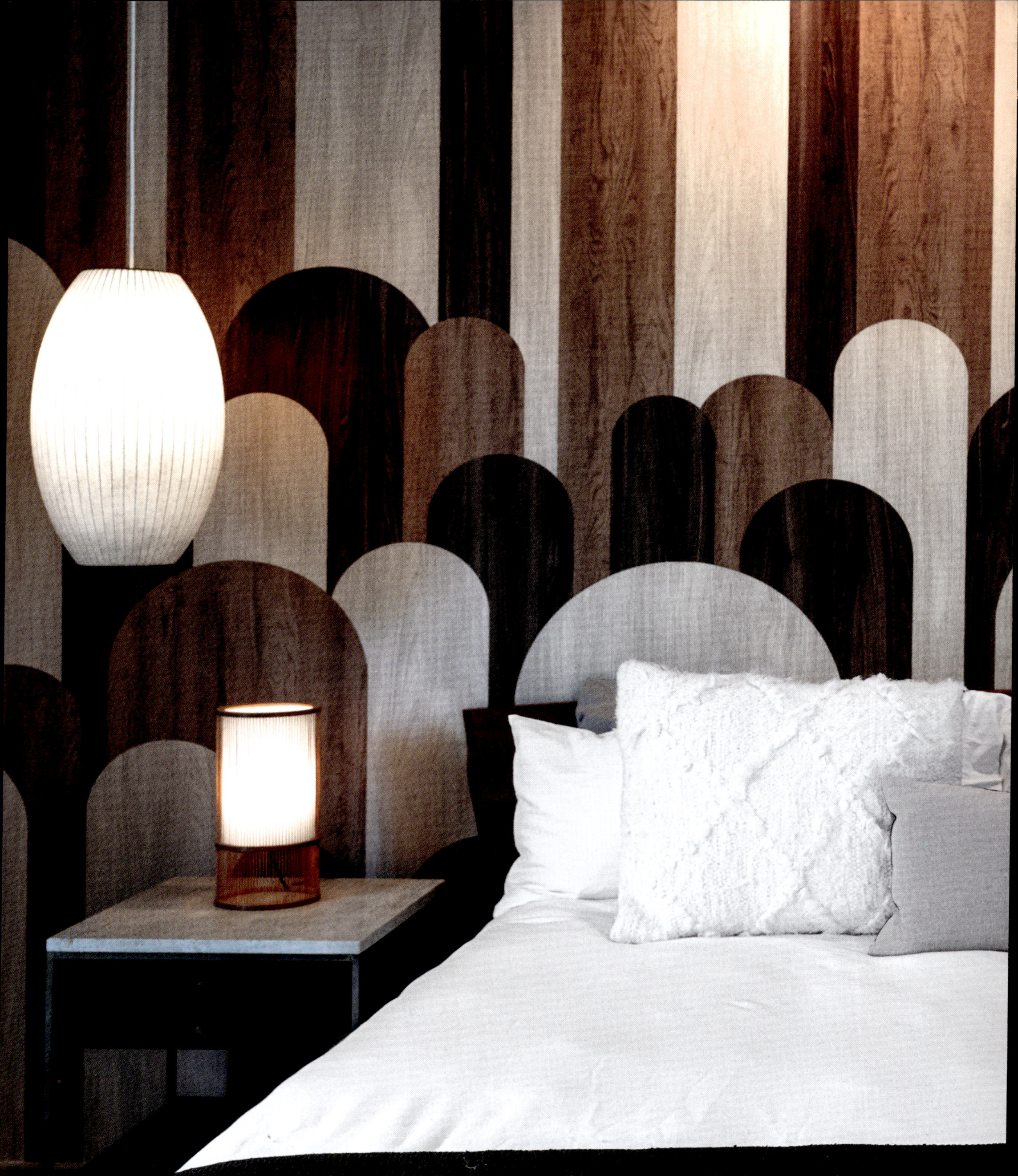

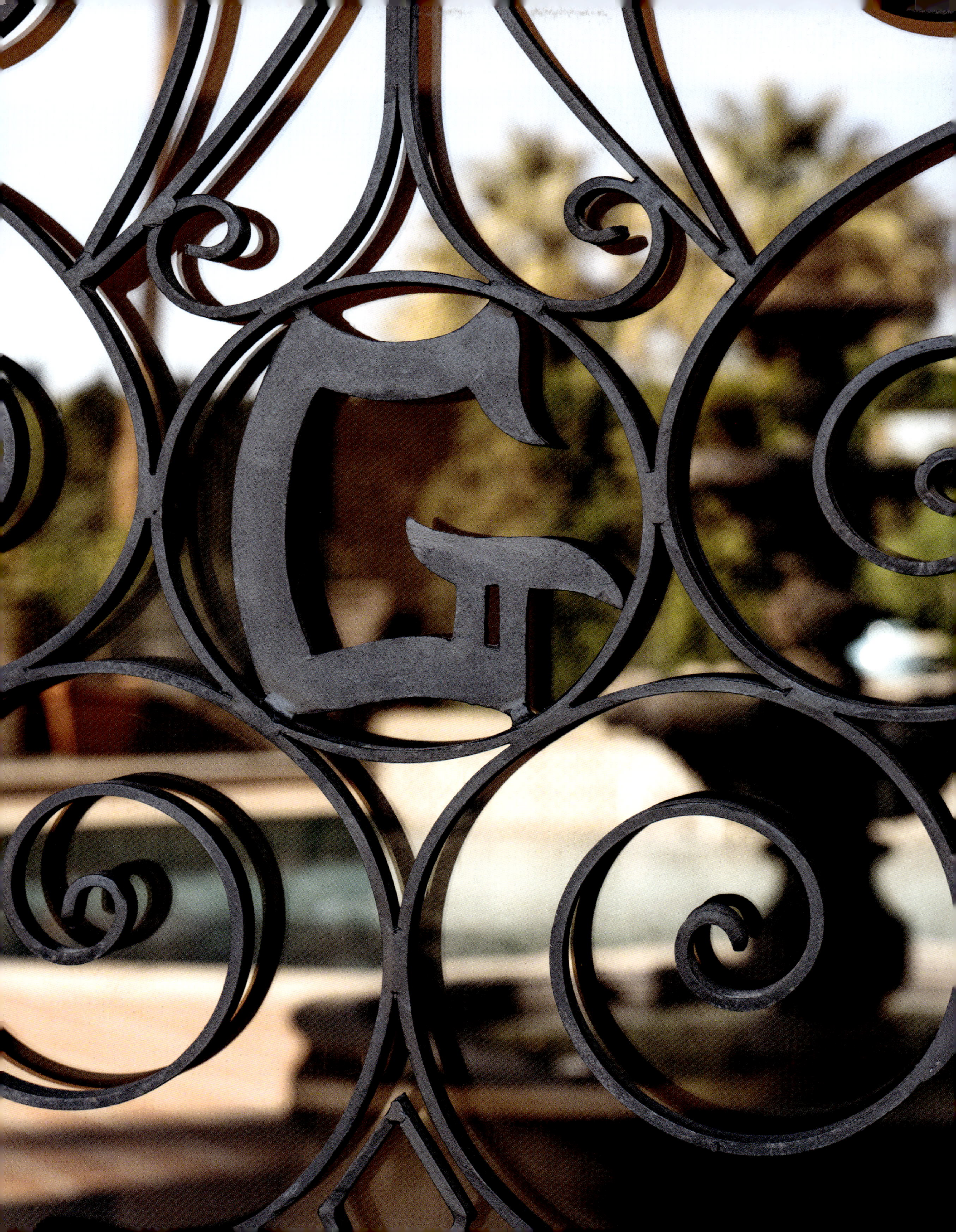

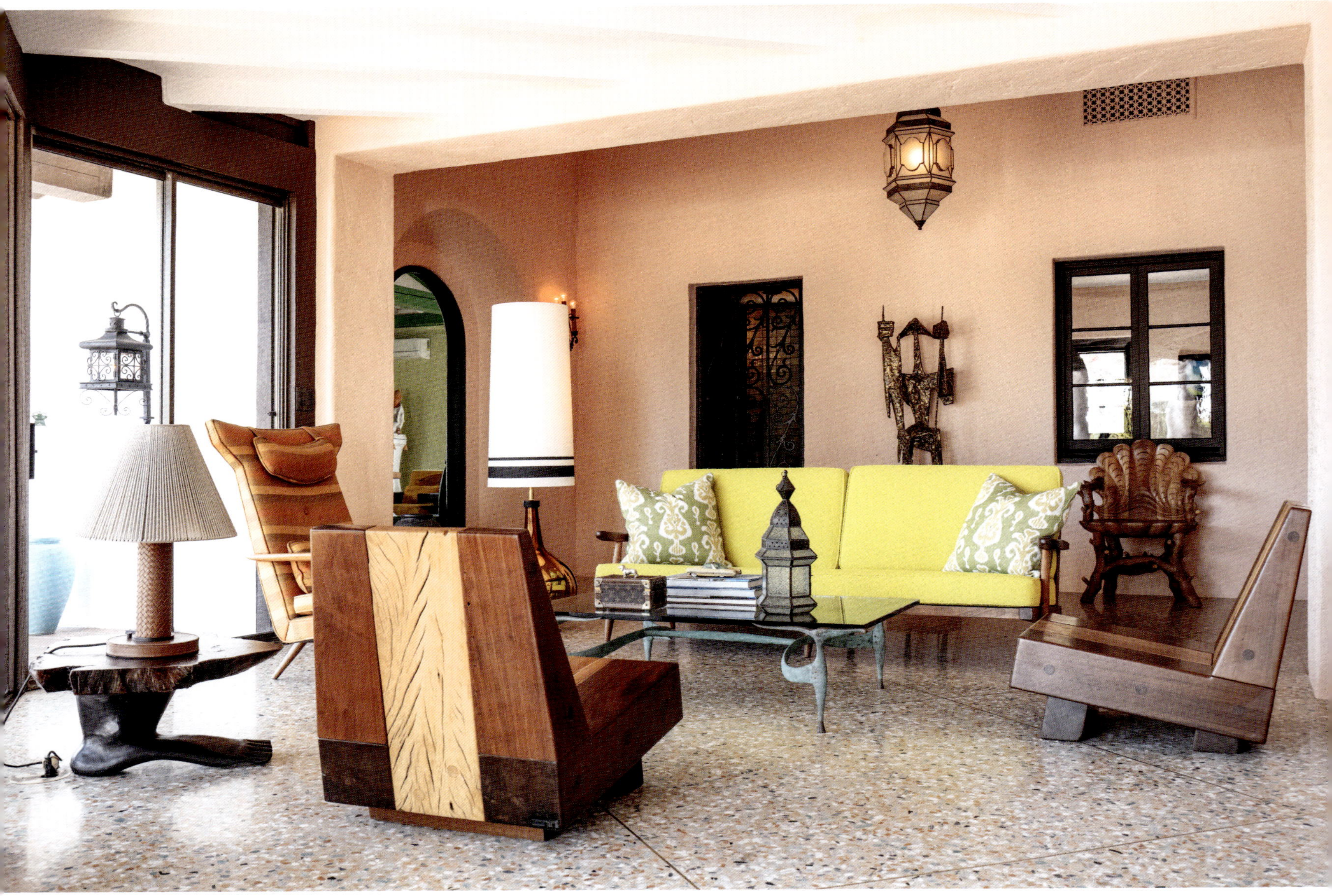

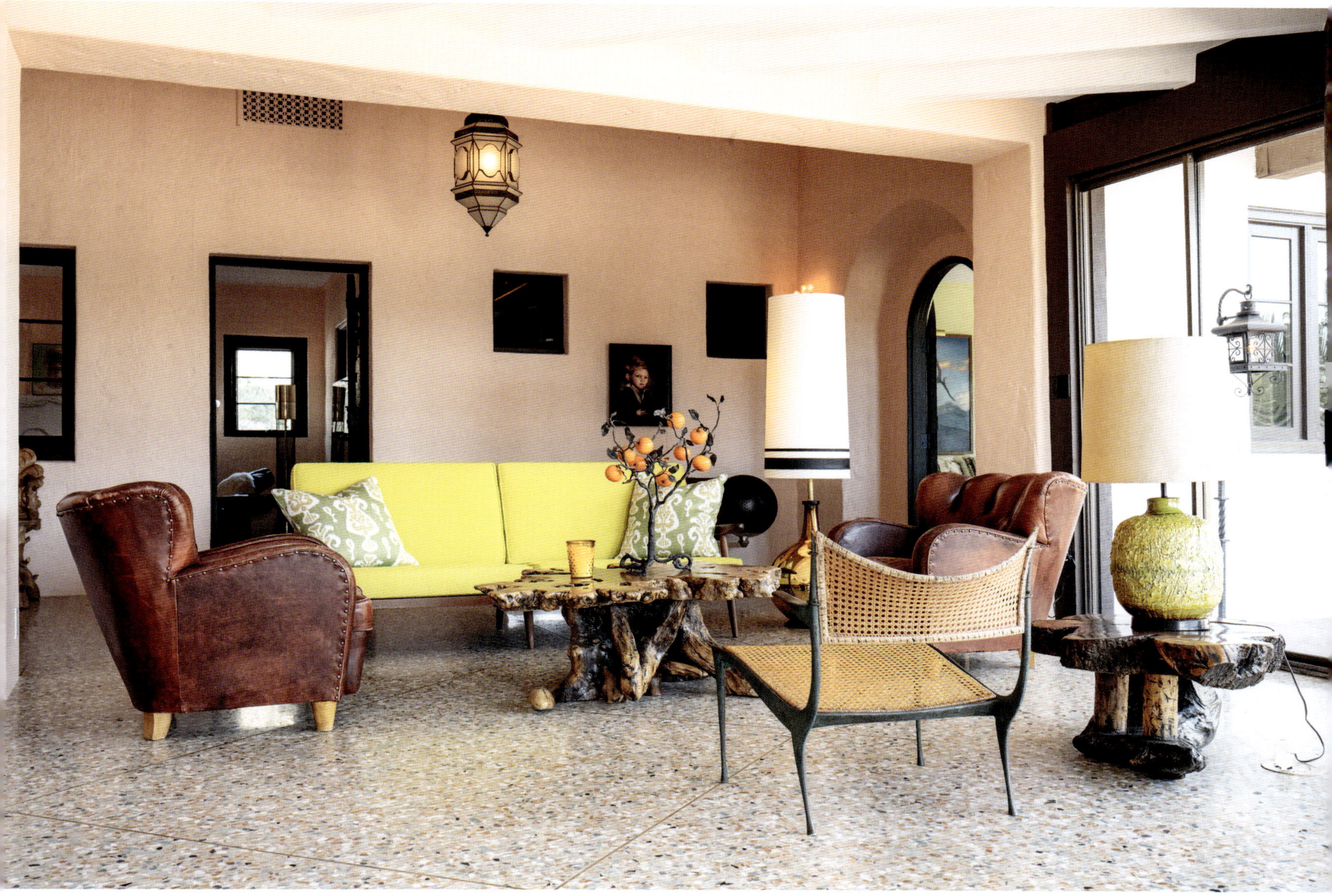

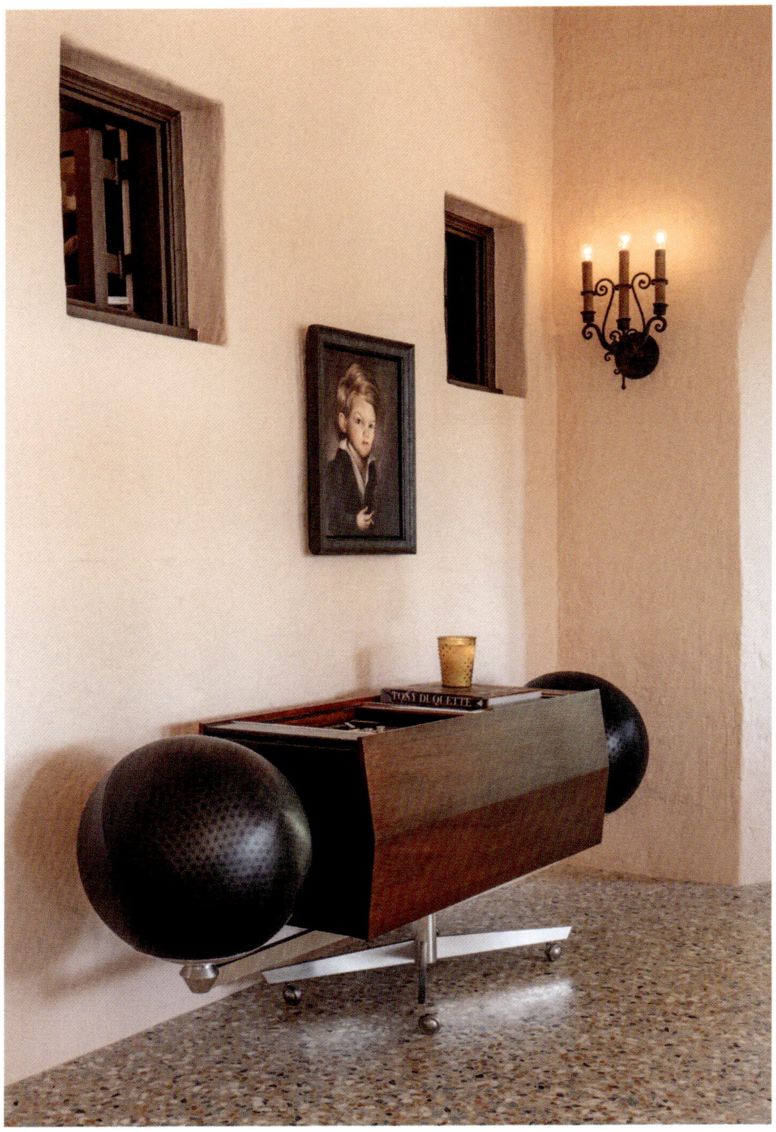
TONY DUQUETTE

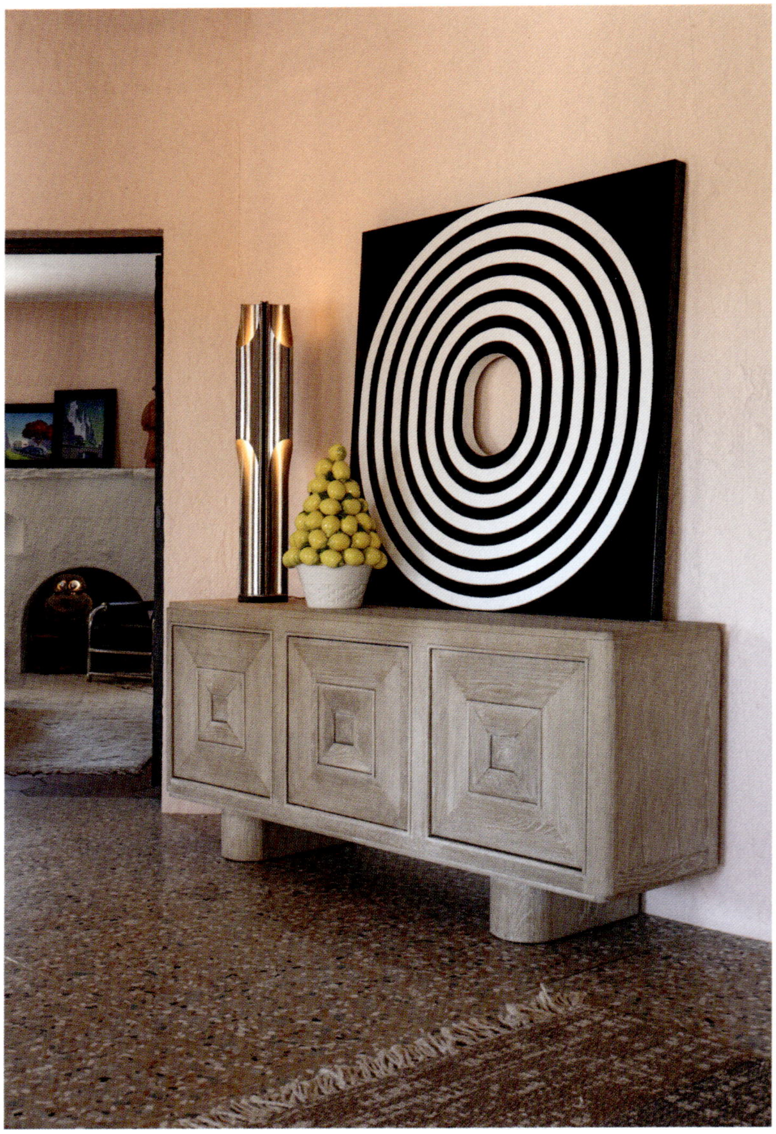

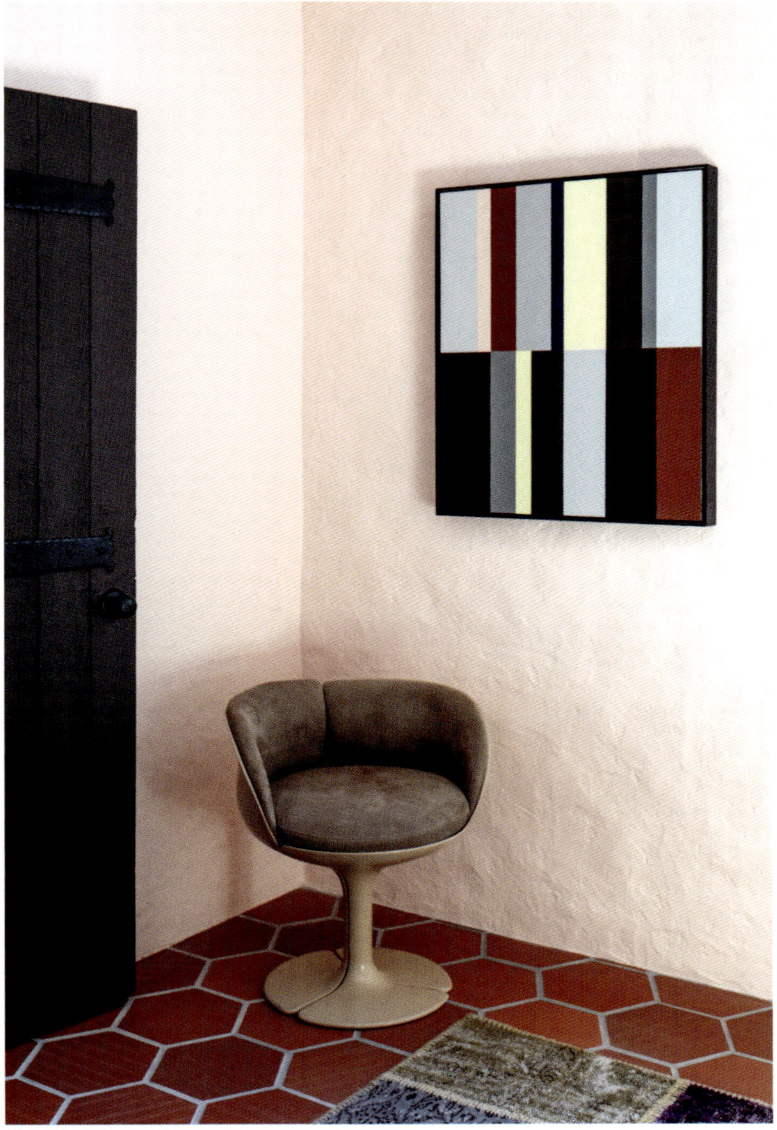

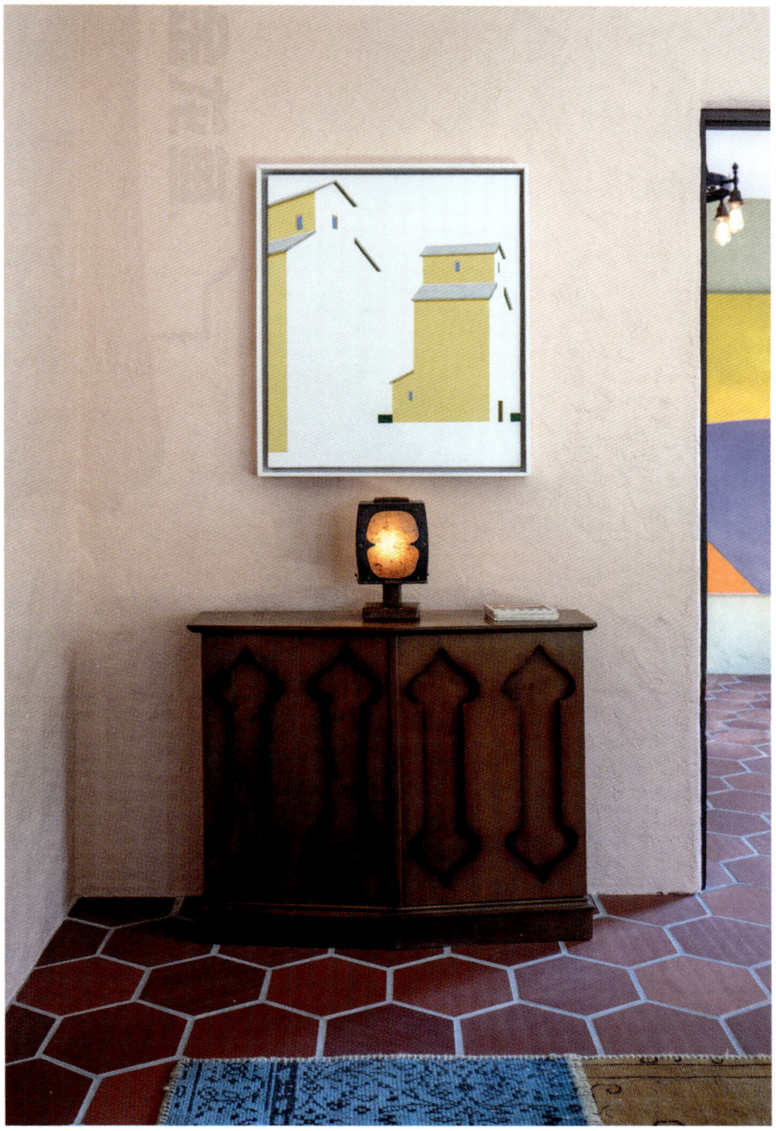

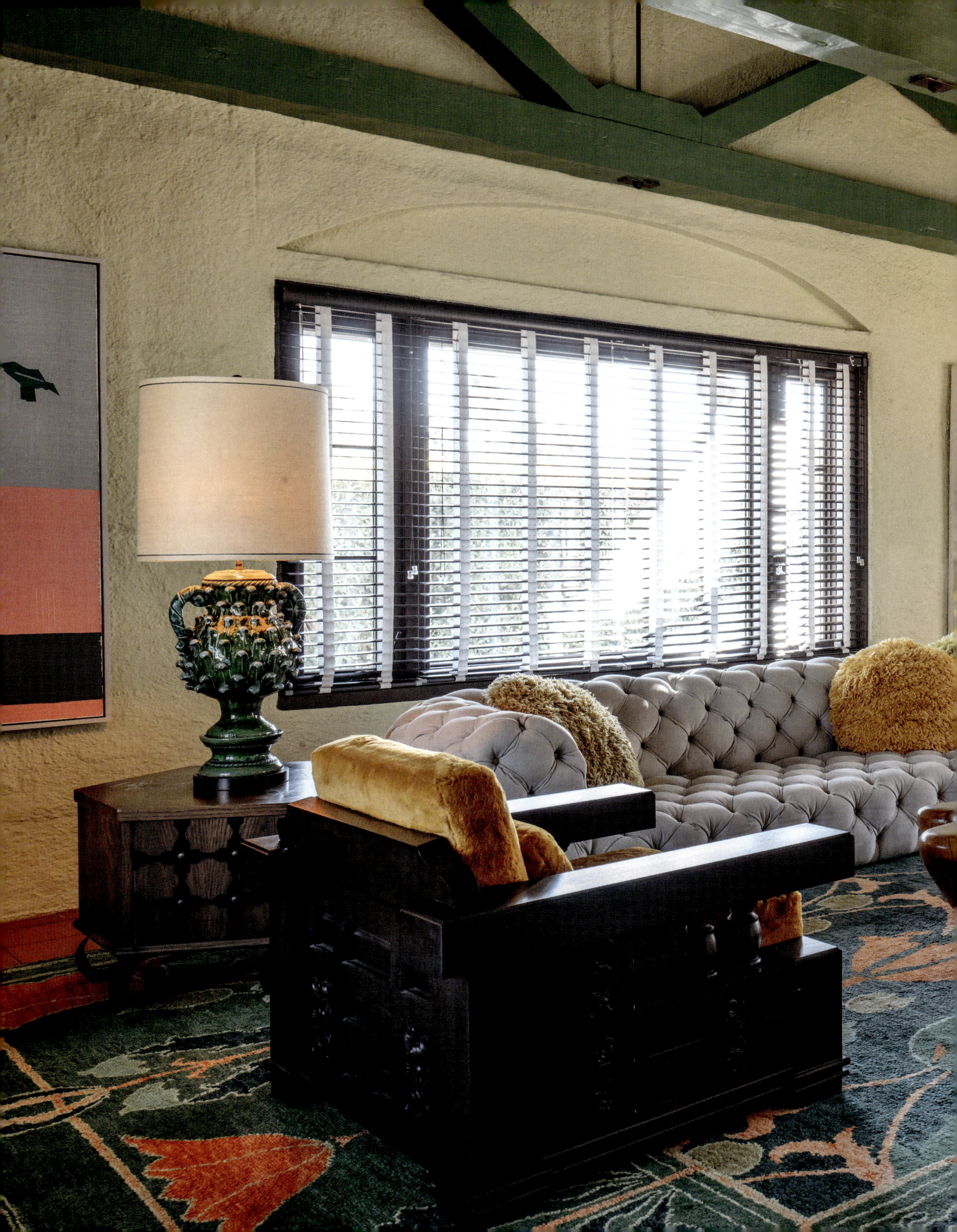

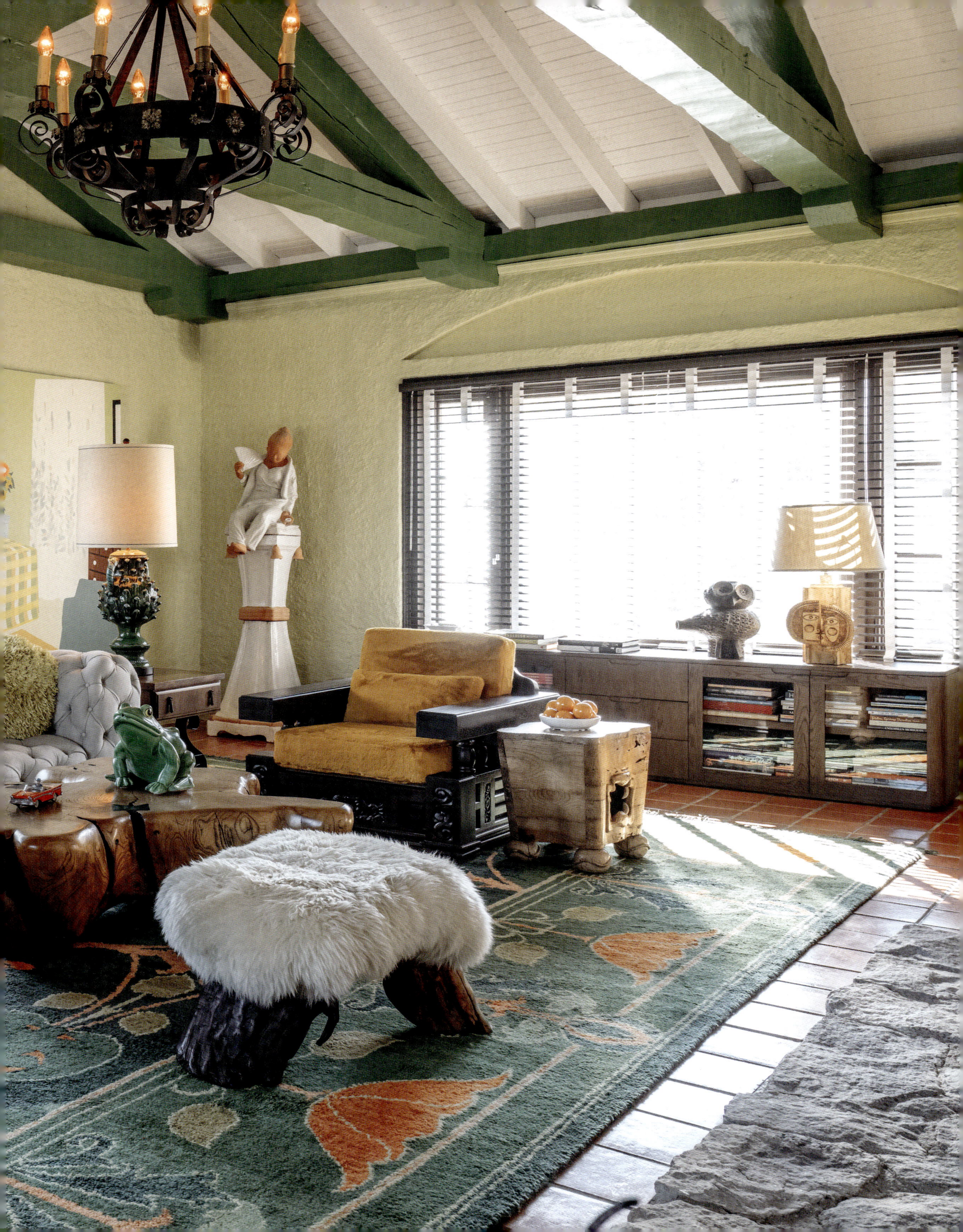

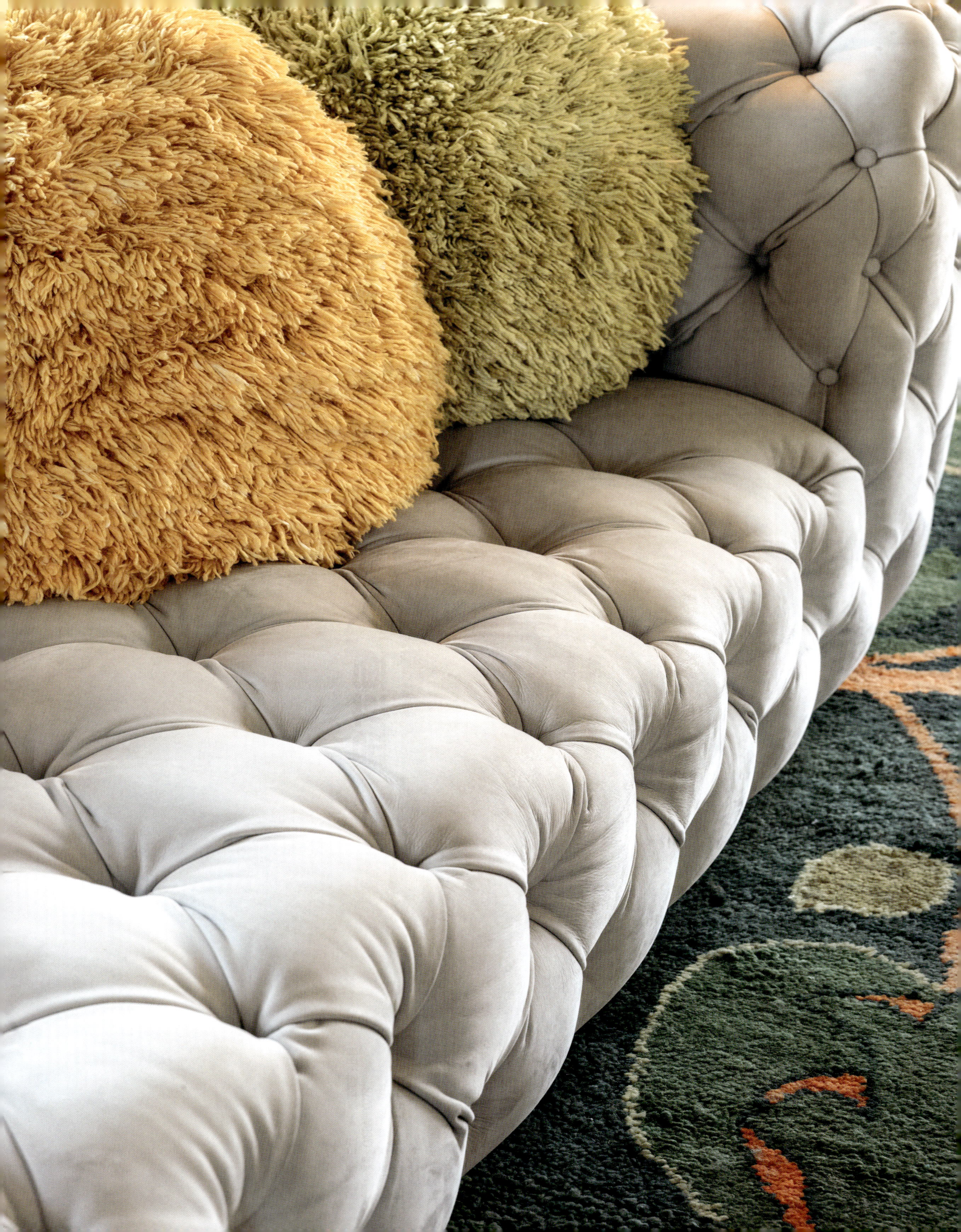

CALIFORNIA ROMANTICA
HITCHCOCK STYLE
CASA MEXICANA
SCOTT SHRADER THE ART OF OUTDOOR LIVING
Jack Pierson
JEAN PROUVE

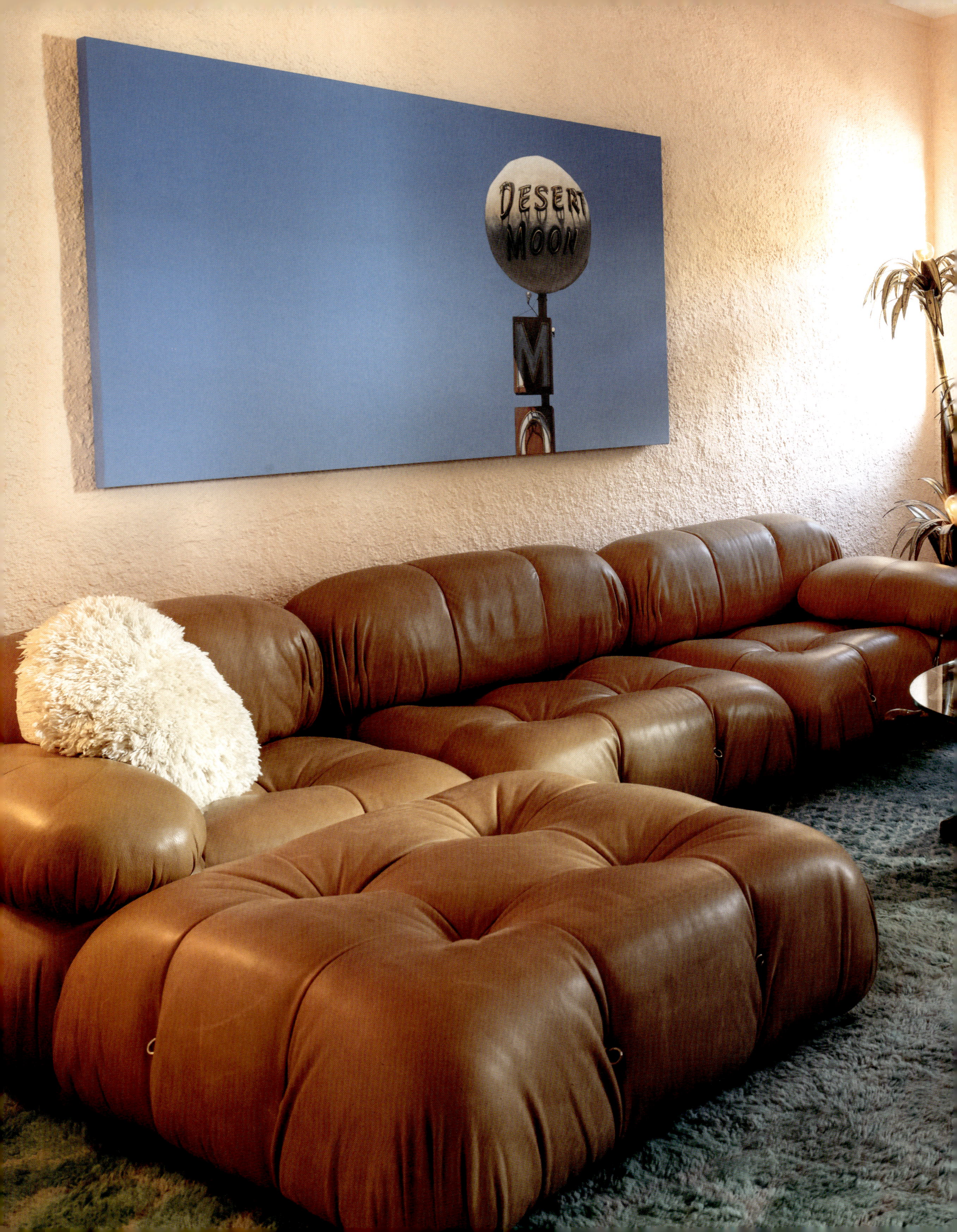
DESERT
MOON
M

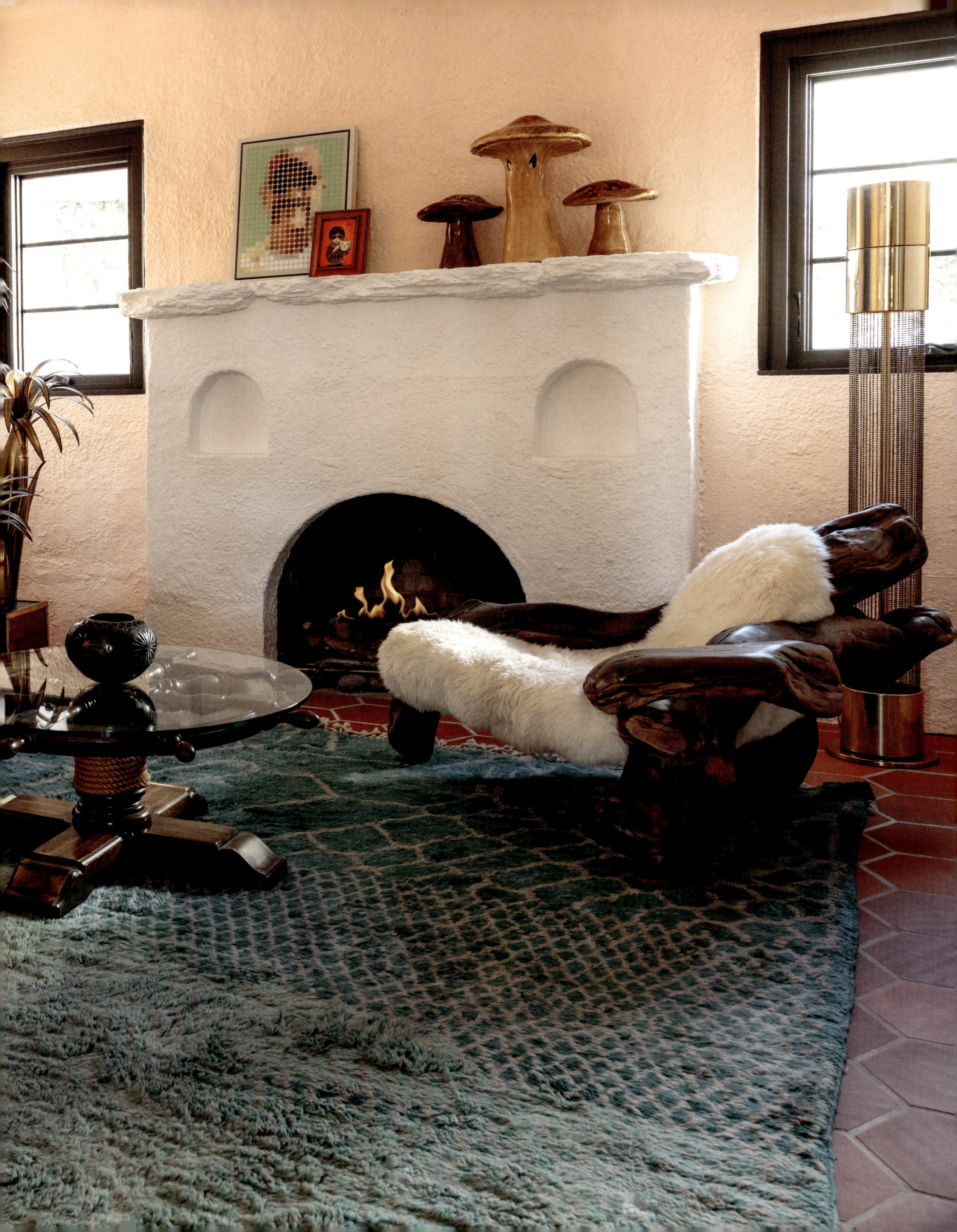

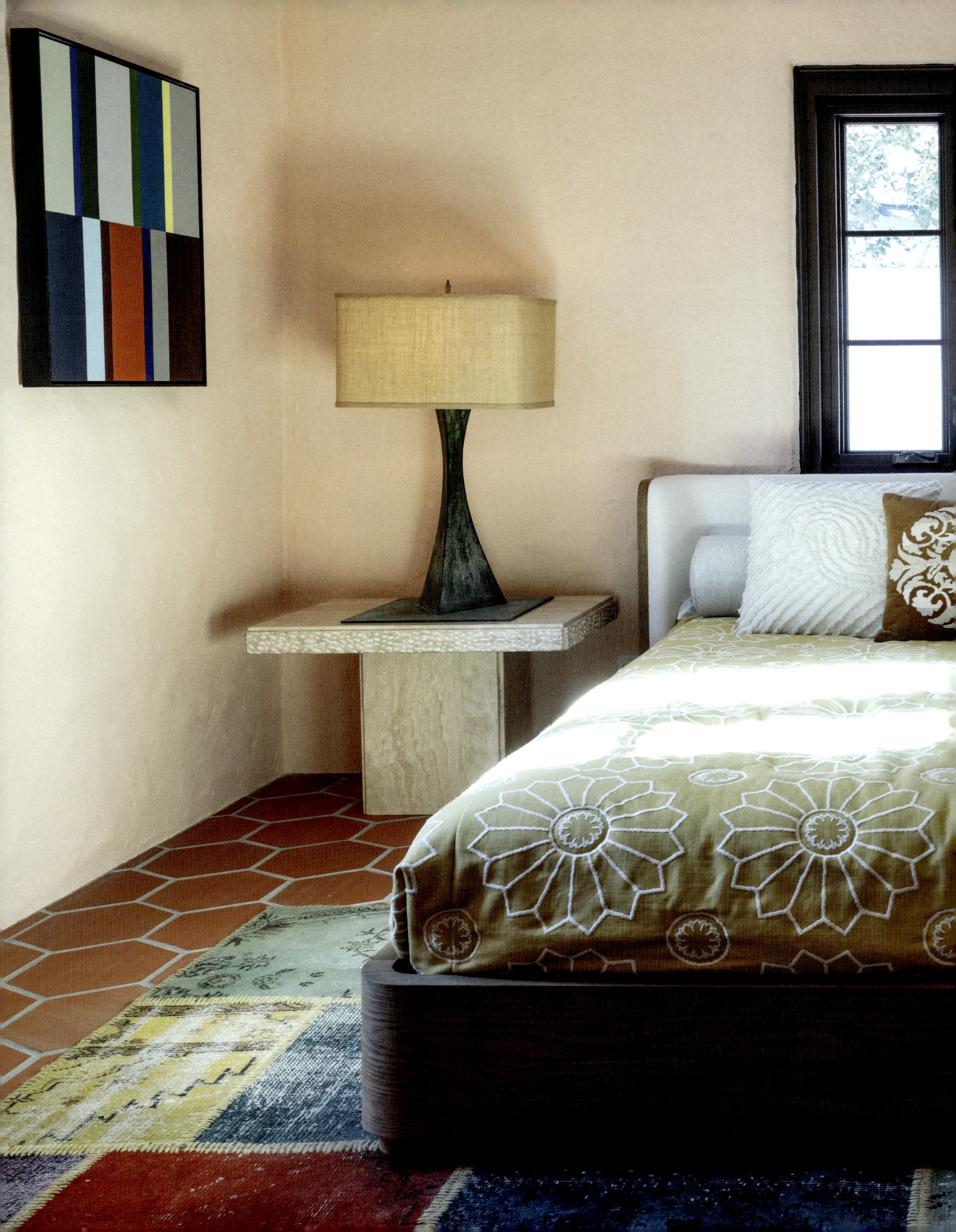

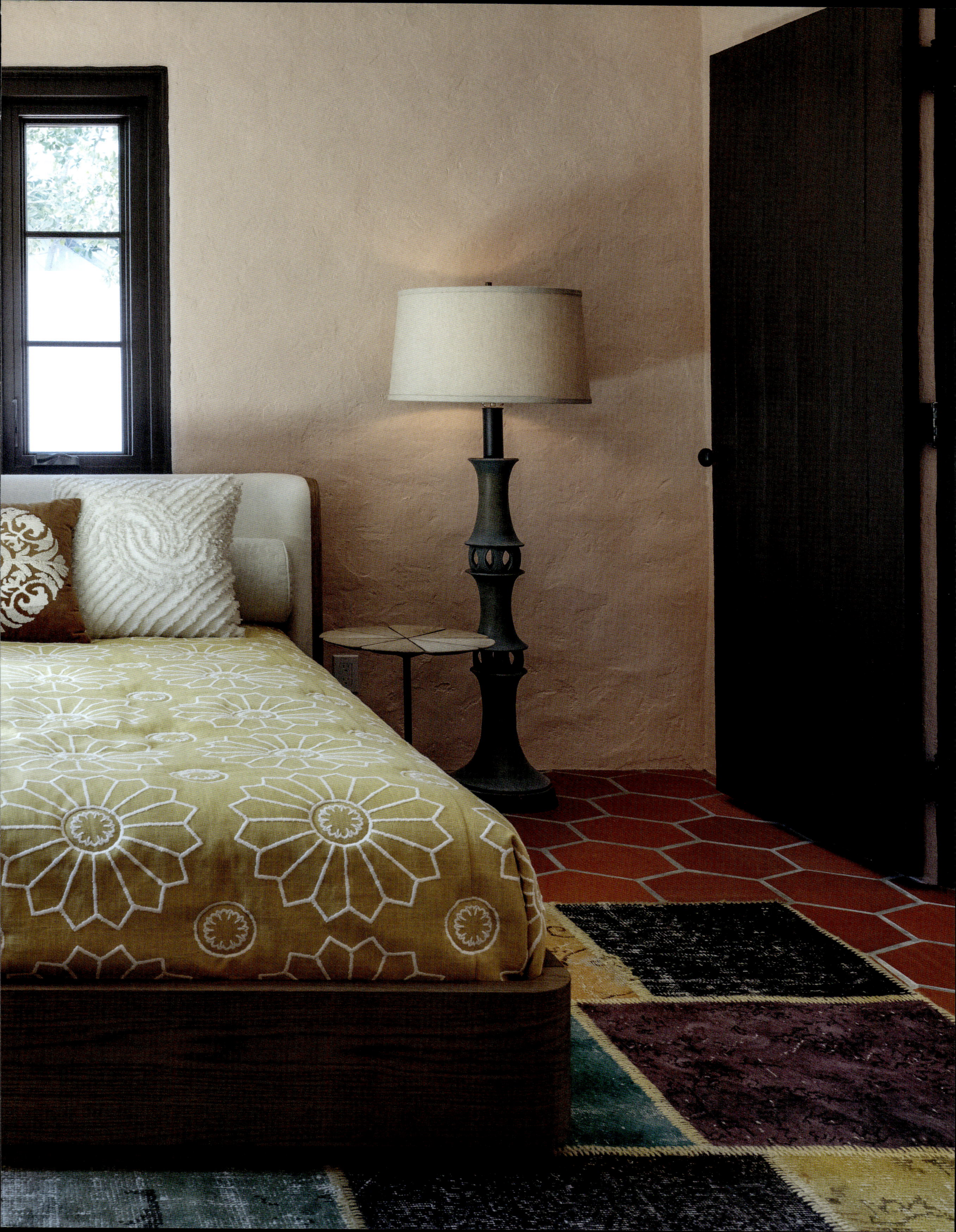

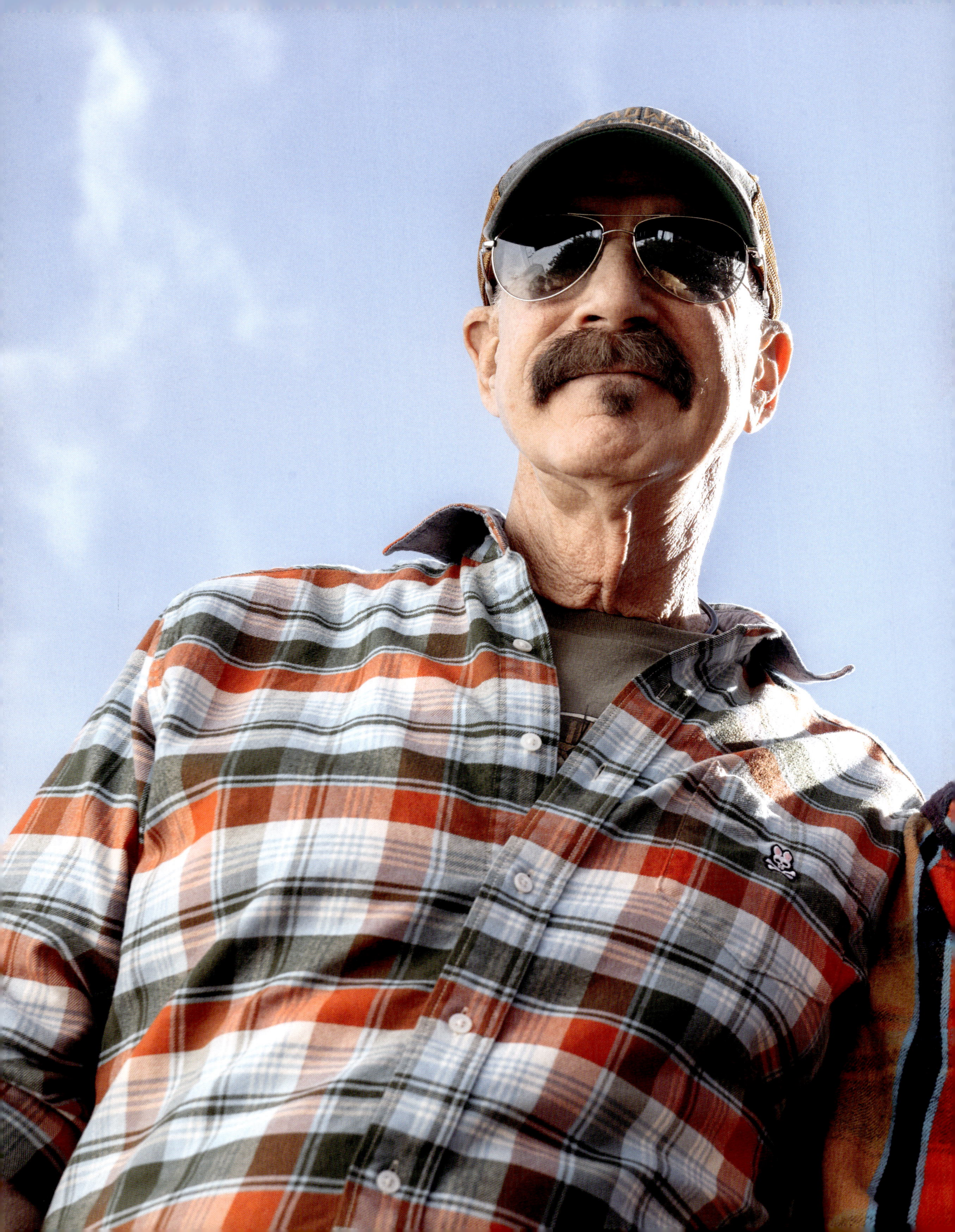

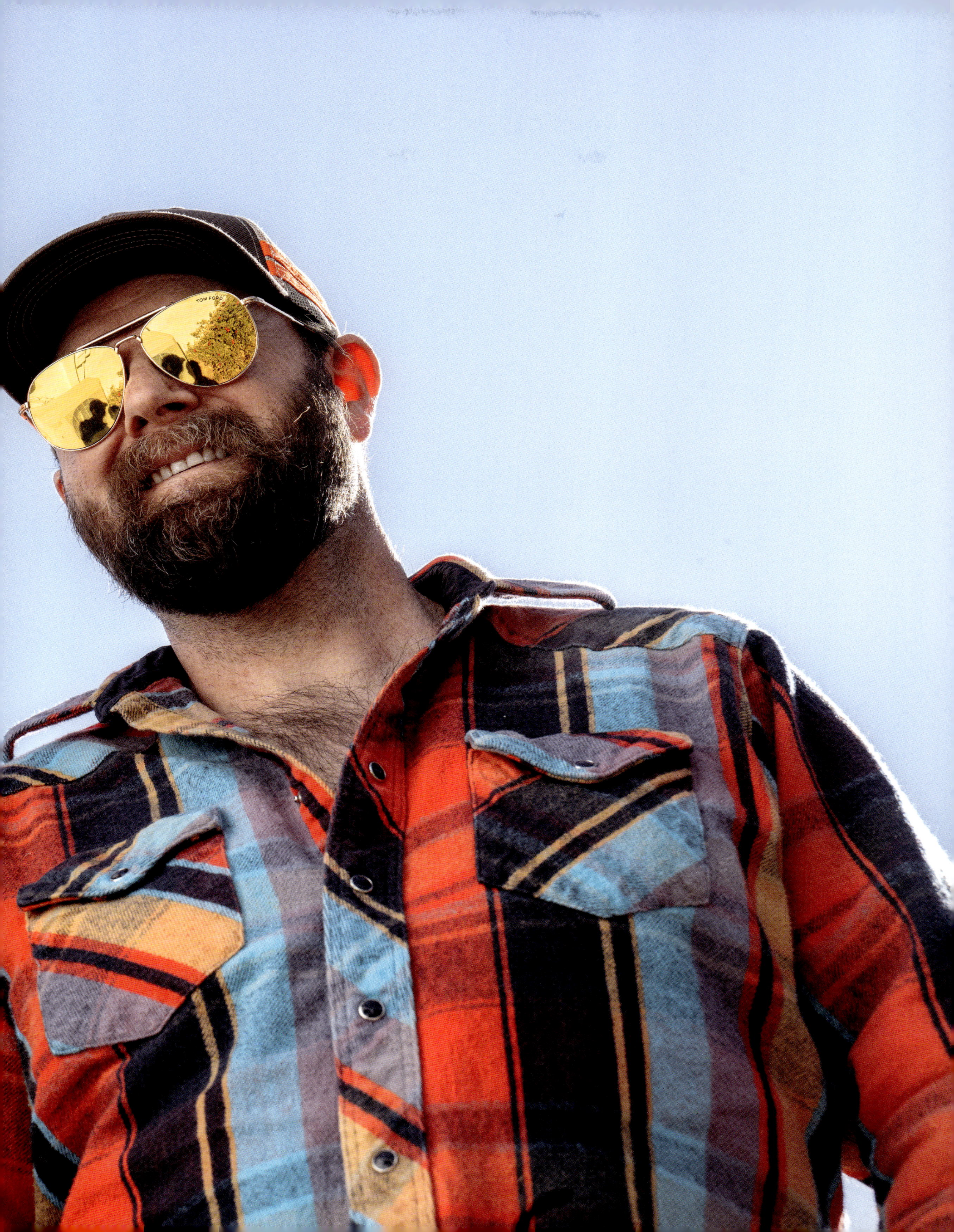
TOM FORD

SOUTH- RIDGE

IN 1969, FLUSH WITH THE SUCCESS OF *Bullitt*, Steve McQueen bought a new pad in the hilltop neighborhood of Southridge—a two-story steel-and-glass house, designed by Hugh Kaptur, with a cantilevered living room to capture the city views. "Decorate it as if it belonged to a bachelor," McQueen urged his interior designer, who stained the pecky cypress walls coffee brown and textured the rooms with woven window coverings and cut shag rugs. Never mind that the actor was married at the time. Against this high-groovy backdrop the "king of cool" indulged his various obsessions: motorcycles, partying, Ali MacGraw (they met in 1972, on the set of *The Getaway*).

McQueen sold the house in the late '70s and passed away in 1980. By 2017, when Lisa Harrison and her husband David discovered it, the place "gave a death vibe," having survived several floodings, among other depredations. Fortuitously, Jeremy Scott, then the creative director of Moschino, lived next door, in John Lautner's Elrod House, and he introduced the couple to Mark Haddawy, who had painstakingly restored the Lautner. Haddawy launched a typically rigorous rehabilitation of the Kaptur house, one that would include remaking the window coverings and Edward Fields rugs, reproducing the original wallpaper, even refurbishing the actor's old weight sets. When new pieces were used, they stuck to "things that felt like they could always have been there," says Harrison: a Hans-Agne Jakobsson brass chandelier, totem sculptures by Stan Bitters, furniture by Warren Platner, George Nakashima, Sergio Rodrigues. Might it all be a little *too* king of cool for a couple from Salt Lake City with four young daughters? Not at all, says Lisa Harrison. "The house just feels like part of the desert to me. I think that's what McQueen got right. Once you're up here, everything else just melts away."

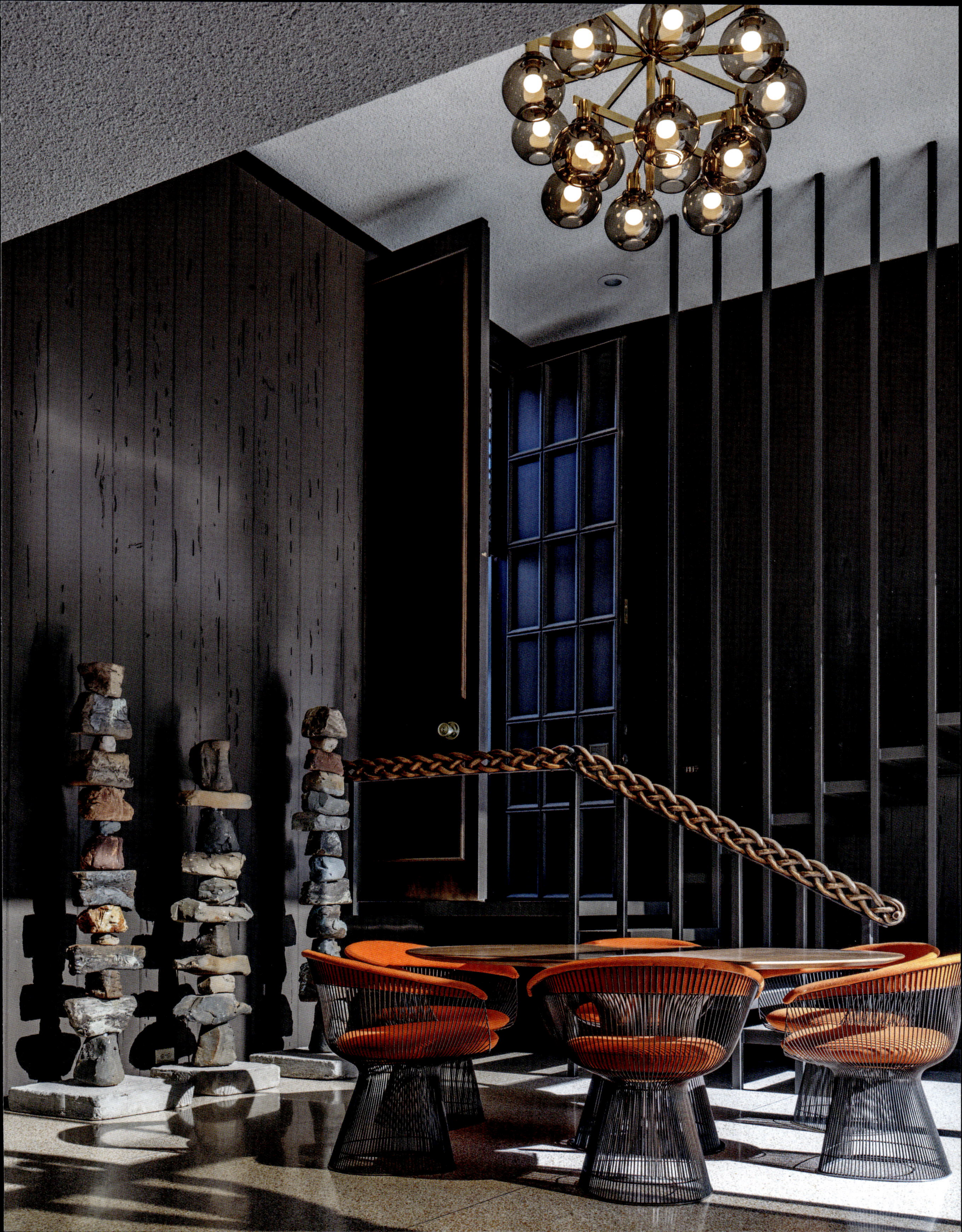

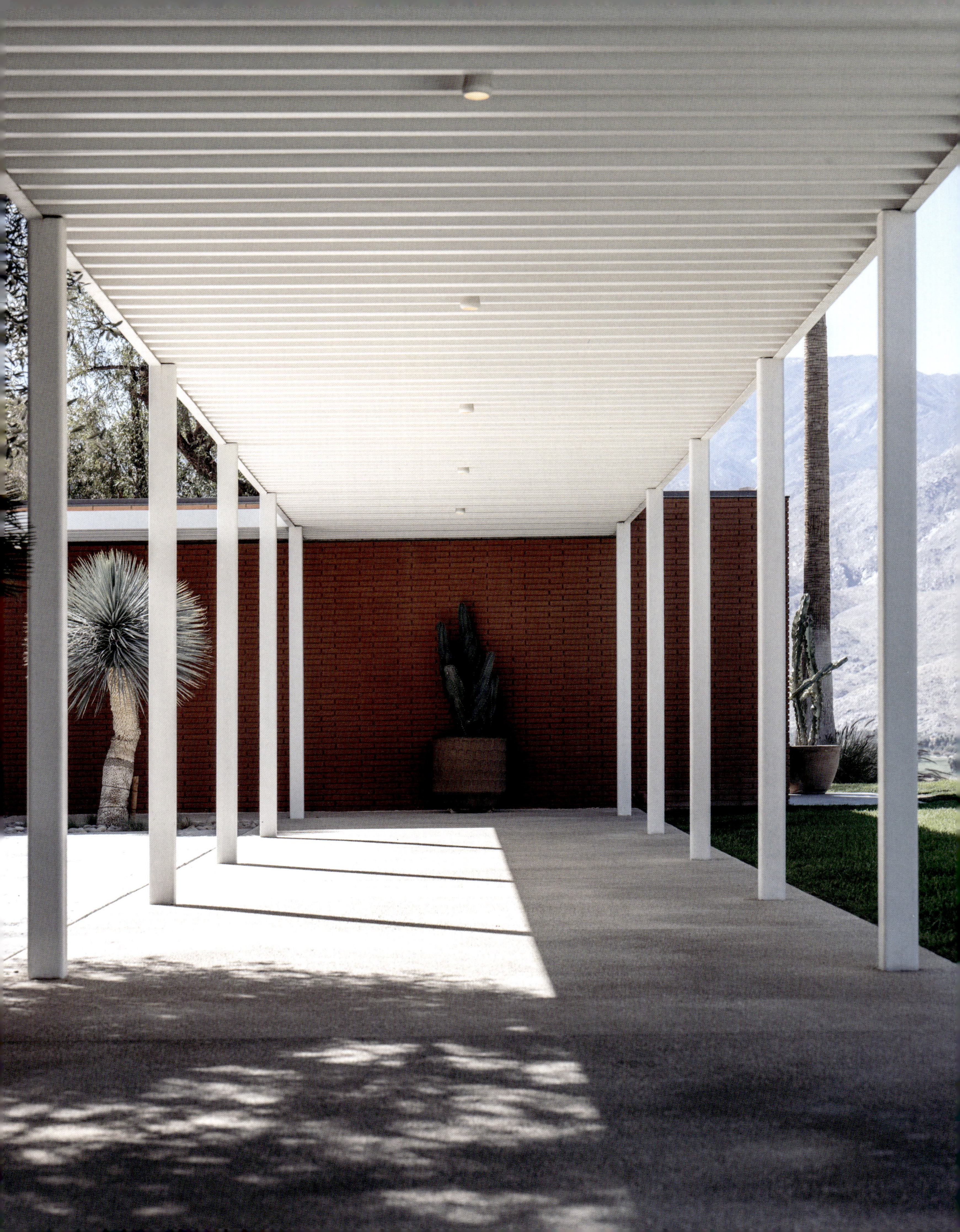

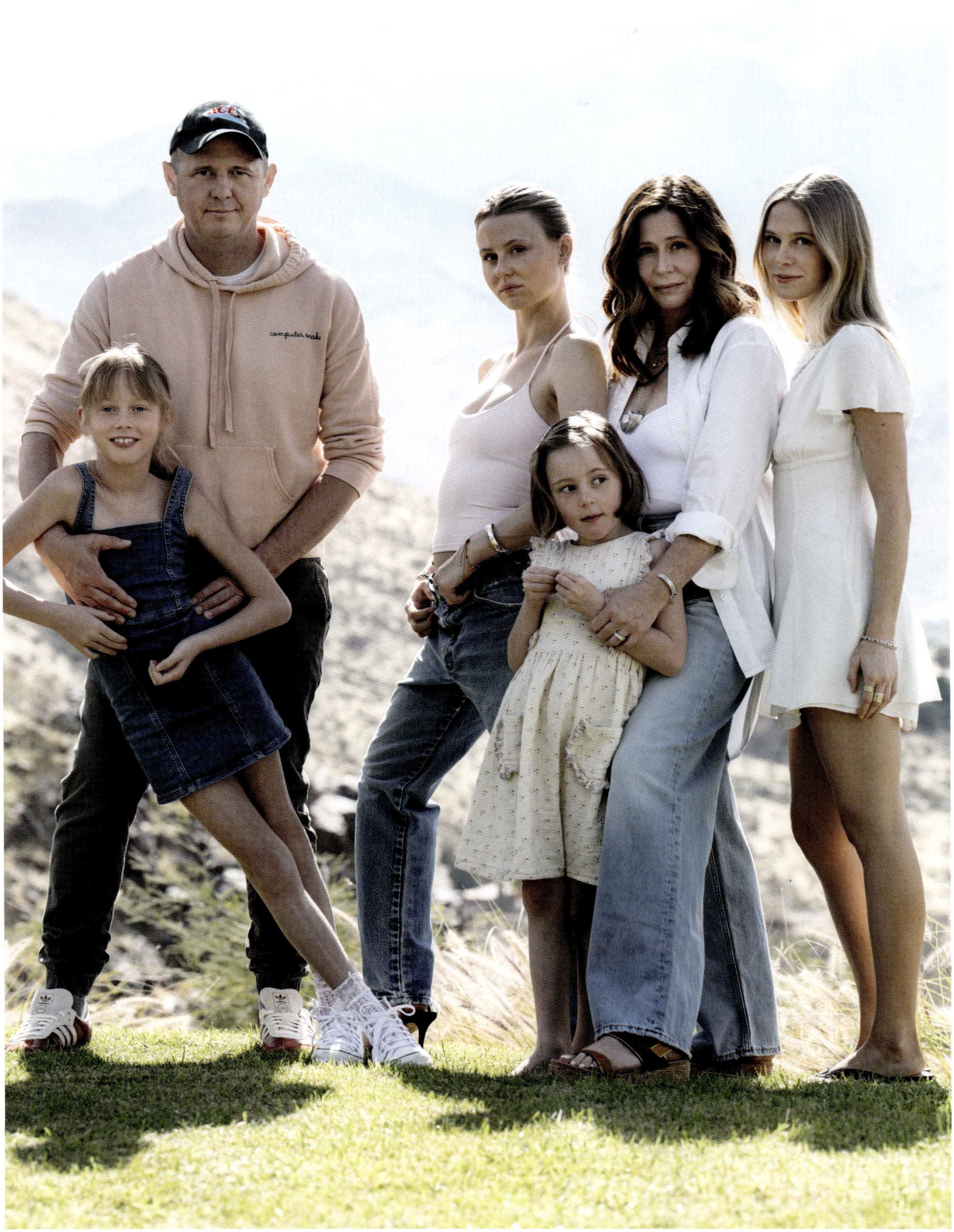

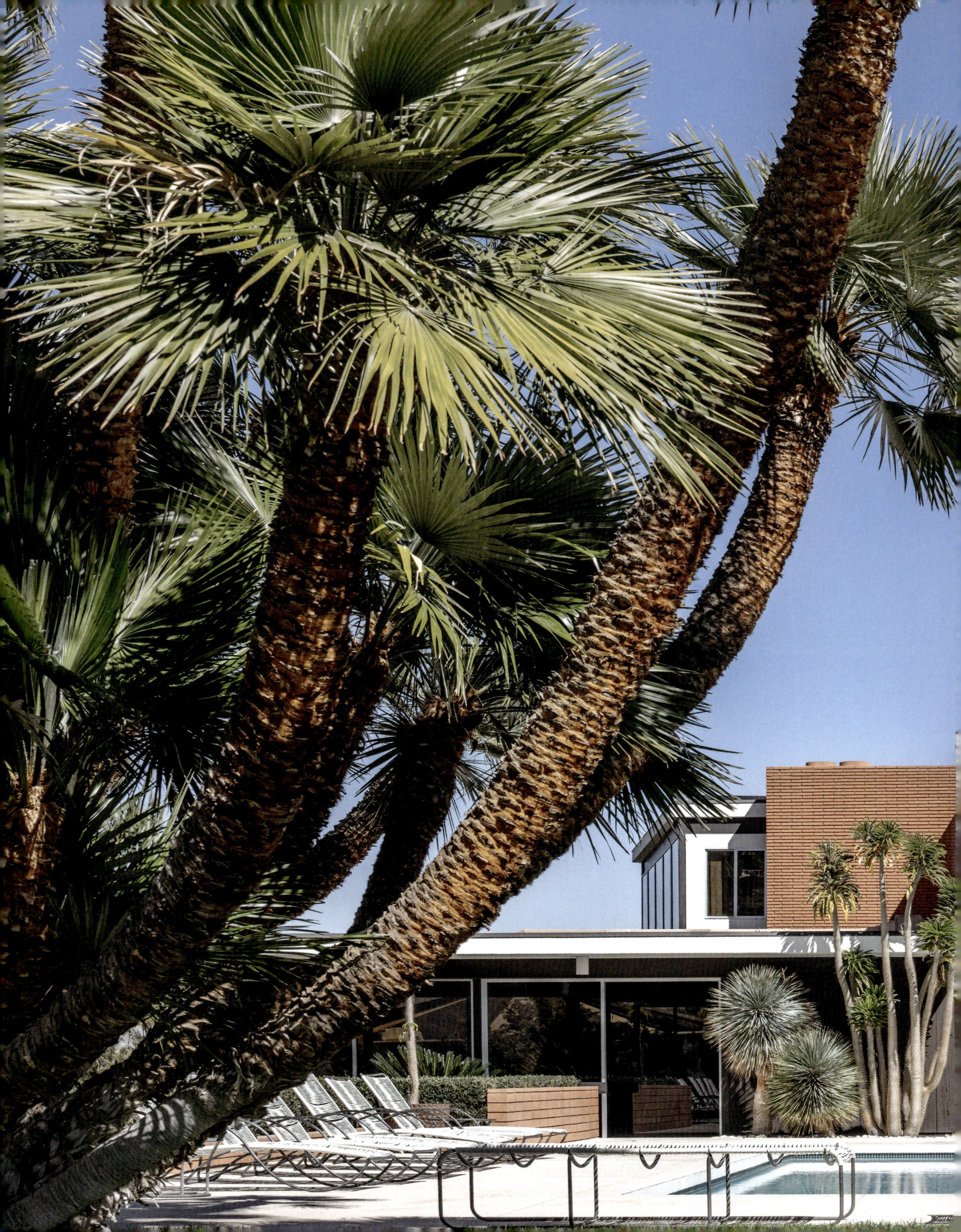

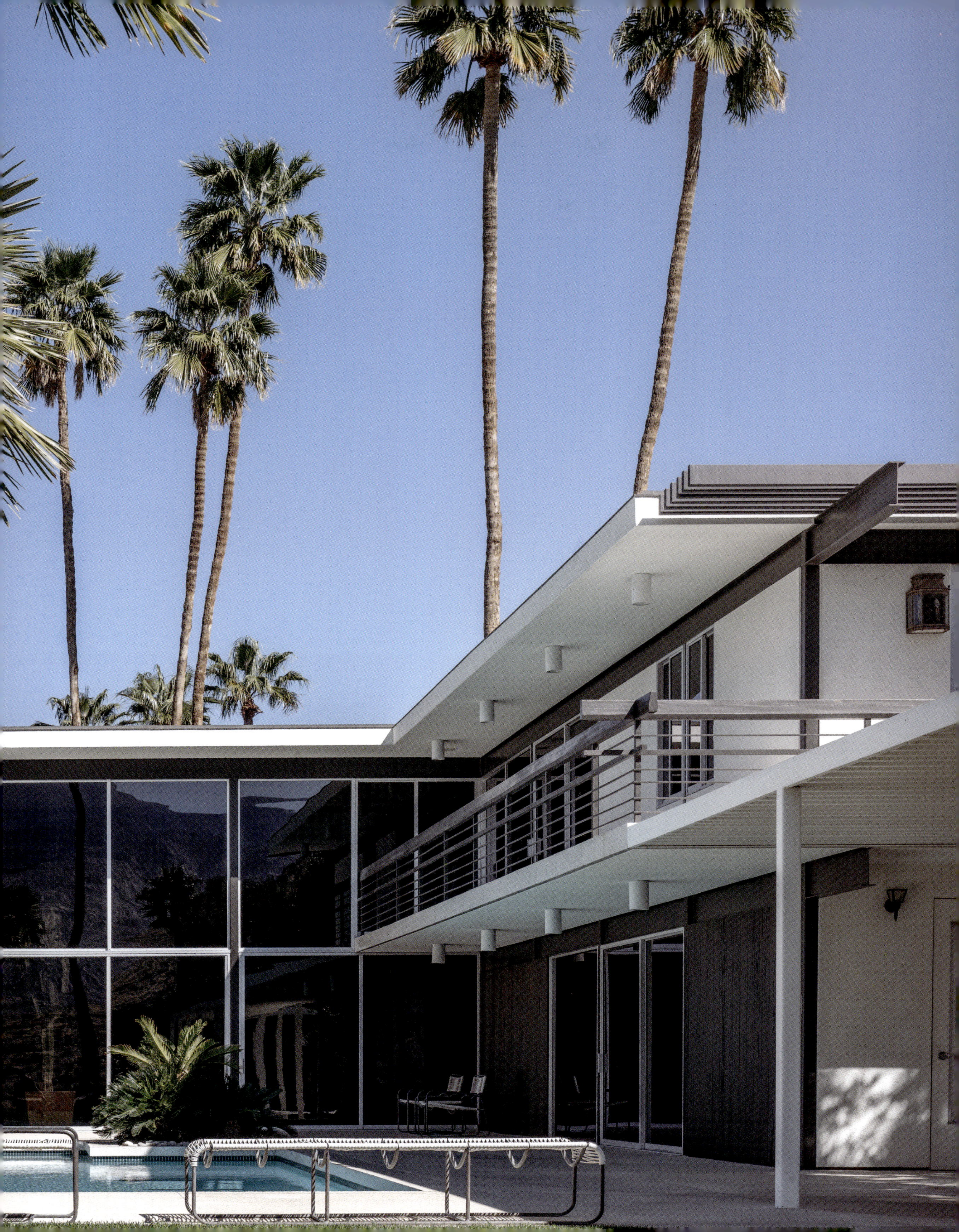

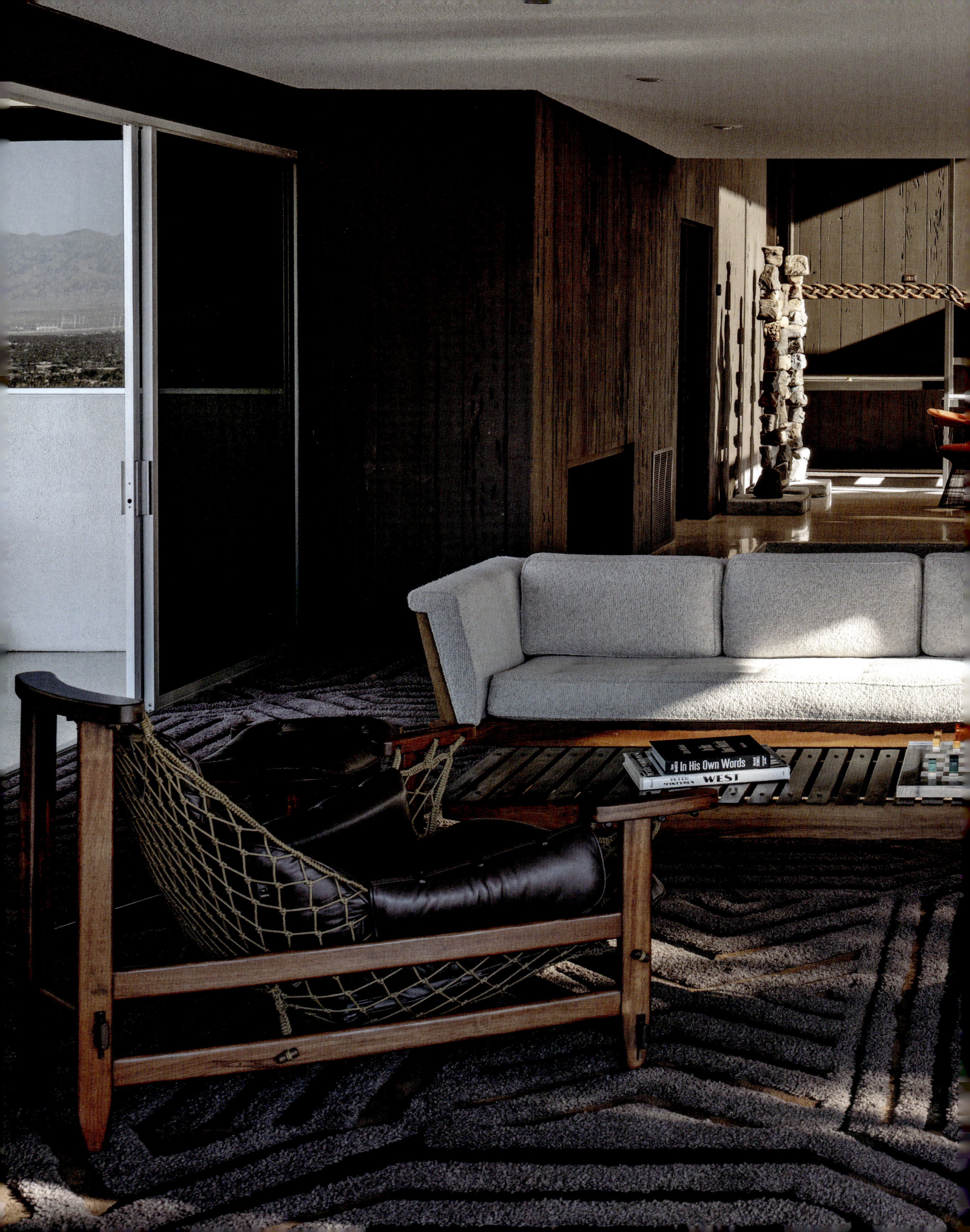
In His Own Words
PETER
WEST

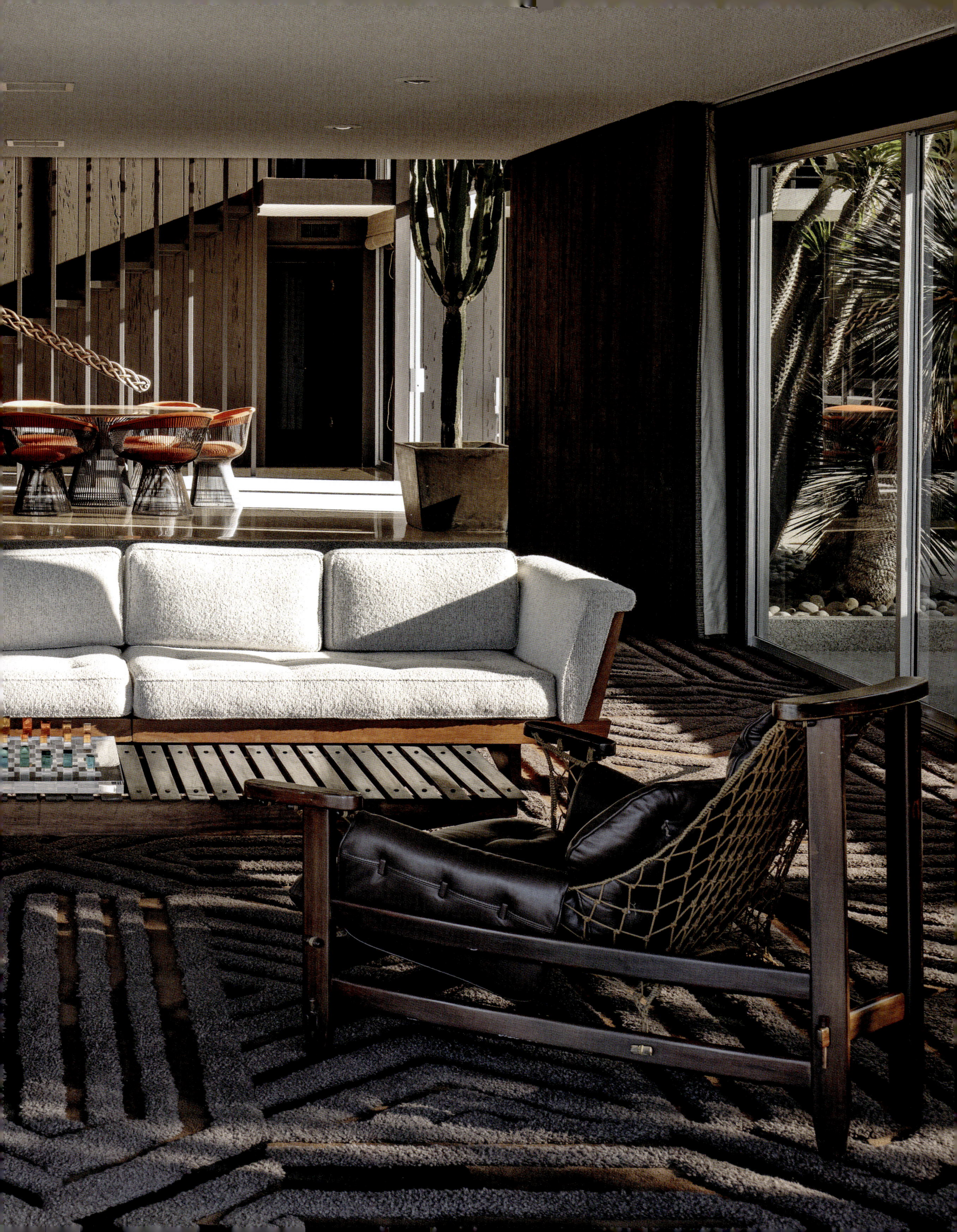

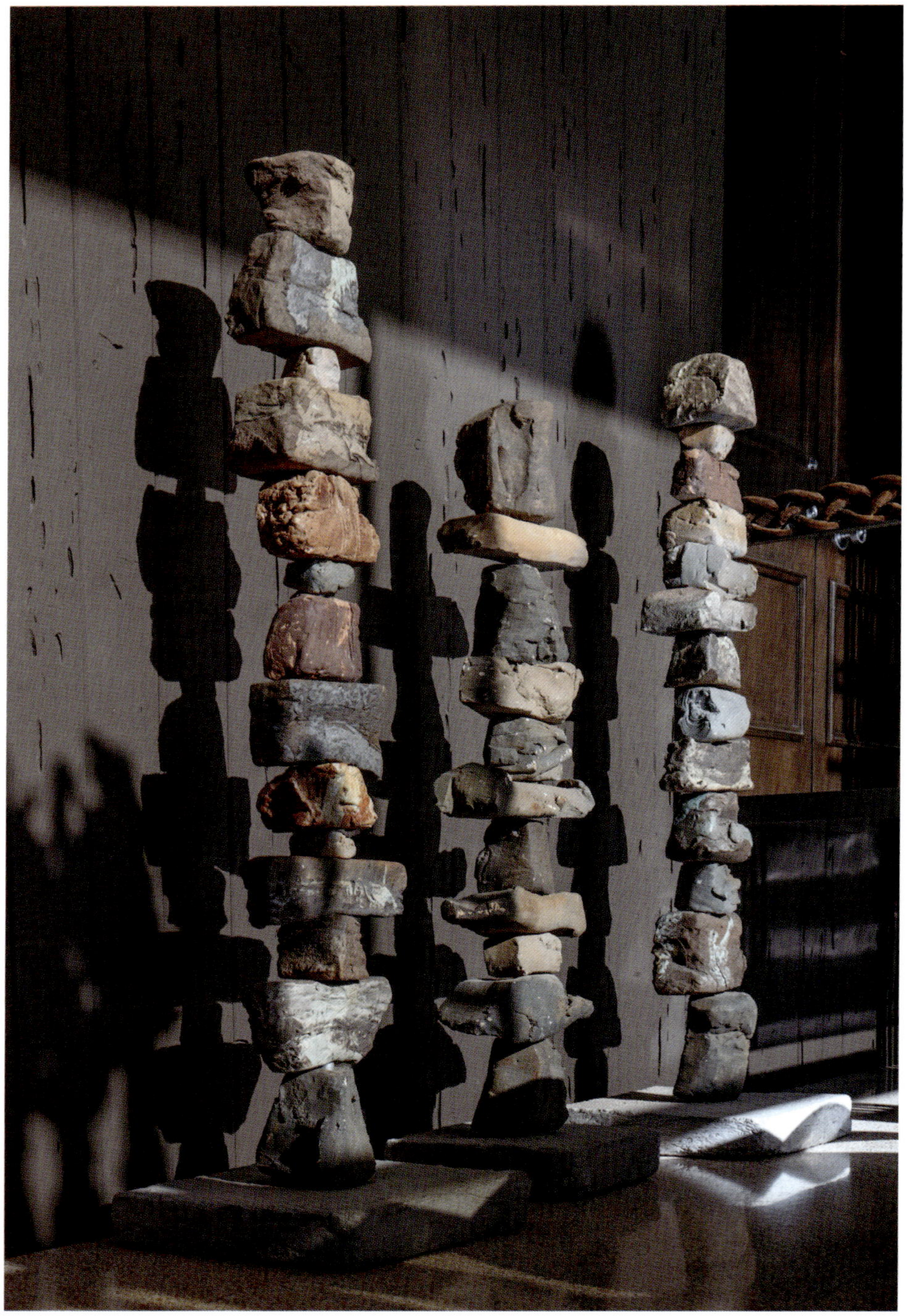

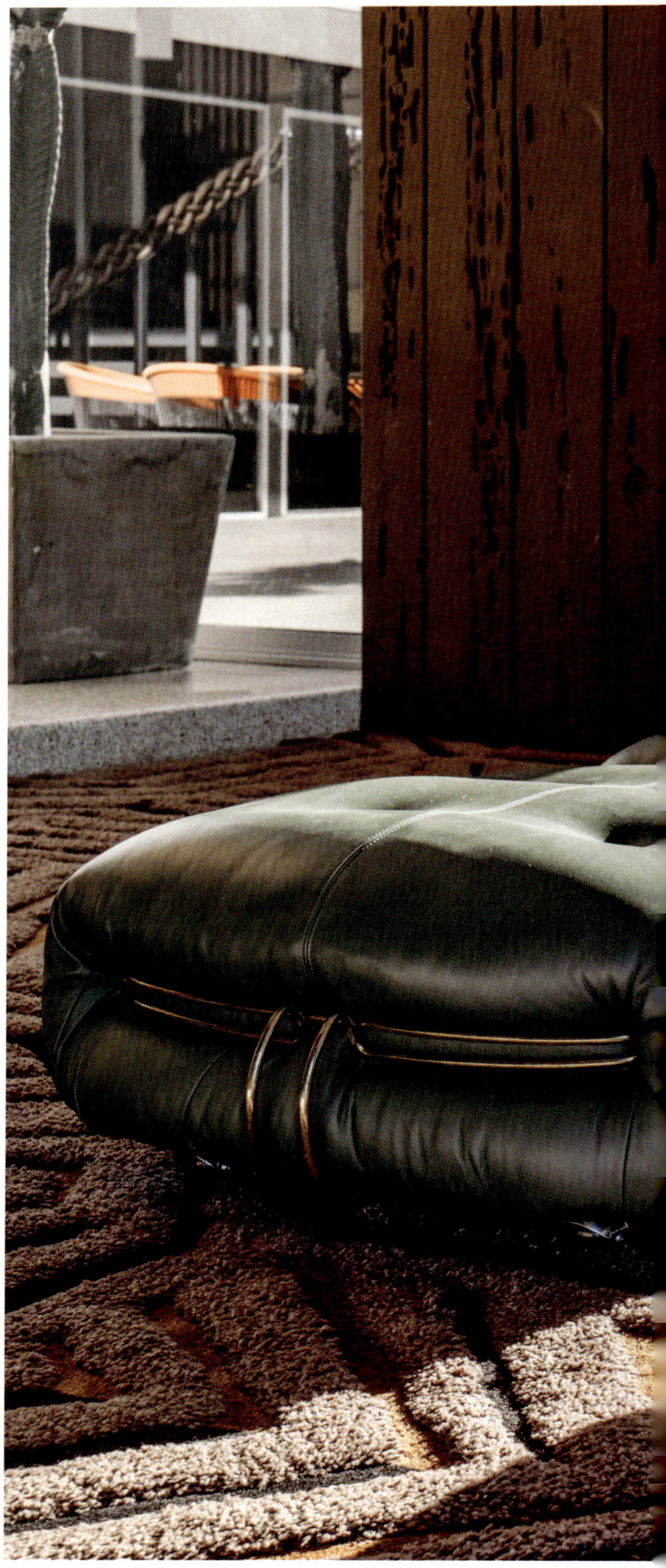

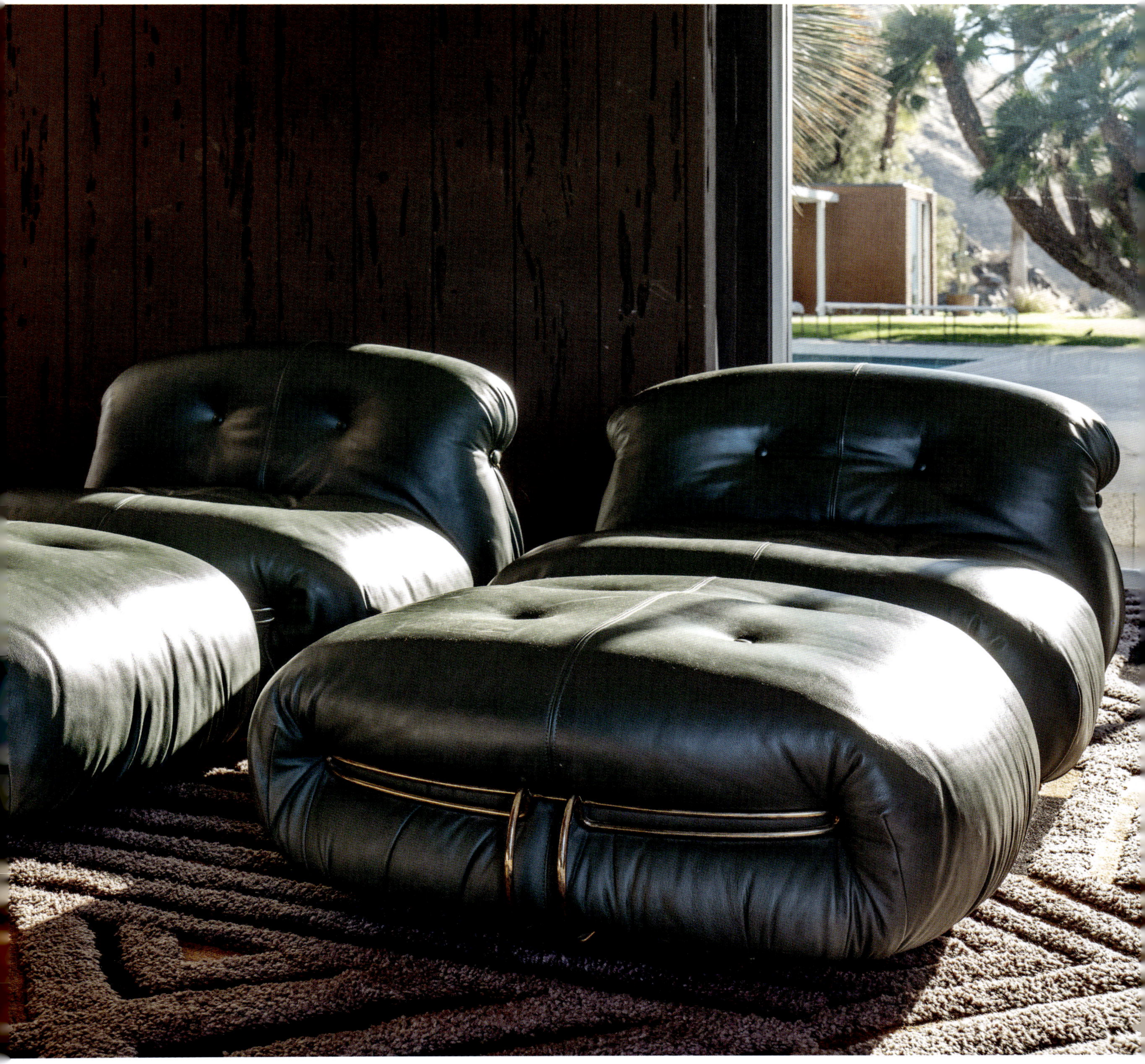

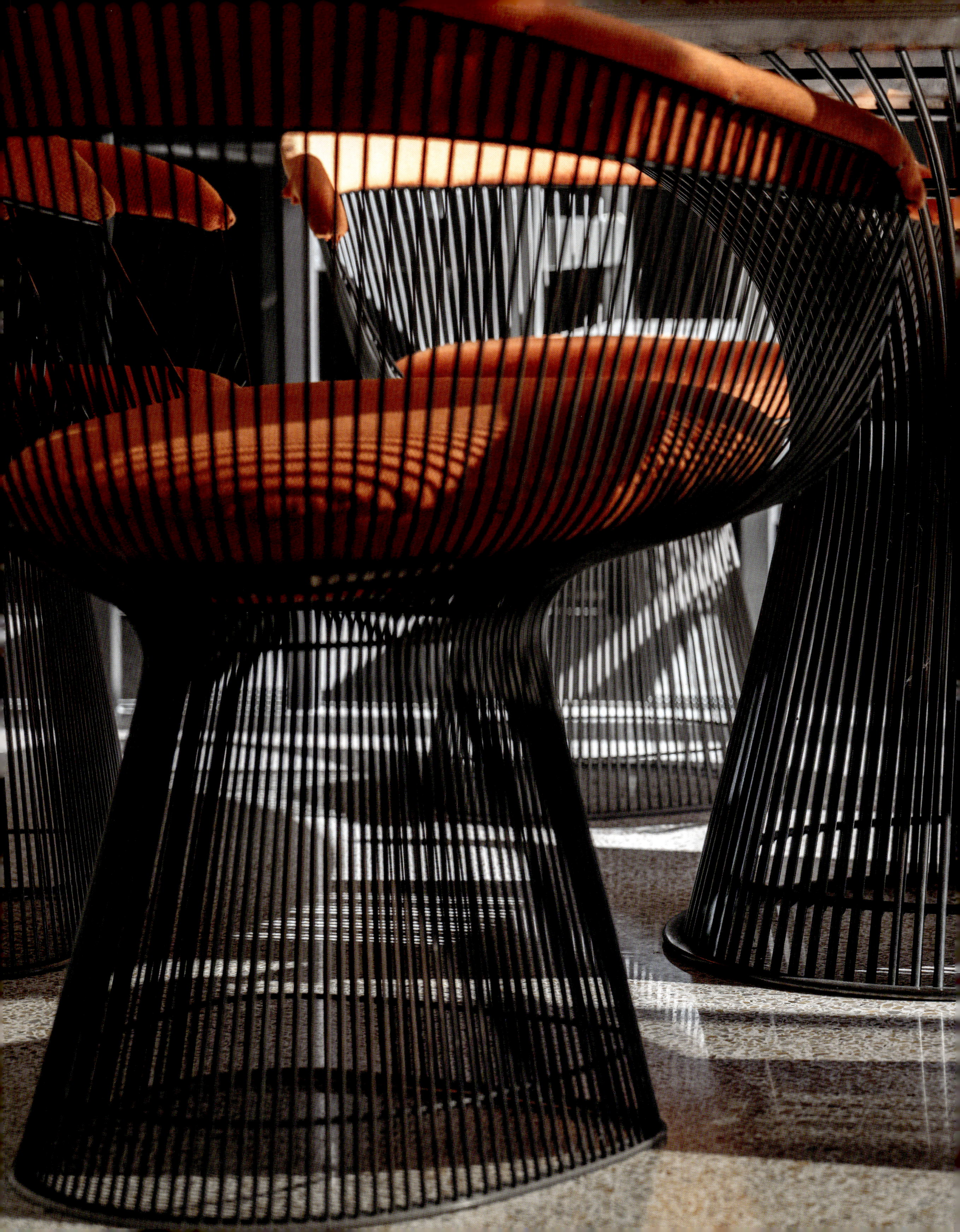

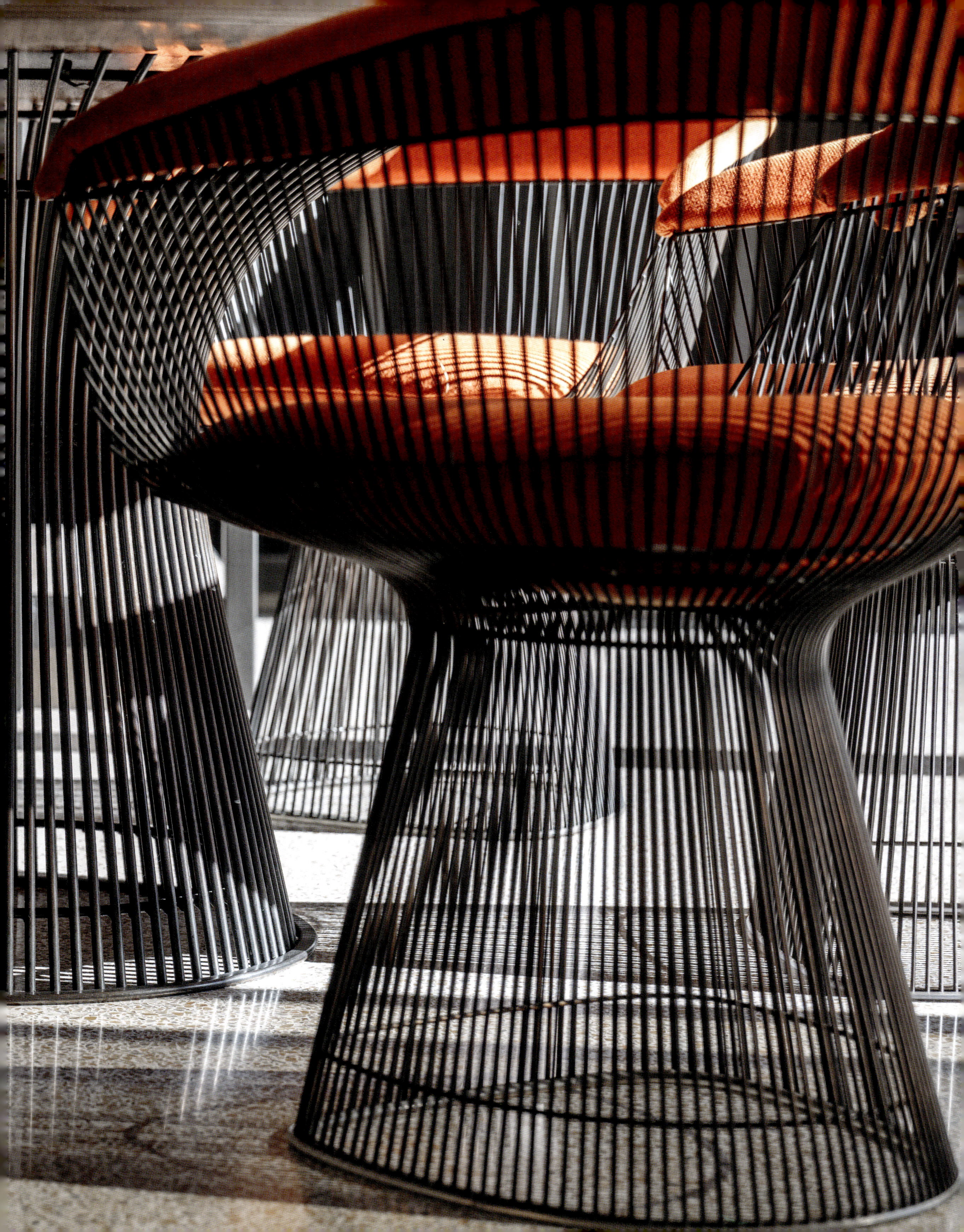

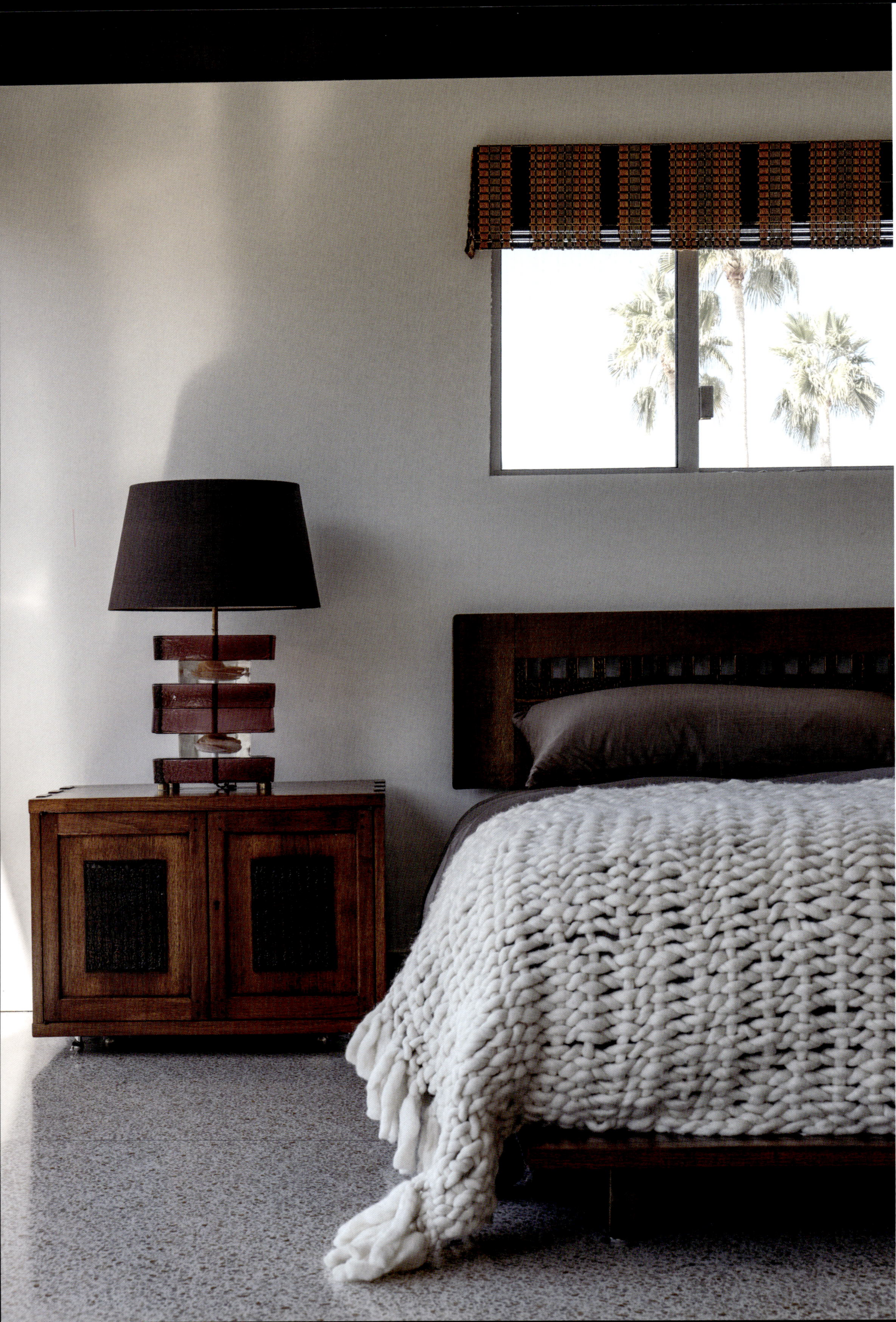

331

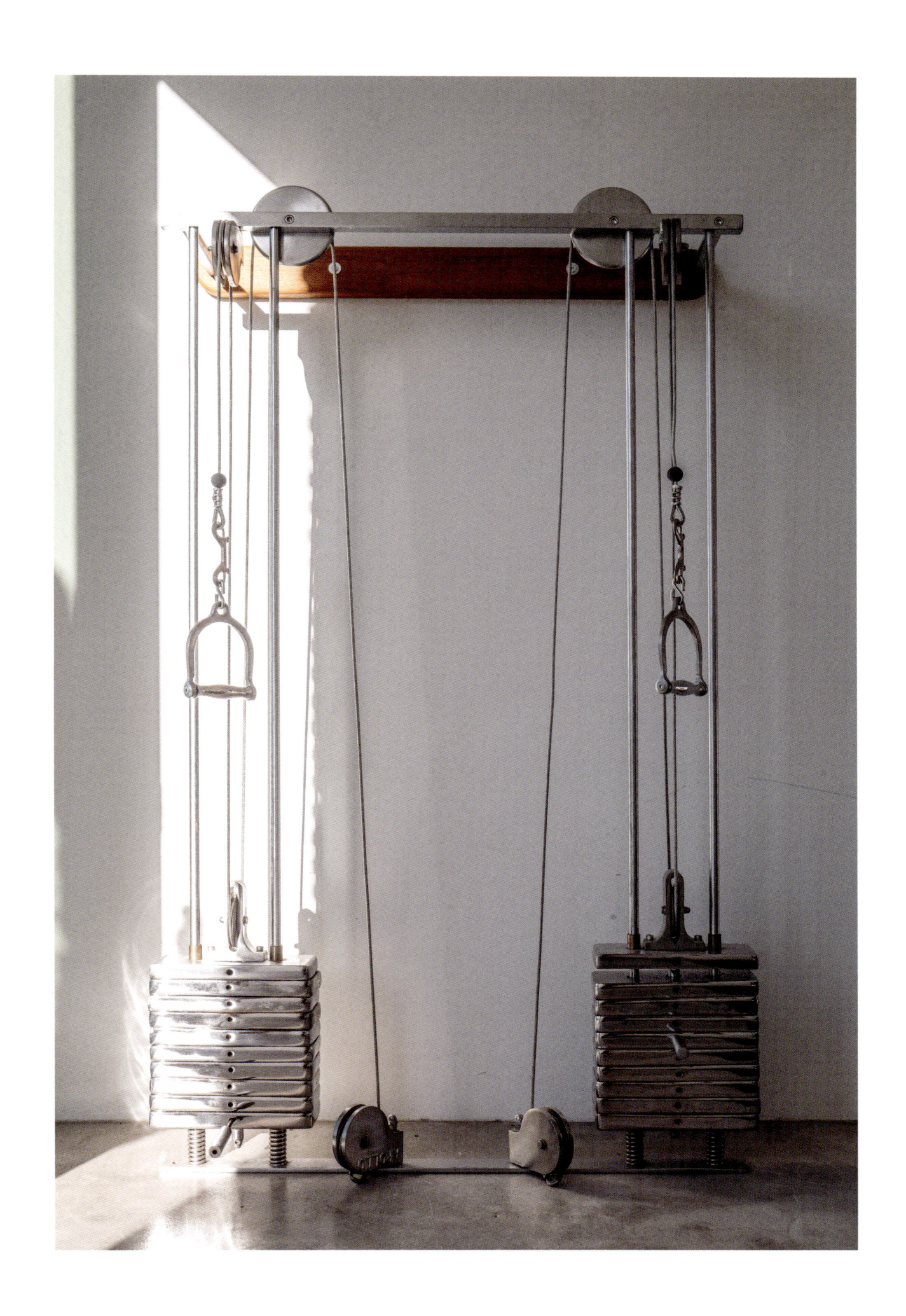

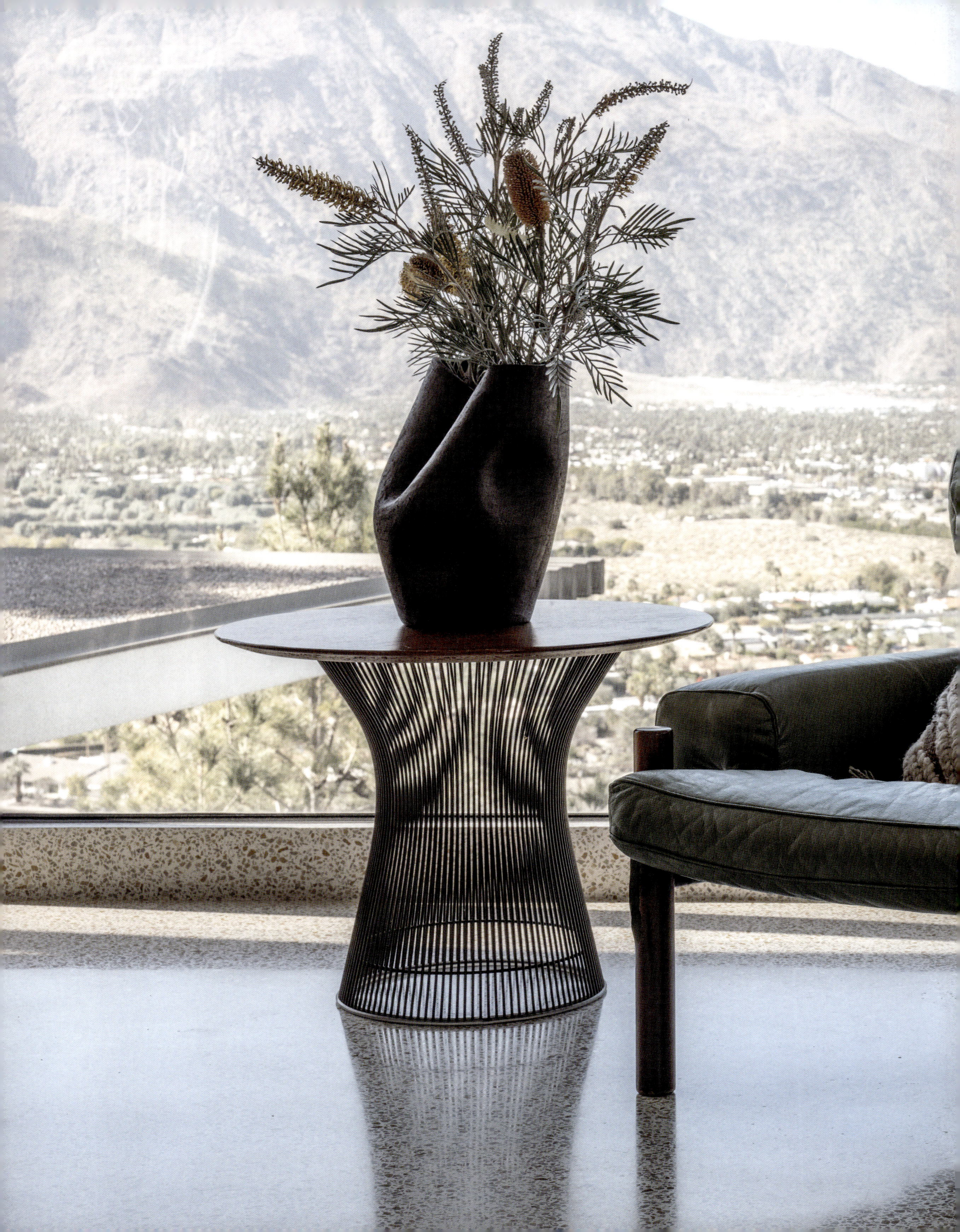

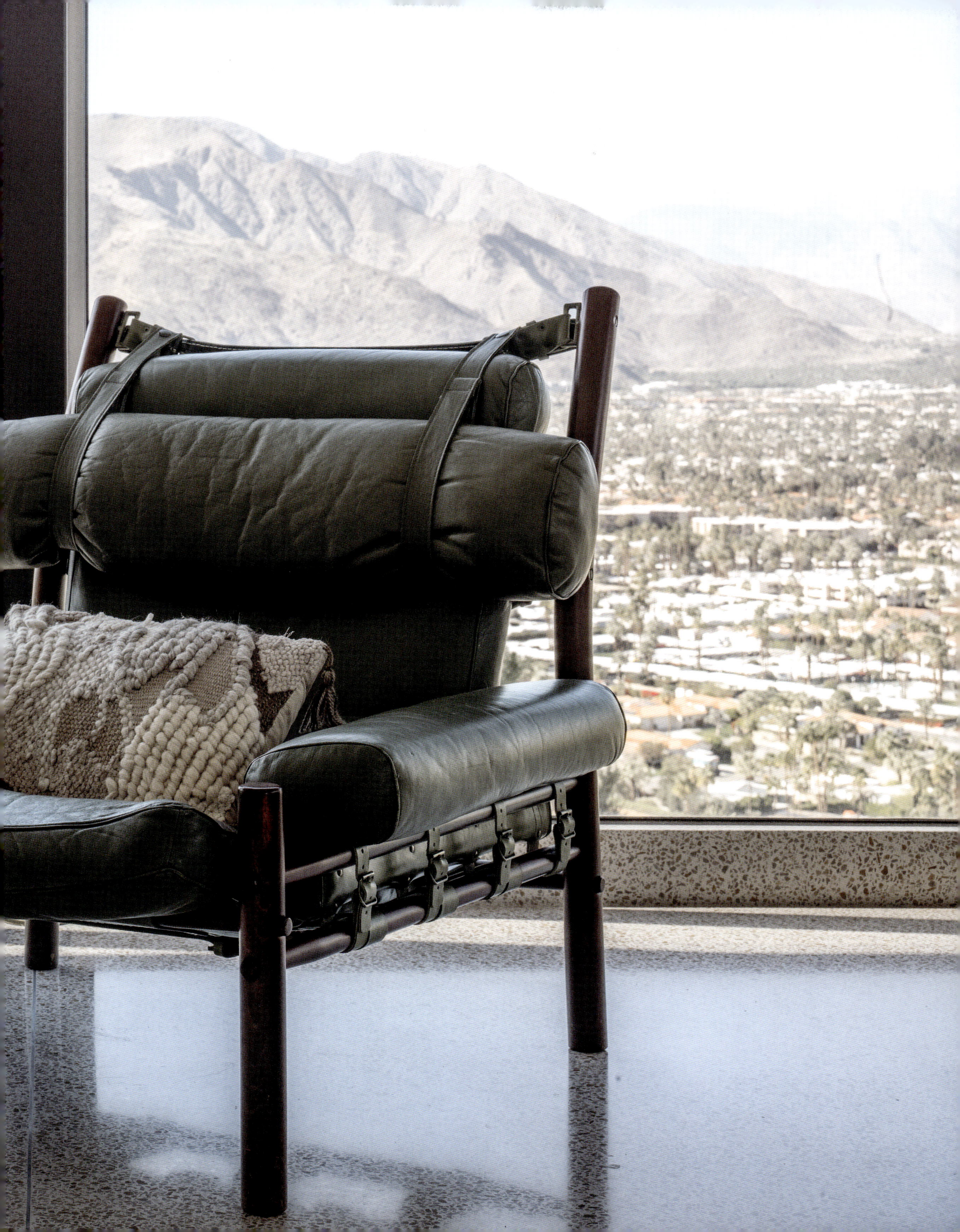

ACKNOWLEDGMENTS

THIS IS MY LOVE LETTER TO A PLACE I CALLED home for many years. Thanks to my desert crew who helped this book to take shape: Carol, James, Nicole, Jim, Tony, JC, Lori, Alfonso. To Robert and Clark for the most incredible and inspiring accommodations during all of my shoot days. To the homeowners who not only trusted me to photograph their homes and their stuff, but also took the extra leap of faith to allow me to photograph them. To Alex Gonzalez, who taught me long ago that shooting a "beauty photo" wasn't only meant for the face. To Ruben, Ella, Edie, and Barrie, my inner circle. And lastly, to my amazing parents who bought me my first Kodak Instamatic 126 when I was ten.

—Don Flood

THANK YOU TO THE FRIENDS WHOSE introductions made this book possible: Liz Armstrong, Anthony Cochran, and Ellen Donaldson; L. J. Cella, Leslie Stewart, and Adam Lerner of the Palm Springs Art Museum, who made the ultimate exception and let us photograph the interior of the Aluminaire House; Sidney Williams, who keeps me serious about architecture; Linda Blank of the Indian Wells Preservation Foundation; Courtney Newman of the Palm Springs Modern Committee; and Gary Johns of the Palm Springs Preservation Foundation, who at Nelda Linsk's house casually handed me a mangled envelope filled with slides stamped SLIM AARONS PALM SPRINGS, CALIF. JAN 1970, leading to my favorite photo in this book (page 165). Finally, thanks to Tom Scheerer, Luke Vincent, and Didona Marcinkevicius for my Marrakesh house, the finest piece of architecture I'll probably ever own.

—Stephen Drucker

Inside Palm Springs
First published in 2025 by The Vendome Press
Vendome is a registered trademark of The Vendome Press LLC

VENDOME PRESS US
PO Box 566
Palm Beach, FL 33480

VENDOME PRESS UK
Worlds End Studio
132–134 Lots Road
London SW10 0RJ

www.vendomepress.com

COPYRIGHT © 2025 The Vendome Press LLC
TEXT Copyright © 2025 Peter Haldeman
PHOTOGRAPHY Copyright © 2025 Don Flood

All rights reserved. No part of the contents of this book may be reproduced in whole or in part without prior written permission from the publishers.

ISBN: 978-0-86565-471-6

PUBLISHERS Beatrice Vincenzini, Mark Magowan, and Francesco Venturi
WRITER Peter Haldeman
EDITOR Stephen Drucker
PRODUCTION MANAGER Jim Spivey
DESIGNER Celia Fuller

Library of Congress Cataloging-in-Publication Data available upon request

Distributed in North America by
Abrams Books
www.abramsbooks.com

Distributed in the rest of the world by
Thames & Hudson Ltd.
6–24 Britannia Street
London WC1X 9JD
United Kingdom
www.thamesandhudson.com

EU Authorized Representative
Interart S.A.R.L.
19 Rue Charles Auray
93500 Pantin, Paris
France
productsafety@vendomepress.com
www.interart.fr

Printed and bound in China

FIRST PRINTING